American Legal Institutions
Recent Scholarship

Edited by Eric Rise

A Series from LFB Scholarly

Alternative Dispute Resolution in Civil Justice Systems

Roger E. Hartley

LFB Scholarly Publishing LLC
New York 2002

Copyright © 2002 by LFB Scholarly Publishing LLC

All rights reserved.

Library of Congress Cataloging-in-Publication Data

Hartley, Roger E., 1969-
  Alternative dispute resolution in civil justice systems / Roger E. Hartley.
      p. cm. -- (American legal institutions)
  Includes bibliographical references and index.
  ISBN 1-931202-36-2 (alk. paper)
  1. Dispute resolution (Law)--Georgia. I. Title. II. Series.
  KFG560.3 .H37 2002
  347.758'09--dc21

2002008584

ISBN 1-931202-36-2

Printed on acid-free 250-year-life paper.

Manufactured in the United States of America.

Table of Contents

ACKNOWLEDGEMENTS vii

INTRODUCTION ix

1: TRIAL COURTS 1

2: RESEARCH FRAMEWORK AND STUDY SITE 29

3: CIVIL JUSTICE IN MOUNTAIN COUNTY 47

4: CIVIL MEDIATION IN MOUNTAIN COUNTY 87

5: THE IMPACT OF MEDIATION ON CASE PROCESSING IN HALL COUNT 123

6: MEDIATION, CIVIL JUSTICE, AND COURT ACTORS 159

7: CONCLUSION 199

NOTES 211

BIBLIOGRAPHY 221

APPENDICES 241

A: CIVIL AND MEDIATED CASE CODESHEET 241

B1: ATTORNEY INTERVIEW SCHEDULE	253
B2: ATTORNEY/MEDIATOR INTERVIEW SCHEDULE	257
B3: JUDGE/ADMINISTRATOR INTERVIEW SCHEDULE	261
B4: MEDIATOR INTERVIEW SCHEDULE	265
INDEX	269

Acknowledgements

This book was the result of a great deal of fieldwork that necessitated the help of a number of individuals. First, I am grateful for the support of the National Science Foundation's Law and Social Sciences Section grant number 96-34453 for funding the costs of this research. Additional financial support came from the University of Georgia's Franklin College of Arts and Sciences Distinguished Graduate Fellowship and from Roanoke College. I am also grateful for the time and access granted to me by the court and mediation officials of "Mountain County." Thanks also go to the following individual, Dr. Herbert Kritzer, Dr. Susan Brodie Haire, Dr. Susette Talarico, Douglas Yarn, Dr. Margaret Herrman, Dr. Arnie Fleischman, Dr. Robert Grafstein, Dr. Herbert Jacob, Dr. Stephen Wasby, and Dr. Gerald McDermott, for commenting on early drafts of this work. Finally, I would like to thank Karen Wilson, Heidi Hanrahan, and Helen Colosimo of Roanoke College and my research assistant Paul Francis at the University of Arizona for their technical and research assistance. I also appreciate the help of my publisher Leo Balk and the series editor, Dr. Eric Rise, for their interest and work on this manuscript.

Finally, I dedicate this book and the years of work within to my loving wife Melissa for her sacrifice and support both emotionally and financially.

Introduction

A controversial policy debate has emerged in the United States surrounding the issue of civil litigation. Civil courts are viewed by some as severely crowded, especially with personal injury suits. The perception of this crisis in the civil justice system has been supplemented by arguments that juries have encouraged the influx of cases by awarding huge damages to plaintiffs. While some recent studies dispute claims of a civil litigation crisis (see Galanter, 1983; Eisenberg and Henderson, 1992; and Eaton and Talarico, 1996), the debate itself has led to widespread efforts to reform the tort system in particular (e.g., caps on damages) and state civil justice systems in general (e.g., efforts at alternative dispute methods).

These reform efforts have long generated interest among legal scholars and more recently have drawn the attention of social scientists. In political science, "public law" scholars have called for more research on trial courts generally and civil courts particularly (see Shapiro, 1993; Jacob, 1991). Until recently, the study of civil law has generated little interest, in part, because of its "private" law status (Dunn et. al., 1995). However, with the declining viability of the public/private distinction and with the political debate surrounding court reforms, new questions have attracted the attention of law and judicial process scholars.[1] Of these, the effect of institutional changes on existing court systems and processes raises interesting questions. In this study, attention is directed to civil courts and one popular institutional change, namely, alternative dispute resolution (ADR). Among the reforms enacted to relieve state civil justice systems is court-connected (or annexed) alternative dispute resolution (ADR). These programs are designed to encourage or mandate mediation and/or arbitration of cases before they reach trial. To date, government-sponsored ADR programs have been added to civil justice processes in most states.[2] The formal addition of ADR as an institutionalized forum for case settlement raises questions about the effects of ADR on the craft, process, and outcomes of civil justice systems

Studying the effects of institutional changes on an existing court system is intriguing because recent theoretical approaches to political science emphasize the importance of institutions (e.g., norms, rules, organizations, and process) as behavioral constraints on individual choice (e.g., New Institutionalism, rational and public choice). ADR could be viewed in this light. Alternatively, as the addition of a new process of dispute resolution to an existing system, ADR might actually "free" individuals by providing other settlement options. The question of ADR program effects, however, is dwarfed by the limited research on civil justice systems as compared with the criminal variety. Related research has examined the organization of criminal courts (Eisenberg and Jacob, 1977) and the "craft" and "community" of these judicial processes (Flemming, Nardulli, and Eisenstein, 1992). However, no such work to date has focused on civil courts from these more original and/or contextual approaches. A thorough understanding of the effects of an institutional change requires a better understanding of civil courts and their role in the provision of justice.

This study provides a neo-institutional analysis of civil justice and ADR. The major goal of this work is to assess how an institutional change (ADR) affects an existing civil justice system. If one views a civil justice system as an existing "web of institutions" and actors (e.g., rules, norms, processes), then the initiation of a new process in the system should change the behavior of system actors and the outcomes of the system. An exploratory study of a single civil court system that has adopted a court-annexed ADR program can provide answers to this question and also a foundation for the more general study of civil court systems. To this end, this study provides an in-depth analysis of civil justice, case processing, and court-annexed mediation in a single Georgia county court system.

To some degree, this case-oriented approach for the study of civil trial courts mirrors the "first generation" of research on criminal court processes (Blumberg, 1967; Neubauer, 1974) that relied on observation, interviews, and analyses of case files. In this sense, the proposed research builds on scholarship developed in the study of criminal courts. Also, the proposed research draws on work in other areas of political science,

… Introduction xi

especially more general conceptions of neo-institutionalism (e.g., congressional and bureaucratic studies).

The study is both qualitative and quantitative. The qualitative dimension consists of direct observation of civil court processes and interviews with key actors in the system (e.g., judges, court clerks, ADR administrators, and attorneys). The quantitative portion focuses on analyses of data culled from civil case records.

There are, then, three primary goals for this book. First, I seek to discover what civil justice looks like. Secondly, I focus on how mediation works within civil justice systems. Finally, using the framework of the "new institutionalism," I seek to assess how mediation as an institutional change affects civil justice.

On the first of these questions, I generally concur with scholars like Kritzer (1991) who argue that civil justice is routine. The vast majority of civil cases are simple actions (e.g, debt collection and uncontested divorces), civil litigants are typically individuals who are represented by a single attorney, and most cases settle before trial and without many formal motions. However, despite the notion of "routine justice", these cases make up a very large proportion of trial court caseloads and are often viewed by judges and court administrators as destructive to court efficiency. To this end, while routine, typical civil cases may require a great deal of intervention by judges and attorneys. I also find that a large portion of civil litigants go unrepresented (pro se), that a significant number of these cases are removed from the system by direct judicial intervention (e.g., motions to dismiss), and that large numbers of cases proceed to trial only to end in a "default" judgment.

On the second question, I find that mediation was institutionalized for the purpose of improving court efficiency (e.g., fewer trials and speedier processing of cases). The types of cases referred to mediation were overwhelmingly domestic, and litigants who were referred to mediation were represented by attorneys. However, these attorneys rarely showed up for the mediation. Interestingly, preliminary comparisons with general civil cases found that mediated cases had higher settlement rates, but also higher trial rates. Additionally, on average, mediated cases were processed slower than general civil cases.

Finally, using more direct comparisons of mediated and general civil cases and analysis of interviews, I argue that mediation may have been oversold as an efficiency program. For example, the low percentage of cases referred to mediation could not have had much of an impact on overall case processing (e.g., speed of disposal). Also, a higher percentage of mediated cases went to trial, and court workloads were slightly higher when compared with general civil cases.

However, consistent with "new institutionalism," mediation did alter the civil justice process, the norms, and the behavior of actors in the system. Judges typically referred a small number of contested, domestic cases to mediation, but these cases were viewed as likely to take more court time. Fewer cases were disposed of before trial by judicial action, and a higher percentage of cases settled "outside" of court. Although mediation was not viewed as improving efficiency in the aggregate, actors in the system made use of the program for distinctly rational ends. For example, judges gained the ability to encourage mediated settlement more formally, attorneys viewed mediation as a method of managing their own caseloads and increasing profits, and most interview subjects argued that mediation promoted satisfaction and empowerment among mediation clients.

In summary, I argue that while the institutional change did not necessarily meet the stated goals of court reformers, the implementation of ADR did change the legal culture among elites in Mountain County. Local actors (i.e., the bar and the chief judge) chose the program and trumpeted goals of efficiency, but other ends were achieved by the implementation of ADR. One of these was the co-option of mediation **into** the adversary system by the actions of "reluctant partners" seeking rational benefits.

CHAPTER 1
Trial Courts and Mediation

Before advancing a new institutionalist perspective in this research, it is necessary to provide a background on trial courts and mediation. A review of social science research on these subjects provides us with good reason to believe that institutions matter to the functioning of trial courts. Institutions, also, affect the choices of individuals and provide a means to assess legal change. What do we know about trial courts and mediation?

Public law scholars have recently called attention to the need to study state trial courts, particularly on the civil side of the law (e.g., Dunn et. al., 1995; Hensley and Kuersten, 1995; Shapiro, 1993; and Jacob, 1991). Our limited knowledge of civil trial court actors and institutions, however, presents problems when considering policy innovations such as ADR and tort reform. For instance, the institutionalization of ADR in state and federal court systems has taken place without empirical knowledge of how civil court systems work (see Saks, 1992 on tort reform). This makes it difficult for policy analysts to assess accurately the potential impact of these new institutions on existing systems.

Also problematic is the lack of theoretical integration in previous studies of trial courts in both civil and criminal arenas. Public law scholars have repeatedly emphasized the need to focus empirical research efforts toward the task of theory generation and hypothesis testing. While much of the recent work on state and federal appellate courts is directed to this objective (Brace and Hall, 1995; Gely and Spiller, 1990; Segal and Spaeth, 1993), similar efforts at the state trial level are limited or lag behind (see again, Hensley and Kuersten, 1995; Shapiro, 1993; and Jacob, 1991).

A considerable portion of this lack of attention may stem from the perception that civil courts are of little importance in policy making. However, recent work by Mather (1991, 1995) suggests that trial courts are important institutions for generating policy alternatives and policy implementation. Further, they play important roles in participant access to justice and dispute resolution.

A more compelling reason for the lack of work exists apart from scholars' interests. It is difficult to study state trial courts. For the most part, trial courts do not provide published opinions as in state and federal appellate courts. This makes access to case records extremely difficult and more laborious in comparison with the ability to download cases from Westlaw or Lexis. Most state courts do not have uniform record keeping procedures, making even case identification problematic and the eventual coding of cases labor intensive. For example, in Georgia, trial court scholars have to sort through docket books and then retrieve case files by hand. Only in the 1990s have states generated computer databases of case files, and when these are available, they only include case records from recent years (Blumstein et. al., 1991). The collection of data in a single trial court jurisdiction, then, is both time consuming and expensive. It is no wonder that large studies of state trial courts are rare and require considerable financial support.[3]

While there is a large body of research on civil and criminal trial courts by legal, public administration, and law and society scholars, political science literature on trial courts as systems is much more limited. This is, in part, due to the intensive effort necessary in studying trial courts mentioned above. Despite this difficulty, existing studies have used a number of approaches to understand trial courts. At the more aggregate level, these approaches have emphasized "organizations, communities, institutions, and time" (Dunn et. al., 1996). In particular, there have been a number of studies on criminal trial courts as systems, studies on various pieces of civil systems, and a large and broad literature on ADR.

Integrating this diverse literature into one theoretical framework is difficult because of the variety approaches employed by scholars. Additionally, this literature needs to be extended in two important directions. Civil courts have not been studied as whole "systems" like criminal courts. One strategy for this proposed by Jacob (1991: 228) was a civil "replication" of Neubauer's examination of the work of criminal courts in a middle-sized city. Relatedly, scholars in the field of ADR have called for studies linking the ADR process to the broader civil system

(Keilitz, 1994). An examination of some of the literature on criminal and civil trial courts and ADR will focus this study toward both of these efforts.

TRIAL COURTS AS COMPLEX SYSTEMS

In a debate at the 1995 American Political Science Association meeting, the late Herbert Jacob and Martin Shapiro considered where the social scientific study of law should move.[4] In response to Shapiro's argument that public law should adopt theories from the broader discipline of political science, Jacob (1995) asserted that the dominant tools of the field (e.g., pluralism, rational choice, voter surveys, etc.) do little to help explain the complex nature of trial courts.

According to Jacob (1995: 2-3), group influences on courts are only marginally related to decision making and do little to provide assistance in implementation or access to courts. Additionally, he argued that individualistic paradigms (behavioralism, rational choice, etc.) explain only portions of trial court activities because sets of actors (e.g., judges, prosecutors, defense attorneys, and litigants) "operate in complex and shifting organizational contexts," not easily explained by individual characteristics and motivations (Jacob, 1995: 3). In this and a more recent piece to be discussed later, Jacob emphasized that courts have special characteristics that need new conceptualization (1995, 1996).

The trial court system, according to these scholars, is indeed quite complex. In the Chicago urban criminal court setting that Jacob (1996) describes, formal bureaucratic institutions exist (e.g., prosecutor/solicitor office, public defender office) along with court administrators (e.g., clerks, formal court administrators) and judges to form a "web" of organizations that routinely interact. Additionally, when crimes occur, police agencies interact through investigation and arrest of offenders. These administrative institutions, made up of personnel with formal rules and norms, are organizations that can be both "loosely" and "tightly" coupled in different trial court circumstances (1996: 1).

Trial court services are also, in criminal court settings, individually driven. The decision-making practices of individual police, judges, and attorneys all affect access to courts, case management, procedural justice, and even case outcomes. For example, access to criminal courts can be impeded prior to the fact by the discretion of police, who act as early "gatekeepers" to the criminal system. Individual officers apply the law through the ability to invoke or not invoke the criminal process (Goldstein, 1960). Studies have shown, for instance, that police arrest practices vary with respect to the relationship of offender and victim and other factors (Berk and Loseke, 1981; Black, 1971). Additionally, judges' decisions on evidence and motions influence the procedures of justice and outcomes via sentencing (Gibson, 1979). Finally, access to trial courts is most often negotiated in the form of plea bargaining between the defense attorney (public or private) and the prosecutor's office.

Jacob (1996) argues that scholarship on criminal courts is explored through two prisms. Some scholars perceive trial courts as governed by the sovereignty of judges who act as autonomous individuals (e.g., Goldman, 1993, 1991 on judge characteristics; Gibson, 1979 on "roles"). Others view them as bureaucracies or organizations (e.g., Blumberg, 1967; Eisenstein and Jacob, 1977; Eisenstein, Nardulli, and Flemming, 1988, 1992).

Each conception has merit in exploring civil trial courts and institutional change by offering different "nodes" to examine. Inherently, the fact that many different units of analysis exist in trial courts shows the need to explore civil systems and actors in some depth, as on the criminal side. Civil trial courts have yet to be explored in this manner and present many similarities and differences on the surface. Viewing civil courts from a "macro" perspective should provide a focus by identifying and explaining these "loose" and "tight" relationships among individuals, groups, and organizations. While criminal courts have been explored from a "macro" perspective, differences exist between criminal and civil courts that merit their examination separately.

One major difference between criminal and civil courts is the lack of formal public organization in civil courts as opposed to the criminal variety (e.g., prosecution, public defenders). Conceptions of civil courts as organizations or bureaucracies, then, may be limited. Also, while bargaining for case settlement seems to drive civil systems and domestic justice, it seems less formal than the sometimes public mechanism of plea bargaining in criminal courts. If we view civil and domestic court process as less formally institutionalized, how does it deliver justice? If civil justice is economically driven and directed by the private bar, what effects might the formal, public institutionalization of ADR have on civil court systems?

TRIAL COURTS AS ORGANIZATIONS

In the debate on the future of public law, it was noted that studies of trial courts are limited and often lack theoretical cohesion. This is, in part, a function of the fact that trial courts have been studied from a variety of disciplines, which, in the social sciences, include anthropology, economics, sociology, political science, and psychology. Despite the lack of theoretical cohesion among these studies, "discernible approaches" from these disciplines offer perspectives on trial courts at the aggregate and individual levels (Dunn et. al., 1996). At the aggregate level, attention has been directed to the importance of organizations, communities, institutions, and time on the behavior of court "actors" and outcomes. Additionally, studies have placed an emphasis on the roles, background, and attitudes of individual "actors" in trial court systems.

One line of research on the structure and work of trial courts has focused on criminal courts as systems. Related research has focused on the actors, institutions, and relationships of criminal courts as organizations. Here, judges, prosecutors, and defense attorneys are viewed as "organized sets of functionally interdependent actors" (Flemming, Nardulli, and Eisenstein, 1992: 4) who interact largely for mutual benefit and not in an adversarial manner. Institutions and norms internal and external to the system affect then, both court behavior and output. In this perspective, the work of the criminal justice system consists of the management and processing of caseloads, the process and outputs of plea negotiations, and the process and outputs of judicial sentencing decisions.

The "first generation" of this line of research focused on single courts in metropolitan (Blumberg, 1967; Skolnick, 1967), as well as more rural, settings (Neubauer, 1974). Blumberg's (1967) work conceptualized criminal trial courts as bureaucracies with judges as quasi-administrative heads. Trial courts were viewed in an almost top-down hierarchy that administrated justice and managed caseloads and sentencing.

Subsequent studies began to expand on the notion that trial court systems were much more complex and less judge driven (e.g., Cole, 1970; Carter, 1974; Neubauer, 1974). Neubauer's (1974) case study, <u>Criminal Justice in Middle America</u> provided an early, in-depth, exploration of a single criminal court. Focusing on the broad question of how criminal courts allocate justice, Neubauer relied on interviews and case records as vehicles for exploration. His analysis illuminated key actors, standards of decision making, the interaction of actors, and the outputs and benefits of the process.

A "second generation" of research on criminal courts provided theoretical focus (e.g., organization theory) and adopted more comparative strategies (Nardulli, 1979: 103-108). The earliest of these "second generation" studies focused on large metropolitan courts (Levin, 1977; Eisenstein and Jacob, 1977) with more recent works analyzing courts of varying size and demographics (Eisenstein, Flemming, and Nardulli, 1988; Nardulli, Eisenstein, and Flemming, 1988; Flemming, Nardulli, and Eisenstein, 1992). These "second generation" studies merit further attention both for approaches to theory building and for the study of trial courts as a whole.

The first of these is Levin's (1977) analysis of urban politics and criminal courts in Minneapolis and Pittsburgh. Relying on both qualitative and quantitative methods, Levin observed and interviewed judges, prosecutors, and defense attorneys and explored their attitudes, backgrounds, motivations, and work. He supplemented this with data on the sentencing of felons (1959-1965). Levin found that sentencing was more lenient in Pittsburgh than in Minneapolis and argued that this variation was a function of differing judicial selection systems. Levin also found that judges (not prosecutors) were the predominant figures in the court system with respect to case management and the primary source of delay in case disposition. Finally, he concluded that most case activity occurred outside of the courtroom.

Particularly interesting is Levin's assertion that judges are the predominant cause of delay in court systems, an argument that suggests that judges, defense attorneys, and prosecutors may pursue self-interested case management strategies. This contrasts somewhat with earlier arguments (Blumberg, 1967; Skolnick, 1967) that describe criminal courts as bureaucratic structures where there is mutual benefit in speedy case disposition.

Eisenstein and Jacob (1977) extended these second generational studies of criminal courts with their organizational study of Baltimore, Chicago, and Detroit courts. Here, the authors applied organization theory to judicial processes in an effort to show that the context of decision making matters and that mutual self-interest is the dominant force in decision making.

> Neither defendant characteristics, nor characteristics of judges, nor features of the felony disposition process such as plea

bargaining, kind of counsel, or pretrial release, provide us with a sufficient explanation of the felony disposition process. Nor can these variables be combined in a simple fashion. But the evidence is strong that each has some effect on the disposition of cases (Eisenstein and Jacob, 1977: 9).

Like Levin (1977), Eisenstein and Jacob relied on both qualitative and quantitative data through observation, interview, and analysis of defendant records. In each of the three sites, they explored patterns in courtroom work-group characteristics,[5] as well as the ecology of courtroom work groups,[6] hypothesizing that the outputs were related to differing characteristics and ecology.

In this perspective, the characteristics and ecology of courts constitute the culture of criminal courts. Statistical analyses demonstrated that while there were similarities in the conviction rates of defendants in each of the sites, substantial differences occurred in sentencing, method of disposition (e.g., guilty pleas, bench trials, jury trials), results of preliminary hearings, and time of case disposition (Eisenstein and Jacob, 1977). These differences were attributed to variation in the courtroom work-groups and court culture particular to jurisdictions.

The organizational works provided a much needed examination of criminal trial courts from a "macro" or systemic perspective. These "macro" examinations underscored the complexity of court systems and hinted at the possibility that variations in trial court outputs could be explained in part by differences in court structure in different jurisdictions. Second generational studies comparing courts of different regions and employing triangular methodologies further solidified the idea that local courts are creatures of local communities.

TRIAL COURTS AND THEIR COMMUNITIES

The organizational paradigm of trial courts was extended in second generation studies to variations among court communities (Eisenstein, Flemming, and Nardulli, 1988; Nardulli, Eisenstein, and Flemming, 1988; and Flemming, Nardulli, and Eisenstein, 1992). Myers and Talarico (1987), for example, provided an analysis of the local community context of criminal trial courts in Georgia. These studies extended the line of inquiry in two major ways. First, the second generation works were more comparative in nature as they expanded to include varying types of jurisdictions (see Flemming et. al., 1992). Second, the works specifically linked environmental, contextual, and individual variables to judicial outputs using both quantitative and qualitative data.

Broadly, Flemming, Nardulli, and Eisenstein (1992) found that the "community" in medium-sized courts is more autonomous than in larger urban courts and is more strongly related to local social and political factors than in larger courts. They concluded, then, that criminal court communities can best be described as complex and pluralistic; however, this structure is dominated by prosecutors.

Similarly, Myers and Talarico (1987) studied felony sentencing in all 159 Georgia counties to see if the specific context of justice mattered. Their research from 1976 to 1985 found that felony sentencing varied by county context even when there were no statewide effects (e.g., race). Overall, their work suggests that local, county-level context outweighs the effects of statewide institutions and characteristics with respect to sentencing.

In another line of inquiry, work on the legal profession has demonstrated differences in how attorneys practice in different community settings (Heinz and Laumann, 1982; Landon, 1990). In his study on country lawyers, Landon (1990) found major differences in the types of practices and legal norms of attorneys in small towns versus city attorneys (see Heinz and Laumann, 1982 on city attorneys). For example, the smaller the size of the city, the more likely are practices to be less specialized (i.e., attorneys practice in civil and criminal arenas). Also, Landon (1990) found evidence that attorney practice was more collegial because of the "repeat player" status of most actors in the system. Thus, in small towns, communities are more homogenized and attorneys are likely to know clients and opposing attorneys. The economic need for repeat business and the necessity of "working with" opposing attorneys is much more important in these communities than in large cities.

Urban attorneys, on the other hand, vary from the very specialized practice in large firms to "local" attorneys who do routine processing of family or basic civil law (Heinz and Laumann, 1982). The emphasis on specialization and the diversity of incomes of urban attorneys provide the possibility of repeat clients, but few repeat performances with opposing attorneys. Justice in urban areas, with the exception of neighborhood attorneys, may be less communitarian and less congenial.

Organizational studies of trial courts, then, emphasize that differences in outcomes could be tied to the size and attitudes of court communities. In this respect, the context or setting of trial courts seems to matter. It is unclear, however, why context or setting makes a difference. Institutions (rules, norms, and process) may vary at the local level and change the behavior of court actors.

TRIAL COURTS AS INSTITUTIONS

Institutional analysis (e.g. rules, norms, processes, and organization) has been uncommon as a means of analyzing trial courts (see Gates, 1991; Smith, 1988). However, research in political science and policy studies has focused on the effects of one or more institutional changes and has identified rules and norms that are important in shaping the behavior of actors in trial court systems. For example, Levin's (1977) research on criminal trial courts found that the selection methods of judges in Pittsburgh and Minnesota correlated with variations in judges' sentencing behavior. Additionally, one norm of district attorneys' offices is the negotiation of criminal settlements in the form of plea bargaining rather than seeking trial (Cole, 1970; Carter, 1974). This use of discretion by prosecutors is said to aid them in managing large caseloads and to save space in overcrowded prisons (among other suggestions). An absence of these formal institutions (e.g., district attorney offices) in civil justice raises questions about what drives civil systems and how institutions affect decisions.

On the civil side, scholars of law and society have paid attention to legal institutions and their effects on civil justice. However, courts have not been studied as integrated systems of institutions. Much of this research has been directed to the effects of policy changes on civil caseloads (e.g., Clarke et. al., 1995; Kobbervig, 1991; McEwen, 1991 on court annexed mediation; Eaton and Talarico, 1994, 1995, 1996; and Eisenberg and Henderson, 1992, on tort reform).

Other strains of research highlight the importance of rules and norms on the functions of civil systems. In their analysis of Rule 11 of the <u>Federal Rules of Civil Procedure</u>, Kritzer and Zemans (1993) found that the use of these effectively controlled litigation at the district level.

With respect to rules, civil justice in federal and state trial courts is most often governed by formal rules of civil procedure. These rules generally differ by state, but all have common institutional procedures. One of the major jobs of attorneys, then, is to instruct their clients on the requirements of the legal process and to socialize them into the role of clients (Sarat and Felstiner, 1986). The formal rules of civil procedure all tend to share the basics of the filing of a complaint by the plaintiff, an answer by the defendant, discovery, pretrial actions (e.g., motions, continuances, leaves of absence, pretrial hearings, and conferences), and trial procedure. Each of these procedures is costly to both clients and attorneys and often result in pretrial negotiations in the "shadow of the law" (see Mnookin and Kornhauser, 1979; Erlanger, Chambliss, and Melli, 1987).

Apart from formal civil procedure, state trial systems often differ in organizational structure. General jurisdiction trial courts in many states function in civil, domestic, and felony criminal cases (see Stumpf, 1988, especially Chapter 3). While jurisdictions vary among states, these traditional courts are generally divided into local counties or judicial districts within states (Stumpf, 1988: 86-87). Additionally, lower courts of limited jurisdiction exist in such arenas as probate, small claims, domestic disputes, and juvenile matters (National Center for State Courts, 1984; cited in Stumpf, 1988).

In addition to rules and structure, norms inside and outside the formal civil process have been viewed by some scholars as instrumental for access to courts and in the choice of forums. Research on dispute formation provides reasons behind the use of formal and informal processes for managing grievances, including the use of adjudication. Stumpf (1988: 285-286), for example, points to important external factors shaping the emergence and transformation of disputes. Among these are (1) relationship of the parties; (2) the structure, jurisdiction, availability, and accessibility of dispute forums; (3) the role of key representatives (e.g., lawyers); (4) the prevailing social attitudes about disputing; and (5) extant legal norms (e.g., do legal rules afford remedies to the type of dispute?).

Each of these external factors aids in the emergence or transformation of disputes and can be viewed as a necessary element in the calculation of how an individual attempts to deal with a dispute formally or informally (Sarat and Grossman, 1975; Sarat and Miller, 1980-81). Largely because of costs, most disputants decide to settle well before the litigation stage is reached (Sarat and Miller, 1980-81).

The key finding of this line of research is that very few of the grievances and claims in society reach formal disputes, and that of those that are formally filed in court, about 90% are settled out of court (Miller and Sarat, 1980-81). Even in the presence of evidence that most disputes end privately, the existence of the formal legal system provides direct and indirect benefits to disputants.

Since most civil cases never reach the court system at all or are settled prior to litigation (see Miller and Sarat, 1980-1981; Mnookin and Kornhauser, 1979; Ross, 1980), system gatekeepers are attorneys. In the civil system, litigants entering the court system are forced to face the economic reality of hiring an attorney or must face civil procedure *pro se*. This alone helps to explain why a large number of grievances are never filed as cases.

One might argue that a formal, state-sponsored system is not necessary for participants to receive justice. However, research demonstrates that among cases formally filed, those that settle do so in the "shadow" of the law. In their analysis of divorce disputes, for example, Mnookin and Kornhauser (1979) argued that over time attorneys exposed to the results of formal adjudication and its structures come to understand and can predict remedies imposed by judges and juries. Additionally, the state legal system has the ability to impose sanctions on individuals who default on agreements. Each of these aspects of law, combined with the costs of legal representation, provide important incentives for litigants and their attorneys to settle disputes rather than trying them.

The concept of the "shadow of the law" as an important factor in case settlement is undisputed, but should not be overstated. The informal structures and procedures referred to by Ross (1980) also can be understood to enhance the choices of litigants and attorneys beyond formal structures. The assumption of a wide "shadow" cast by the law depends on how many legal barriers (or institutions) are in the way and the strength of the law being applied. Here, Erlanger, Chambliss, and Melli (1987) emphasize that most divorce settlements are "rubberstamped" by judges, that litigants' knowledge of judge's expectations for remedies is limited to attorney interpretation, and that attorneys often acknowledge that these outcomes are uncertain. Thus, the "shadow of the law" is not very expansive.

Work by Kritzer (1991) and Jacob (1992) provides additional qualifications on the "shadow of the law." In his study of attorneys in civil litigation, Kritzer (1991) argued that in tort law there are two "shadows" that are perceived to give more bargaining power to a single litigant. These shadows are appellate court cases (which provide little information on monetary damages in a case) and the ability to impose costs on the opponent (73-75, 103-04, and 132-33; see Macauley, Friedman, and Stookey, 1995). According to Kritzer, neither impacts settlements because tort appellate cases provide little predictive power in terms of legal shadows. Also, the contingent fee system equalizes costs to plaintiffs versus corporations and insurance defendants. Jacob (1992), in addition, argued that the shadow of the law depends on many conditions, including the language in which a claim is framed, the manner in which attorneys are used, and the success of personal network consultation (see Macauley, Friedman, and Stookey, 1995).

This discussion of dispute formation and norms in settlement provides an important basis for the exploration of civil courts and the impact of ADR. These studies suggest that informal norms are integral to case settlement outside the formal procedures of law.

Formal rules, norms, and institutional structure, however, impose costs and incentives for individual behavior. If nothing else, they provide arenas in which individuals can negotiate or make decisions about disputes. As we will see, ADR originated as an informal process and was applied outside of state legal systems for settling disputes. Court-annexed ADR programs are those ADR institutions formally adopted by courts into the legal system. By considering the impact of "formalizing" informal ADR procedures into court systems, one can assess whether existing case processing norms change and the system and behavior of individuals who act within it.

RESEARCH ON LITIGATION TRENDS, CASELOAD, AND OUTCOMES

The largest portion of the empirical work on civil courts has been in response to recent policy debates about the litigation crisis, tort reform, and alternative forms of dispute resolution. In this fashion, institutional changes such as tort reforms are studied, most often in the form of limited caseload analysis or more normative assessments of specific policy proposals. Here, some argue that courts are overburdened with increasing civil disputes fueled by "runaway" juries (e.g., Clarke, et. al., 1988; Olson, 1991), especially when there are "deep pocket" defendants. On the other side, scholars argue that there is no civil litigation crisis, that litigation trends mirror increases in population, and that most cases never make it to trial (e.g., Catenacci, 1989; Galanter, 1983, 1986).

Largely because both legislators and the public seem to subscribe to the crisis argument (see Neubauer and Meinhold, 1994), states have enacted several reforms in the civil justice system (e.g., caps on damages, penalties for frivolous suits) and advocated the use of ADR as a relief to court congestion (e.g., court-annexed arbitration or mediation). These reform efforts have generated policy debates of their own and have fueled some empirical work on policy formation and impact (e.g., Elliott and Talarico, 1991; Lipincott and Stoker, 1992).

This line of research has produced a mixed bag of evidence. First, it seems that most civil disputes are never filed, and of those that are, 88% settle out of court (see works by the Civil Litigation Research Project; Trubek et. al., 1983; Miller and Sarat, 1980-81; Felstiner et. al., 1980-81). One of the most comprehensive of these research efforts, the Civil Litigation Research Project also concluded that among the disputes examined (including torts), stakes were modest and a fairly small group of litigants accounted for a disproportionate number of cases. This last finding supports Galanter's proposition that the justice system is dominated by "repeat players" (1974).

There have been a considerable number of longitudinal studies of both appellate and trial court caseloads (see Munger, 1990). These include Daniels' (1988a; 1988b; 1990) study of litigation in four Illinois counties from 1870-1960, Stookey's (1990) work on the effect of crises on litigation trends in four Arizona courts, and Eisenberg's (1982) analysis of Section 1983 litigation and related doctrine. These works compared trial court litigation patterns over time and found changes in dockets to be related to political, economic, and local institutional factors.

Related research on civil filings (Rottman, 1990; Hensler et. al., 1987; Daniels, 1988a, 1988b, 1990) emphasizes minimal changes in litigation patterns. There are, however, exceptions. For example, Hensler and colleagues (1987) indicated that "high stakes" litigation such as mass torts, medical malpractice, and products liability were rising at moderate to high rates. However, recent research in Georgia found that these types of torts were very few in number, especially as a proportion of tort cases and as compared to the dominant auto claims (see Eaton and Talarico, 1996; Dunn et. al., 1995). Two studies of civil litigation conducted by the National Center for State Courts and the Bureau of Justice confirm these patterns to be generally consistent across 45 urban jurisdictions of the United States in 1992 (DeFrances et. al., 1995; Smith et. al., 1995). For the most part, these longitudinal studies provide little evidence on micro-level trial court procedures or other forms of dispute processing (see Dunn, et. al., 1996: 5). In a Law and Society Review issue devoted to the longitudinal study of trial courts, scholars argued for a focus on more explanatory models of civil systems (see Reiss, 1990), organization of trial courts (Seron, 1990), trial court culture (Yngvesson, 1990), and the procedural nature of dispute processing in trial courts (Mather, 1990). An analysis of courts as "systems" could provide relevant internal case processing dynamics of importance to caseloads, pace of litigation, and outcomes.

Recent works by political scientists have begun to examine trial courts and outcomes from a more integrated and systemic perspective. For example, research in Georgia focuses on civil case procedures with an eye toward the creation of an explanatory model of case outcomes (Dunn et. al., 1995). Generally, Dunn and colleagues found that tort outcomes were somewhat uniform across the four counties studied (1995). Therefore, local organizational culture may not affect outcomes as originally assumed by scholars of criminal trial courts. Second, the preliminary results demonstrated that measures of case complexity (e.g., presence of multiple defense attorneys) were correlated with case disposition, suggesting that attorneys may act strategically and place more manpower on cases with complex issues, high stakes, or those that seem bound for trial. Also of interest was the fact that wrongful death claims were more likely to settle and property cases more likely to go to trial. This finding suggests that in cases with higher stakes, it may be more rational for attorneys to settle. Defense attorneys avoid potentially large jury verdicts and plaintiff attorneys receive a contingency fee with less effort.[7]

In a follow-up study by Dunn et. al. (1996), differences in case disposition (settlement or trial) were analyzed against case characteristics, jurisdiction, and indicators of case complexity and uncertainty. In related multivariate analyses, they found that case disposition patterns did not vary significantly across the four counties in the study. In general, the study found that "repeat player" activity among attorneys and case type (e.g., auto) were significantly correlated with the settlement of civil cases.

Research from the Georgia project also focused on patterns in tort litigation with an eye toward assessing tort reform. In this study of four counties in Georgia, Eaton and Talarico (1996) found little evidence from case files to support claims of a tort "crisis" in Georgia. Torts constituted a small portion of state dockets, the trend of tort filings was stable over the four-year period of the study, and the vast majority of cases settled before trial (average trial rate was about 7%). Finally, cases were processed within in a year, and damage awards at trial were found to be modest when plaintiffs won these suits.

Additional work on civil courts systems by the National Center for State Courts and the United States Bureau of Justice parallels the Georgia research (DeFrances et. al., 1995 and Smith et. al., 1995). In a descriptive profile of civil justice in 45 selected urban jurisdictions in 1992, researchers found that civil case processing and outcomes were generally consistent.

The research highlighted above provides a good beginning for understanding the work of civil court systems and some of the factors that drive them. Studies on caseloads over time have found that economic and other societal factors lead to caseload change. However, how these changes occur is often left to question. Scholars have called for more research on the internal process of civil justice, as well as the earliest stages of disputes over time. One interesting question relates to this study: how does civil justice change with respect to changes in the process? Does the formal introduction of ADR to civil justice systems impact caseload over time? Does it change disposition patterns? Time to disposition? Case outcomes? Do cases referred to mediation settle earlier than similar cases without mediation?

INDIVIDUAL ACTORS IN TRIAL COURTS

While the literature reviewed has examined trial court actors as participants in systems or constrained by institutions, a separate line of research has viewed court actors from a more singular perspective. The most common of these studies focus on judges as political figures in trial courts with some recent attention to civil attorneys.

Judge-centered conceptions of trial courts specify that they are the dominant players in criminal court systems and that they act virtually unimpeded by their organizational context (Jacob, 1996: 1). This line of research has focused primarily on the links between a judge's background, characteristics, and ideology, and his decisions (e.g., Goldman, 1991, 1993; Martin, 1993, 1990; see Jacob, 1996). At the U.S. Supreme Court level, scholars who subscribe to the attitudinal model argue that judges' decisions are shaped primarily by their attitudes toward the policy or issue under consideration apart from institutional factors (Segal and Spaeth, 1993). At the trial court level, judges may be more constrained by local, federal, and state institutions (e.g., precedent from courts above, formal litigation procedures). Work by Gibson (1979) on criminal trial courts emphasized that the role of judges in adhering to or breaking precedent shapes decisions in sentencing. Institutional constraints (e.g., precedent, local legal culture) at lower court levels are probably much more pronounced than on the highest court in the land, where rulings on policy matters are much more common. Additionally, the judge-centered research tends to ignore the administrative functions of trial courts as organizations delivering justice. Wearing the hat of court administrator, a judge may indeed make decisions or rulings for the purpose of caseload management (see Blumberg, 1967). Additionally, work on plea bargaining found evidence that other actors in the process have extremely powerful positions, especially the prosecutor (e.g., Cole, 1970; Carter, 1974). These concerns led scholars to study trial courts as organizations with judges as one of several actors in a complex administrative process (e.g., Blumberg, 1967; Levin, 1977; Eisenstein and Jacob, 1977; Nardulli, Eisenstein, and Flemming, 1988).

The role of judges in civil court systems has been explored much less than in criminal courts. For the most part, this has been driven by the difficulty in obtaining measures of civil justice outcomes. Judges are involved in a very small percentage of cases, and in these, juries often decide the outcomes at trial (unlike criminal sentencing). One could analyze the outcomes of bench trials, but they are less common in civil cases (with the exception of domestic cases).[8]

Additionally, most cases settle prior to trial, so an analysis of judicial decisions only gets at a relatively small portion of the civil justice caseload. Judges' influence on settlements is also difficult to determine because most outcomes are "sealed" and known only to litigants and attorneys. However, examination of the early procedures of justice may account for how a case is disposed (see Dunn et. al., 1996). According to Kritzer (1990), a judge's ruling on motions often sets the stage for whether a case remains in the justice system or not. At the most extreme level, a judge who grants a motion for summary judgment disposes of issues in a case if not the entire case itself when the evidence is shown not to support a claim. Additionally, judges have the power to reduce jury verdicts or even overrule a jury in a "judgment notwithstanding the verdict." Even if judges are not central figures in the civil arena, their rulings and management of caseloads merit attention.

Since the majority of civil and criminal cases settle, attorneys have been the focus of research. Their work in large and small settings (Heinz and Laumann, 1982 ; Landon, 1990), and their role as "actors" in case processes (e.g., Mnookin and Kornhauser, 1979; Ross, 1982) has been examined.

Of this work, the most comprehensive on civil justice actors and institutions is Kritzer's (1990, 1991) study of lawyers in ordinary litigation. Relying on data collected in the Civil Litigation Research Project, Kritzer (1990) looked at the characteristics and work of attorneys, and probed the outcomes of litigation. Here he argued that much of the work of attorneys is broker-like rather than professional. Attorneys, then, can be viewed as intermediaries who, for a fee, aid in transferring money, property, or other arrangements between parties.

Kritzer (1990: 76) also provided preliminary evidence of the "repeat player" characterization. Plaintiff attorneys, in particular, responded that they expected future relationships with opposing attorneys (often those who represent insurance companies). In civil cases other than torts and in the case of defendant attorneys, expectations of future relationships with other attorneys were less pronounced. However, a substantial minority of respondents did affirm that relationships with opposing attorneys were likely. Kritzer (1990: 71-72) even went so far as to say that "routine players" may be a better description of some attorneys who work within the system on a regular basis (e.g., insurance attorneys).

Interestingly, Kritzer (1990) found that while attorneys did not have personal, working relationships with judges, they did expect future dealings with them. This is not surprising considering that there are normally few judges per attorney in most jurisdictions. What is surprising is that Kritzer found that even though very few cases are heard by a judge at trial (7%), a much higher percentage of cases are directly affected by judges. Twenty-nine percent of the cases analyzed showed direct judge involvement when dismissals, summary judgments, and rulings on motions were included as adjudicatory functions (75). Therefore, even though most cases are settled privately, judges are still heavily involved in the civil system, and the behavior of attorneys may reflect the influence of judges.[9] For instance, attorneys may be aware of how judges respond to particular motions and may choose to file or not file as a tool to aid in the game of settlement.

In a related study, Let's Make a Deal, Kritzer (1991) presents a portrait of how ordinary civil cases are negotiated and argues that settlements can be understood with reference to game theory, economics, and negotiation. Again, lawyers are viewed as "insiders" who interact with other actors in the process. Negotiation skills and professional knowledge are, then, what clients purchase when they engage a civil attorney.

Kritzer also found that attorneys are more apt to act as brokers when they work as "repeat players" for organizations. Attorneys are less likely to serve as brokers and apt to act as professionals for individual plaintiffs who are "one-shotters." Here lawyers operate more autonomously and provide instructions to clients, generally on a contingency fee basis. In each situation, the calculus is rational. When working for an organization which is apt to be a repeat player, an attorney works to maximize client interests and is paid by the hour. When working for an individual, "one-shot" client, an attorney is more apt to provide instruction and act autonomously in order to maximize either a settlement or trial verdict. In each of these cases, outcomes are based on the attorneys' perception of the "stakes" of a case. Settlements will likely occur when the negotiation leads to a figure within the range of "stakes" of both parties.

One very important hypothesis generated by Kritzer (1990, 1991) is that case settlement is driven by bargaining that may be outside Mnookin and Kornhauser's (1979) "shadow of the law." Attorneys may understand the stakes in the case, but can rarely predict what a jury will award. Settlement often occurs because of this unpredictability and the costs of taking a case to trial (e.g., costs of discovery, court time, etc.). Justice may be perceived as "routine" in that attorneys find it more profitable to settle a large number of cases quickly for lower fees or awards than the risk of taking a large dollar case to trial.

More recent work by Kritzer and Pickerill (1996) examines the role of contingent fee lawyers in civil justice systems. The authors view contingent fee lawyers as "gatekeepers" to the system through their use of case screening. In an examination of the process and results of the case screening process, they found that lawyers screen out more cases than they accept (19). The largest factor in this decision is economic self-interest, where lawyers take cases that "will yield fees at least equal to what they could earn from either non hourly fee cases or from other contingent fee cases" (19). In this respect, contingent fee attorneys can be viewed as controlling access to courts for clients, and for those clients accepted, they often act as "risk managers" (see also Kritzer, 1996).

Contingent fee attorneys as "repeat players" accept the costs of the system as a "risk" (like a portfolio manager) for clients who are most often "one shotters." In this way, the disadvantages of "one shot" clients (e.g., financing the costs of litigation) are mitigated by the contingent fee attorneys (1996: 86).

Individual studies of trial court actors are numerous and often focus on the roles, behavior, and decisions of judges. The studies mentioned above do not constitute the only studies on individual actors in trial court system, but highlight approaches and important findings. It should be emphasized that much less work has been performed on civil court actors, although Kritzer and colleagues do enlighten us on the importance and roles of attorneys in that system. However, studies that highlight the relationships of actors to the institutions of the system have yet to be performed. A system-wide study might provide more knowledge on how actors in the system interact, behave, and what institutions matter the most.

The potential impact of ADR on civil court systems could be important when considering the evidence presented by Kritzer. How does ADR affect the work of lawyers? Do attorneys find benefits in using ADR? Does ADR form workgroups or provide formal structure to the civil justice system? The implications of answers to these questions might transform how scholars have viewed civil justice systems and how ADR affects civil justice.

COURT-CONNECTED ADR

An interesting, institutional court reform movement is court-connected alternative dispute resolution (ADR). The history of ADR in America is often a story of groups who turn to the settlement of disputes in a fashion that is outside the formal authority of law (Aeurbach, 1983). Auerbach, in fact, argues that much of the history of the movement includes the use of mediation and arbitration by early religious communes, immigrant communities, and merchants who feared the authoritarian culture of American law. Mediation, in these formats, served the interests of these groups by emphasizing personal responsibility for the dispute and by keeping disputes private and within the norms of the community. However, the use of ADR was never institutionalized in American culture because of the individual rights orientation of the legal system (Auerbach,

1983). Justice in America, according to Auerbach, could never exist "without law."

Interestingly, though, Auerbach details an important alteration in the movement of ADR beginning in the 1980s. The legal establishment, in conjunction with scholars of ADR, began to emphasize the connection of ADR to the courts more formally. In part, this was out of a need to preserve mediation programs that had been perceived to be failing (i.e., a lack of cases). These ADR programs have been implemented in the federal court systems and the states as a way of achieving greater efficiency in case management (see Schwerin, 1995; Hermann, 1993). Additionally, state justice systems have incorporated ADR as a more appropriate mechanism for solving certain types of cases and problems (e.g., minor civil cases, domestic disputes, and some minor criminal cases). As advocated, minor cases would be taken out of crowded civil court systems, thus freeing judges and other court personnel to focus on more complex cases. Therefore, a process that was viewed traditionally as "alternative" to law became more integrated with the legal system (or even co-opted by it).

Just prior to "annexing" ADR to courts, mediation programs around the country primarily existed in the form of local, volunteer-oriented, neighborhood and community justice centers (see Harrington, 1985; Schwerin, 1995; Merry and Milner, 1993). These programs (still in existence today) process a range of civil and criminal matters through non-judicial forums (Neubauer, 1996). Community justice centers generally receive cases from walk-ins or referral, and focus on the goal of increasing accessibility to justice *outside* of the formal legal system (1996).[10] These programs, then, do not focus on ADR for reducing caseloads, but on improved dispute resolution that is of less cost to disputants, increases accessibility to poor and middle classes, and transforms communities into more peaceful places to live (1996: 54-57).

Neighborhood justice centers and "multi-door" courthouses provide similar mediation centers but are more connected to courts (Neubauer, 1996: 10-57). In addition to walk-in clients, these centers take case referrals from courts or prosecutors and seek to improve the civil justice system by removing minor cases from courts (10-57). According to Neubauer, these procedures "in a sense...convert criminal matters in to civil ones" by processing cases between individuals instead of the state versus the defendant (10-57). Harrington (1985) argues that these centers reflect a return to informal justice procedures that existed in courts before structural changes such as court unification.

Similar to the neighborhood justice center is court-annexed ADR, where cases are formally referred by the court system and mediation is often supported by government funds or case processing fees. The most common ADR programs annexed by courts are mediation and arbitration. At a minimum, mediation is a process in which two disputants (with the aid of third-party intervention) are brought together to craft their own agreement (see Schwerin, 1995). Here, the mediator encourages the disputants to tell their sides of the story. The mediator may hold a private caucus with each of the parties in which possible conflict resolutions are generated. Finally, the parties are brought back together and common ground is discussed with hopes of achieving a mutually satisfying agreement. The process, however, can be more complex than discussed here (see Folberg and Taylor, 1984; Bush and Folger, 1994). Under court-annexed mediation, an agreement does not have to be reached by the parties. The disputants have the option to continue in the traditional justice system if no agreement is reached.

Arbitration differs from mediation in its quasi-court character. Arbitrators conduct hearings in which parties "present arguments, submit exhibits, and cross examine witnesses" (Hanson and Keilitz, 1991: 1). On the basis of the evidence presented and reviewed, an arbitrator then renders a decision for one side or the other.

Mediation has a variety of constituencies and correspondingly varied rationales. For example, Harrington and Merry (1988) argue that there are three different models of mediation with very distinct ideologies: court-affiliated, community-based, and social-service-agency affiliated programs.

Court-affiliated programs emphasize better and more efficient delivery of dispute resolution. Underlying this are assumptions that courts are too slow, that cases are costly to disputants, and that some cases are inappropriate for litigation. Mediation, as an institution, is seen as a way to provide efficiency to the system and is commonly called a forum that better fits the "fuss" (Sander, 1984). Community-based mediation emphasizes empowerment, decentralized judicial decision making, and the potential for societal transformation. Finally, the social service model emphasizes the personal growth and the development of the disputants.

Although one should not discount the possibility that these approaches overlap in the different models, it is important to recognize that an emphasis on a particular conception has consequences. Hermann (1993) argues that dispute processing found in court-annexed programs has led to poorly trained mediators and poorly run mediation. She also argues that an emphasis on efficiency has detracted from the original empowerment values to which mediation advocates subscribed. From her viewpoint, mediation is now a part of the formal justice system that was formerly viewed as insufficient for some types of disputes. Hermann (1993) argues, then, that mediation faces a serious crisis if a balance is not reached between efficiency and the original altruistic properties of mediation.

RESEARCH ON COURT-ANNEXED MEDIATION

There has been a very large body of research on court-connected ADR program types (see National Center for State Courts and State Justice Institute, 1994; MacCoun, Lind, and Tyler, 1992), with numerous evaluations of both programs and effects, particularly of court-ordered arbitration (e.g., Clarke, Donnelly, and Grove, 1991; Hensler, 1992) and elements of ADR (e.g., Ellen, 1995a; Boersema, Craig, Hanson and Keilitz, 1991). Additionally, studies have been performed assessing the impact of particular types of ADR procedures and uses (e.g., Hensler, 1992; McEwen, 1992; Hanson, 1990; Pearson, 1991; Umbreit and Coates, 1993; and McEwen and Maiman, 1984). These are just examples of the diversity of research on ADR in the United States. This review provides a summary of studies relating to court-annexed mediation, the focus of this study.

Ellen (1995a; 1995b) has extended ADR research on court-annexed mediation in her study of the North Carolina civil mediation program. Here she found that the idea of mediation had been co-opted by the bar association for its self-interest (see also Menkel-Meadow, 1991). In North Carolina, most mediators are attorneys, and all participants must be represented by counsel. Non-attorney mediators in the North Carolina system are quite rare and were only introduced into the process in 1994. Even then, Ellen (1995a) notes that the requirements are quite stringent (e.g., bachelors degree, 20 hours of basic training, 5 years experience as a mediator, and additional training on civil procedure).

Ellen (1995b) likens this co-optation to a defensive effort by attorneys and judges to respond to court reforms by producing "incremental, socially innocuous reform" (16). Thus, one might conclude that mediation was established in North Carolina as something of a preservation strategy. Attorneys and judges benefit by producing more work for attorneys (as mediators) and by placing "privatized" justice within the legal establishment.[11] Apart from these potential advantages to attorneys, survey results reported by Ellen (1995a) show that North Carolina attorneys are enthusiastic about the program and mention several benefits. These include reducing the likelihood of trial, speeding up discovery, giving litigants greater control of cases, and encouraging settlement *before* a pending mediated conference (1995a: 4).

Interestingly, a related evaluation of mediation in North Carolina emphasized that the change did not decrease the number of disputes going to trial and did not improve the settlement rate (Clarke, Ellen, and McCormick, 1995). It is ironic that this system, which was directed to efficiency and privatization concerns, now places state authority over case settlement that was originally private (Ellen, 1995b: 16).

It should be noted that evaluative studies of other programs have produced more positive findings (Kobbervig, 1991; McEwen, 1991; Schultz, 1990; and Fix and Harter, 1992). Here, research did find evidence to support the efficiency expectations of state officials. In several jurisdictions, case processing time decreased in mediation cases, court workloads were lower, trial rates were lower, and settlement rates, on the whole, were higher.[12]

EFFECTS OF COURT ANNEXED MEDIATION

Despite the research on mediation and litigation pace and case disposition, a number of questions are still relatively unexplored. First, if mediation does not produce significant changes in settlement rates, does it lead to cases settling earlier? One might argue that the referral of a case to mediation may lead parties to begin talking and to initiate settlements before or early after a failed mediation attempt. Second, what is the organization of mediation within the civil justice process and its effects on system actors? How do these players use (or abuse) the process of mediation for their own ends? How far along in a case's development is mediation likely to be effective in terms of cost reductions and case processing efficiency? Finally, does mediation occur with or without the benefits (and expense) of formal discovery? These questions and others could be answered in an in-depth study of the effects of the mediation process on the justice system. Such a study requires that case records before and after the introduction of mediation programs be analyzed to gauge case processing such as delay, court workload, and type of disposition.

The institutionalization of mediation programs in court systems also raises interesting questions about the role of mediation, and how it was adopted and implemented. Some have argued that ADR does not equate with (and should not be equated with) the expectation of efficiency (Hermann, 1993). The expectation of efficiency has the potential to undermine its other benefits (i.e., empowerment of participants, transformational politics, and the opportunity for long-lasting, peaceful agreements). Of particular concern on this point is evaluation research which shows mediation to be inefficient at speeding case processing (e.g., Clarke et al., 1995).

If not efficiency, then what other motives exist for court-annexed mediation? First, they could be viewed as an attempt to place more state authority behind private settlements from community mediation. Similarly, scholars have argued that co-optation of local mediation efforts has occurred as a way to protect the monopoly of legal services held by attorneys (see Ellen, 1995a, 1995b; Menkel-Meadow, 1991).

Whatever the motives of program proponents, what effect has the addition of this institution had on the justice system? Neo-institutional theorists might argue that ADR institutions should produce changes in behavior and outcomes. Indeed, previous research on civil court case processing shows that attorneys and judges engage in strategic behavior by encouraging case settlement (Kritzer, 1990, 1991). When combined with a system of mediation as an alternative forum for disputes, the civil justice system and the behavior of its actors might produce interesting changes in strategic behavior. For example, the expanded use of mediation could lead to less formal adjudicatory activity to the advantage of repeat or routine players. Also, a formalization of case settlement via mediation, as opposed to non-mediated settlements, might provide the structure necessary for court work groups to form. The behavioral changes in response to court-annexed mediation and the effects of these changes constitute the focus of this study.

CONCLUSION

What have we learned from the aforementioned literature review? First, it is obvious that trial court systems are quite complex. Much research has been performed on criminal courts, including their actors, institutions, and how they function as systems. The "first" and "second" generation studies on criminal courts showed that outcomes are linked to differing institutions (social and political factors) inside and outside the courts (sponsoring organizations). Second, courtroom organizations or work groups are made up of actors with both different incentives and mutual interests. The interactions of these actors (judges, prosecutors, defense attorneys) and the constraints placed upon them by their environments help to explain the process and outcomes of criminal courts. So, despite the fact that judges are very important actors in the system, court work groups and institutional constraints provide us with more information on the workings of trial courts than focusing on judges alone.

Finally, these studies have generated hypotheses for a "third" generation of research for criminal courts, one that will eventually rely on larger data sets and provide multivariate, integrated models of judicial behavior and processes at the criminal court level.

The portrait of civil justice is much less clear. To date, there has been no study of civil courts from a "macro" perspective or as systems. Jacob (1991) argued that a "first generation" study of civil courts much like that of Neubauer's on the criminal side would be necessary to understand the complexity of these trial courts. Existing efforts to study civil courts, while piecemeal, do suggest that there are differences between civil and criminal trial courts. Most importantly, civil justice systems seem to lack much of the formal organization and institutionalization of criminal courts. In one sense, it may be difficult to view the "court" as the center of civil justice organization since most cases settle outside of courts. Additionally, there are no formal local "offices" dedicated to civil justice except for that of the judge. Even though many state courts serve as forums of general jurisdiction for both criminal and civil cases, civil system actors seem to have functional workgroups that interact for mutual benefit (as do government prosecutors and public defenders). Law and society scholars, however, have found evidence of important informal "norms" of behavior that aid in the work of court actors and the efficiency of the system (e.g., Mnookin and Kornhauser, 1979; Ross, 1980; and Kritzer, 1990, 1991, and 1996).

Collectively, one conception derived from these works is that civil justice is more privately oriented and more likely to be driven by economic interests. For instance, attorneys can be viewed as rational actors who compete to maximize self-interest (i.e., pursuit of fees and a winning environment for future clients). The importance of informal norms (e.g., case screening, settlement procedures) and "repeat-player" relationships among some attorneys, clients, and judges is also evident. Lawyers, then, can be understood to maximize their self-interest within particular institutional constraints. This conception of civil courts is not unlike those found in criminal court literature, except that the institutions of civil justice are less formally organized.

Kritzer's (1990; 1991) research on attorneys and ordinary civil litigation draws attention to the importance of informal institutions, but also provides evidence of the self-interested motivations of court actors. It may be that the less formally organized nature of civil justice systems merits attention to alternative explanations of the function of these courts. A "macro" focus, including the motivations of other civil actors (beyond lawyers) and the context of justice, then, highlights important differences between the administration of civil and criminal law (Flemming, 1992).

The works noted here also suggest that institutional changes affect the behavior and outcomes of trial courts and their actors. Admittedly, some of the research reported does not seem to support this. Preliminary evidence from the institutional reform of tort reform and court-annexed mediation, for example, suggests that system outcomes did not change to meet the expectations of reformers (e.g., Eaton and Talarico, 1996; Clarke et al., 1995). However, neither study examined how these reforms changed the work of civil justice systems and their actors. It may be that the institutional changes were not effectively designed to assess what changes in norms or behavior of actors might result from the reform. For example, did the implementation of court-annexed mediation in North Carolina reinforce the power of attorneys in the civil justice system by mandating that mediators be practicing attorneys?

By studying civil courts from a system-wide perspective, it is difficult not to include the impact of ADR, particularly where states have formally annexed or connected courts to mediation or arbitration. Studying civil justice systems, then, also provides an opportunity to study alternative dispute resolution. Apart from the general research focusing on civil justice, inquiry on alternative dispute resolution exists, but is limited theoretically. ADR research has focused on types of alternative dispute resolution, underlying justifications, and the ways these programs may be incorporated by state and federal courts. As such, descriptive and explanatory research on ADR has been interdisciplinary and has recently moved toward efforts at program evaluation.

One idea for incorporating the role of ADR with that of civil court systems is to study them together under a single unified framework. As noted earlier, such a study would necessarily focus on three questions. What does civil justice look like as a system? How does ADR function in the general civil justice system? How does an institutional change in civil courts like ADR affect civil justice outcome, system norms, and the behavior of system actors? These questions can be answered by offering a profile of civil justice and by exploring the role of one form of ADR, mediation. These questions are set against a new institutionalist framework, a subject that is considered in the next chapter.

CHAPTER 2
Research Framework and Study Site

In order to study civil trial courts and the impact of court-annexed ADR, it was necessary to review existing knowledge of criminal and civil trial courts and that related to ADR. This review indicated that there has been little theoretical integration of trial court research.[13] Criminal trial courts have been studied separately from the civil variety even when the systems are integrated in a single court of general jurisdiction. While studies on the criminal side have attempted to generate explanatory theories, attention to civil courts has been piecemeal with no similar attention.[14] Finally, even though ADR has been added formally to court systems at all levels, no study has included ADR within a system-wide study of civil or criminal courts (Keilitz, 1994).

In addition to this theoretical vacuum, there are several other reasons for a study of civil justice and ADR. First, no study to date has even offered a picture of the civil justice system as a whole or the way ADR programs interact with the civil justice system (Keilitz, 1994: 31). According to Keilitz and the National Center For State Courts (1994), such a study is needed to "enable courts to better integrate ADR into their case management systems (31).

The results of studies on criminal court systems suggest that a more general examination of civil trial courts would identify institutions and provide behavioral explanations that are missing in studies of only portions of the system. Flemming (1992), for example, suggests that a more "macro" focus on civil courts would highlight differences in types of civil cases and in the structure and dynamics of "communities of negotiators." An exploratory study of this type, then, will help to identify key civil justice actors, institutions, and their relationships. Such a study will also generate specific hypotheses about the decision process and outcomes of trial courts in general.

RESEARCH FRAMEWORK

The research on judicial politics in general, and criminal courts in particular, provides a number of theoretical avenues for exploring and explaining civil court systems. Some explanations of trial court behavior have focused solely on their bureaucratic functions, such as the processing of disputes (Blumberg, 1967; Skolnick, 1967). Other studies have provided individually based frameworks for the analysis of trial courts and their culture. For instance, Gibson's (1979) work suggests that individual attitudes of decision makers (e.g., judges) are tempered by professional roles (e.g., attention to precedent).

Organization theory, as applied by criminal courts scholars, also provides a potentially viable framework for study (e.g., Eisenstein and Jacob, 1977; Nardulli, 1979). Consisting of interactions of individuals and groups, organizations are seen to produce outcomes of mutual interest. Organization theory provides a richer portrait of the functioning and outcomes of courts by giving attention to individuals, groups, and the institutions in which they interact. Gibson (1979), however, argues that organization theory stops short of assessing the individual motivations of actors and instead focuses on shared or mutual benefits.

Jacob (1995, 1996) attempted to reconcile this problem in papers on trial courts as loosely coupled organizations. This conception of trial courts takes into account that some parts of the justice system are formally institutionalized (e.g., district attorney office) while others involve individuals or loosely packed groups (e.g., juries, private attorneys, litigants).

The behavior of actors in the system also may be explained in terms of self-interested motivations (e.g., profit maximization of civil lawyers, see Kritzer and Pickerill, 1996). Axelrod (1984) suggests that individuals or groups may come to "mutual benefits" through the pursuit of self-interested outcomes. An example of this in the civil system might be case settlement negotiations between civil attorneys (see Kritzer, 1990, 1991).

None of these conceptions, however, provides a sufficient framework for the study of civil justice systems. In a sense, all of the conceptions have merit and tell us something about how trial courts work. However, an integrated theory is still needed to at least explore civil trial courts by incorporating the best of each of these perspectives. One recent approach that blends an organizational approach with the decisions and actions of individual actors is new institutionalism (March and Olsen, 1984, 1989; Smith, 1988, 1989).

NEW INSTITUTIONAL PERSPECTIVES

The new institutionalism focuses on the interrelationship of institutional structure (e.g., organization, rules, and norms) and the behavior and decisions of individual actors. The phrase "new institutionalism" was coined in a landmark article by March and Olsen in 1984. They suggested that, in contemporary theories of political science, institutions (i.e., legislatures, the legal system, etc.) had "receded in importance" and that under the study of behavior, "social institutions ha[d] come to be portrayed simply as arenas within which political behavior...occurs" (1984: 734). Previous study of institutions as structural or functional determinants of political behavior gave way to theoretical conceptions of individualism (i.e., rational choice) and pluralism. While not denying the importance of the "social context of politics and the motives of individual actors," March and Olsen's (1984) new institutionalism insisted on a "more autonomous role for political institutions" that is more than just a mirror of societal forces (738-739). Institutions, then, are viewed as both coherent, autonomous, and as "political actors in their own right" (738).

The new institutionalism requires that scholars focus not only on the social and economic conditions that affect democracy, but also on the design of institutions. In this regard, March and Olsen (1984) identify three factors that drive poltical outcomes: (1) the distribution of preferences among political actors; (2) the distribution of resources; and (3) the constraints imposed by the rules of the game (739). Each of these, according to March and Olsen, can be considered as exogenous to the political process by modern political theorists:

> That is, preferences are developed within a society and transmitted through socialization, resources are distributed among political actors by some broad social processes, and rules of the game are either stable or change by a revolutionary intervention exogenous to ordinary political activities (739).

However, the new institutionalism as a theory proposes that each of the three functions of the political process are more endogenous. For example, as to preferences:

> The new institutionalism...argues that preferences and meanings develop in politics, as in the rest of life, through a combination of education, indoctrination, and experience (739).

Therefore, the distribution of preferences, resources, and the constraints imposed by the rules of the game are all viewed as developing within the context of political institutions.

Following March and Olsen, Rogers Smith argued that this new institutionalism should become the future of the study of public law (Gillman, 1997). According to Smith:

> institutions are expected to shape the interests, resources, and ultimately the conduct of political actors, such as judges, ... The actions of such persons are in turn expected to reshape those institutions more or less extensively. Ideally, then, a full account of an important political event would consider both the ways the context of background institutions influenced the political actions in question, and the ways in which those actions altered relevant contextual structures or institutions (1988: 91).[15]

Just how institutions affect political behavior and outcomes in the judicial arena is, however, in debate. Among law and courts scholars, (see Epstein and Knight, 1997; Gillman, 1997) the new institutionalism is based on the two traditions mentioned by Smith (1988), rational or public choice and neo-marxist approaches (91).

The rational/public choice approach views legal and political institutions as products of self-interested behavior where these decisions are constrained by existing institutions (see Buchanan and Tullock, 1962; Epstein and Knight, 1997; Shepsle, 1989). This variation of new institutionalism calls attention to the strategic choices of individuals who exist within an institutional framework. In a rational choice perspective, institutions as Knight (1992) reminds us, can be:

> viewed as a structure of formal or informal rules that shape the strategic calculations of actors who are self-consciously pursuing

a set of presumably fixed, exogenously determined, short term preferences (Knight, 1992; see Gillman, 1997: 7).

In this context, institutional settings provide for bargaining and are "parameters of choice" (Ethington and McDonagh, 1995: 89; see Gillman, 1997). Thus, according to Shepsle (1989), rational actors settle for the highest preference level possible given the constraints of the rules. In this perspective, then, the choice of institution (i.e., rules or norms) can also be viewed as an exercise in preference maximization under constraints. Even though judges, as in the attitudinal model, may indeed be voting their policy preferences, they do so within institutional constraints (i.e., precedent; see Epstein and Knight, 1998). Individual choices, then, may be strategic, but actual preferences are tempered by the consideration of these other factors or constraints.

The second variation in new institutionalism is derived from neo-marxist historicists and Parsonian structural functionalists. Advocates here stress the relative autonomy of political and legal organizations, especially as they are products of economic relations or the functional needs of social systems (see Almond, 1960; Easton, 1953).

In more recent years, this approach has evolved from the structural-functionalist notion to more complex conceptions of institutions that do "matter" but that exist as more than just a product of society or of rational, individual action. Those who adhere to this modern conception of institutions refer to themselves as "historical" and "interpretivist" institutionalists (see Gillman, 1997; Skocpol, 1995; Skowronek, 1995).

The difference between the historical/interpretivist camp and the rational choice camp is primarily based on the premise that institutions can "prescribe action, construct motives,and assert legitimacy" (Skowronek, 1995: 94). In other words, by focusing only on the rational interests of individuals within institutions, one loses sight of the fact that institutions have a legitimate function and that actors often fall back into a sense of duty when making policy choices.

In a debate with advocates of rational choice, Gillman (1997: 8) asserts that "mission" has priority over the presence of rules. In this respect, he argues that institutions are organized through the use of ceremonies and rituals that are designed to perpetuate an attachment to the mission of the institution. These provide maintenance and legitimacy to authoritative institutions while related principles are not captured by "being governed or constrained by a rule or procedure" (8). He further asserts that we might lose sight of the genesis, significance, and importance of institutions by focusing only on rules and procedures apart from the mission. Finally, Gillman (1997) argues that the rules that are discernible might be designed to distract from the actual mission that is motivating actors. Therefore, one must try to interpret the state of mind of these participants.

In sum, Gillman (1997) argues that rational choice institutionalists provide a conception of politics that is underinclusive but simultaneously overinclusive. With regard to the latter, he argues that rational behavior can be used to describe any emotion such as love or acting in the interest of the public good (8).

The differences between the competing branches of new institutionalism may be subtler than proponents acknowledge. Indeed, the debate between rational choice and historical/interpretivist institutionalists may be too simple. Scholars have made some strides toward reshaping the importance of institutions beyond the debate above (Grafstein, 1992; Sproule-Jones, 1993). Grafstein (1992) criticizes each of the variations of new institutionalism as under-inclusive, while Sproule-Jones (1993) focuses on the importance of "rules-in-use".

Grafstein (1992) challenges the "conventionalism" of institutional theory and argues for what he calls "institutional realism." Furthermore, he emphasizes that conventional theories (including new institutionalism) do not provide a satisfactory understanding of why institutions matter. In criticizing the existing forms of institutional analysis, then, Grafstein (1992) asserts:

> When social science respects the power of institutions to constrain, it largely ignores their status as human products. When social science emphasizes the role of participants in the creation of institutions, it does so at the expense of institutional constraint. Together these problems reflect the failure of social science to resolve the delicate problems of institutional ontology (7-8).

Instead, Grafstein's (1992) "institutional realism" attempts to create a better understanding of institutions that, in a way, marries the two conceptions. In short, he asserts that institutions are like the rules of a game. They are "ultimately conditions within which--not on which-- actors operate" (1992: 7). Thus, institutions can be considered physical entities in which individuals are embedded. In this perspective, it is not certain that individuals understand their institution and that there is "homogeneity in their beliefs, behavior, and perceived alternatives," as assumed by conventionalists (7). Rather, we should let "actual behavior rather than postulates guide psychological imputations" (7). Sproule-Jones (1993), in his study of the regulation of Canadian water rights, focuses on the institutional "rules of the game" like scholars of the new institutionalism. However, he "stresses...that more than one rule tends to operate in most settings and that rules-in-use are developed by participants in both public and private settings" (Ostrom, 1995: 176; on Sproule-Jones, 1993). Rules-in-use are those that are followed at a particular time and place to structure relationships around a particular policy process. These are distinguished from rules-in-form which might include constitutional arrangements, institutions, or a policy change (e.g., legislation, regulations, etc.). Of importance to this study, Sproule-Jones (1993) argues that in order to assess the outcomes of policy changes, one needs to understand what the rules-in-use are. This, he argues, cannot be done without substantial empirical research on the ground using intensive field research and "not by studying formal legislation and committee reports" (Ostrom, 1995: 176; on Sproule-Jones, 1993). Like Grafstein (1992), then, his work suggests that studying the affects of institutions on individuals is quite complex and that the behavior of actors must be the focus.

From these last two sources, we learn a great deal for the study of ADR as an institutional change. Since individuals are imbedded in institutions and institutions are real, the behavior of individuals may not always be constrained, but might be, in fact, freed by institutions. Conversely, individuals who choose new institutions might be constrained by existing institutions in these choices. This is important in the study of institutional change or reform when one tries to assess whether a new law or program has had any impact as institutional realism gives us reasons why policies and reforms may not always produce their intended effects.

Understanding why and how institutions matter could help us understand why institutional changes do or do not achieve intended goals. Why is this? If institutions are created by humans and if they constrain individuals, then why do policies fail? One might suggest that individuals do not always behave as policy adopters predict or that the rules-in-use differ from the rules-in-form (see Sproule-Jones, 1993). Individuals may not understand the new institution, individuals might prefer the old institutions, or individuals might rationally use the rule changes for their own preferences or objectives.

ADR AS NEO-INSTITUTIONAL CHANGE

A focus on institutions and their effects on political behavior and outcomes can provide an interesting perspective for a study of civil justice and ADR systems. One can easily argue that the civil justice system and its culture constitute a "web" of complex institutional arrangements that fulfill the function of dispute processing while maximizing the opportunity of individual actors to benefit from the process. The traditional conception of ADR as a non-adversarial mechanism for dispute resolution also lends itself to institutional interpretation. Because new institutionalists emphasize the importance of behavior that is endogenous to institutions, the addition of ADR to the civil justice system should, then, alter the system and individual behavior within it. Also, the political choice of adopting ADR provides a potential policy objective.

We can learn a lot about how ADR and the civil justice system are linked, then, by operating from a neo-institutionalist framework. Under new institutionalism, the addition of ADR to civil courts can be viewed against three fundamental propositions that March and Olsen (1984: 739) emphasize: the distribution of preferences, resources, and the constraints of the rules of the game. First, ADR adoption can be viewed as a function of the rational interests of diverse actors in both the ADR movement at large and "elites" within the local legal culture. Here, the preferences of actors in both camps led to ADR as a court reform. For reasons explained later, these "reluctant partners" institutionalized ADR within courts for the rational purpose of keeping the ADR movement "alive" as well as the co-option or control of this movement by legal elites. As March and Olsen (1984) suggest, "leaders interact with other leaders and are co-opted into new beliefs and commitments" (739). In the interaction of ADR and legal elites, ADR was advanced as an efficiency effort and a means of professional enhancement.

Second, it is clear that existing political institutions "affect the distribution of resources, which in turn affects the power of political actors, and thereby affects political institutions" (March and Olsen, 1984: 739). Policy alternatives are shaped, then, by those who hold office or by existing administrative agencies, both of whom provide participation rights, the distribution of power, and access (739). ADR's success or failure as a policy depends on the support of those who most easily wield resources. In this case, then, the legal "elites" who dominate the existing dispute resolution institutions drive the adoption, implementation, and the success of this policy change.

Finally, new institutionalists recognize the importance of the rules of the game on the behavior of actors. Some suggest that individuals act within the rules of the game and that choices are constrained by these rules (Shepsle, 1989). However, scholars also recognize that institutions are adopted or chosen for reasons that can emerge from rational self-interest (see Shepsle, 1989; Epstein and Knight, 1997) or as a sense of fulfilling the societal mission or duty of the organization (see Gillman, 1997). In each conception, however, institutional change provides new constraints to some actors and a mechanism (or freedom) of new choices to others (see Grafstein, 1992). With this in mind, I propose that the adoption of ADR in civil courts was a product of the self-interest of policy advocates from both the ADR movement and the legal system. In each case, however, the adoption of this new institutional process provided new opportunities for court actors and constrained the decisions of some clients or consumers of litigation.

THE IMPACT OF ADR ON CIVIL COURTS

In addition to understanding how ADR and civil courts function, I am also interested in the effect of ADR on civil courts as a policy change. Scholars of policy implementation from a "top down" perspective have emphasized that policy change often leads to results that are different from the original goals of the proponents (see Pressman and Wildavsky, 1984). Others do not see policy change as happening from "above", but, rather, from the political behavior of individuals and groups in agencies below. These "bottom-up" scholars suggest that, ultimately, policy change and its implementation occur at the local level through the strategic interaction among multiple actors in a policy network (see Mazmanian and Sabatier, 1989). Some (e.g., Stoker, 1991) describe policy implementation in a similar manner but focus on the rational interests of policy actors. Stoker (1991) discusses how policy is often implemented by the cooperation of "reluctant partners."

Indeed, a number of policy evaluations reviewed in the previous chapter suggested that court-connected ADR has not lived up to the efficiency goals of legal reformers. "Top down" scholars might argue that this is yet another example of failed policy, while "bottom up" scholars would argue that we need to look deeper and consider the implementation problems that those at the top did not foresee. Whatever the vantage point, new institutionalism and that of Grafstein's (1992) institutional realism imply that changes in institutions do lead to changes in both the behavior of actors and policy outcomes.

One change suggested by March and Olsen (1995) concerns "changes in the environment [that] produce dislocations in the political system which are translated into new political coalitions, institutions, and policies" (42). Complaints from the legal establishment about the litigation crisis combined with the social change movement advanced by ADR advocates produced a "legal discourse" on the use of ADR within civil courts. The new political coalition predicted by March and Olsen is, then, what Harrington and Merry (1988) refer to as the court-affiliated ideology of ADR which fostered a political coalition of unlikely bedfellows. These "bedfellows" produced an institutional change by adopting ADR as a formal policy change to civil courts.

In addition to new institutional perspectives, principal-agent theory may help us understand the relationship between ADR and the more general civil justice system. Principal-agent theory is based on an economic understanding of market activity of firms (see Alchian and Demsetz, 1972) and has been applied to the hierarchical control of other organizations (Moe, 1984; see Songer, Segal, and Cameron, 1994: 674). This theory is based on the principle that individuals who are "agents" will not always obey or act in the interests of a "principal" who has power over them, largely because economic theory suggests that acting in the interest of another may contradict economic self-interest (1994: 674).

As Songer, Segal, and Cover (1994) suggest in their application of this theory, agents have discretion to act in their own interest when there is "difficulty in monitoring the actions of subordinates, asymmetric information in the form of expertise, or transactions costs in overturning the actions of subordinates" (674). Under some organizational structures, there may be great congruence between the wishes of principals and the actions of agents (674). However, in other structures or settings there may be considerable room for discretionary actions or "shirking" but still be great responsiveness "to changes in the desires of principals" (674).

Principal-agent theory, then, might provide an explanation for why policies that are implemented from the "top" do not necessarily fulfill the goals of the principal reformers. As a final proposition, then, ADR may not fulfill the efficiency goals of reformers because of the "loosely coupled" nature of civil courts. Indeed, the loose structure or organization of trial courts might make local rules and norms more important than policy directives from above. Therefore, local actors may "shirk" the widespread use of ADR while using it enough to be responsive to the interests of principals. Alternatively, though, what if the principals have great control over the implementation of the program (i.e., a "bottom up" design)? If the program still falls short of the intended policy goals, then one might suggest that other rational interests might be at stake for policy actors who implement the program and who signal interests to "agents."

In order to shed light on the above propositions, I offer (1) a profile of civil justice in a single jurisdiction and (2) explore the role of mediation in this civil justice system. In each case, I explore the existing institutions of civil justice and provide an analysis of institutional change brought about by mediation. In this analysis of institutional change, I do not set out to adopt any specific variation of the new institutionalism but will attempt to reconcile which of these theoretical approaches best applies to the reform in Mountain County. I also intend to make use of the principal-agent model (along with the new institutionalism) in evaluating the impact of ADR in the same jurisdiction. Furthermore, the exploratory and triangular nature of this work follows suggestions by Sproule-Jones (1993) about the importance of studying rules-in-use in assessing policy change.

RESEARCH SITE

This research explores the institutional structure and process of civil courts and provides a preliminary test of new institutionalism propositions related to ADR (see Smith, 1989; Gates, 1991). As a method of inquiry and exploration, a triangular research strategy is employed using both qualitative and quantitative data collection. These techniques are applied to a single Georgia county court system, re-named Mountain County for anonymity. Mountain County (pop. 95,000) includes the city of Mountainville (pop. 18,000) and is a medium-sized jurisdiction. The county has considerable industry and serves as a finance center for the northeastern region of Georgia. The county population is quite diverse racially and economically, with African-Americans, Latinos, and whites from both Mountainville and the outer mountain areas of the county. Mountain County also serves as an outer suburban area for the city of Atlanta, with a number of upper-middle-class developments on near-by

Lake Lanier. As such, the county can be viewed as growing in population and economy.

Mountain County is an appropriate study site because its 1992 implementation of court-annexed mediation (upon recommendation of the Georgia Supreme Court) allows for evaluation. The Ninth District Mediation Program serving Mountain County (and fifteen others)[16] is one of the most established court-annexed programs in the state of Georgia and is applied to a diverse caseload, including family disputes, general civil cases (e.g., torts and contracts), and minor criminal cases referred by the county solicitor's office. Focusing on a single county court system provides the opportunity to explore the institutions and behavior of court actors in some depth.[17] As a "first generation" study of civil trial courts and mediation, a single jurisdiction is appropriate for both exploration and the generation of hypotheses. Additionally, since the mediation program has been in existence since 1992, its effects on the system (e.g., caseloads) can be studied before and after the policy implementation.

BACKGROUND: ADR IN GEORGIA

In 1983, a new Georgia state constitution took effect and a provision mandated that the state judicial branch provide speedy, efficient, and inexpensive resolution of dispute and prosecutions. This was drafted in response to mounting evidence of a litigation crisis in the state. The total caseload in 1991 "in the Superior courts exceeded 300,000 cases, over 2000 cases per judge" (Supreme Court of Georgia, 1993). Since 1987, the caseload increased 30% in total civil filings of which domestic filings increased 40%, criminal findings 35%, and felony cases 55%.

With the evidence of a litigation crisis looming over the Georgia courts, the Georgia Supreme Court in September 1990 established the Joint Commission on Alternative Dispute Resolution. This commission studied the feasibility of implementing a system of court-annexed or court-referred ADR (Supreme Court of Georgia, 1993: 1). The Joint Commission on ADR gathered information and set up pilot mediation programs in the state. These efforts eventually led to the promulgation of rules by the Supreme Court of Georgia that established a statewide plan for the use of ADR systems.

The state plan for the implementation of ADR consists of the establishment of the Georgia Commission on Dispute Resolution as the central authority over the statewide program. The commission is charged with the following duties: developing guidelines for the certification of

Research Framework & Study Site

ADR programs; certification of local court programs; and developing criteria for training, qualifications, and conduct of mediators (Supreme Court of Georgia, 1993: 5-6). The plan also established the Georgia Office of Dispute Resolution that serves the Commission by implementing the guidelines and certifying mediators. The office also collects data on mediation programs throughout the state.

In general, the plan encourages every court in Georgia to adopt an ADR program and submit it to the Commission for approval. It should be noted that the plan does not mandate any particular form of mediation, but rather gives courts the discretion to create a program that fits the specific needs of the community. The program need only meet the general guidelines set forth by the Supreme Court's rules of ADR.

General guidelines for approval of a local program include specific rules related to referral of cases to ADR; exemptions of litigants from ADR; appearance at an ADR conference or hearing; qualifications and training for mediators; confidentiality and immunity for process participants; communications between mediators, the program, and the court; enforceability of agreements; selection of mediators by the court; and collection of data necessary for evaluation of the program (Supreme Court of Georgia, 1993: Appendix A). These guidelines (generally stated here) were designed to promote eventual uniformity of rules in the programs developing around the state.

Funding for the state programs comes from a filing fee surcharge on cases and by fees on certification and recertification of mediators (Supreme Court of Georgia, 1993: 8). These fees fund the work of the Commission and operation of the local ADR programs. Permanent funding for these programs was authorized through the 1993 ADR legislation, which includes a filing fee of $5.00 per case.

ADR IN MOUNTAIN COUNTY, GEORGIA

Mountain County, Georgia is served by the Office of Dispute Resolution for the Ninth Judicial Administrative District, consisting of fifteen counties in northeast Georgia. The Ninth Judicial Administrative District Mediation program has the purpose of finding "a mutually acceptable resolution of the dispute through cooperative attempts to solve the problem which presently separates them" (Ninth Judicial Administrative District, 1993b). The program allows for a less contentious alternative for solving disputes than the formal, adversarial legal system of negotiation and litigation. Proponents of the program argue that when cases are settled through mediation, the costs to the court system decrease, especially in terms of caseload.

The mediation program in the Ninth District is a system of court referral that includes the 15 counties of Cherokee, Dawson, Gwinnett, "Mountain", Forsyth, Pickens, Gilmer, Fannin, White, Lumpkin, Townes, Union, Stephens, Rabun, and Habersham. Cases are initially filed in the superior, state, magistrate, and probate courts of these counties and are then screened and referred to mediation by the presiding judge. The referrals are made on a case-by-case basis, and the discretion to refer is left with the judge.

The Ninth District Mediation Program processes disputes referred by judges in primarily State and Superior courts in a variety of case types (domestic, general civil, misdemeanor criminal). Generally, judges refer cases to mediation at pre-trial hearings. These cases are then sent to the Office of Dispute Resolution where a mediator (or neutral) is assigned by the program director. In the Ninth District program, the neutral assigned can be an attorney or non-attorney, but both must have at least 20 hours of training to do general civil cases. Additional training is required to mediate family law disputes. If an agreement is reached in mediation, the case is sent back to the civil system for final disposition. If an agreement is not reached, cases go back into the court system and continue through the regular process.

DATA AND GENERAL METHODS

The quantitative portion of the research is based on two data sources: (1) a probabilistic sample of cases filed in Mountain County civil courts from 1989 to 1995--three years before and after the implementation of ADR and (2) the population of civil cases filed in Mountain County that were referred to mediation from 1992 to 1995. For the general civil sample, a random, systematic, sample of 200 cases per year was drawn from 1989 to 1995 and included both domestic and general civil cases. The yearly sample was stratified by court type by drawing 100 cases randomly from state and Superior courts.[18] This procedure yielded a dataset of 1,400 general civil cases.

Additionally, I examined all mediated cases (civil and domestic) filed since the program's beginning in 1992. The mediated cases analyzed included those that were referred to the program through the ending date

Research Framework & Study Site

of 1995.[19] This design of research is, then, non-experimental and raises external validity questions that are associated with non-random selection. However, in this study, mediated cases were examined primarily to describe the types of cases that are selected by judges for the program. Mediated cases were identified from the records of mediation referrals accessed at the Ninth District Mediation Office in Mountainville, Georgia. Mediated case files did not include the information found in a general civil case file. Therefore, these cases were tracked back through the system by examining the full case file at the Court Clerk's office. In the time period above, I was able to identify 627 mediated cases for analysis.

In each of the mediated and general civil cases, I coded case type, system actors (i.e., attorneys, judges, and litigants), procedures (i.e., motions and pre-trial hearings), and outcomes (i.e., disposition type, who wins/loses, and damages).[20] In addition, more specific information particular to the mediation process was drawn from cases referred to mediation (i.e., date of mediation; attorneys in mediation).[21]

The quantitative phase of the project yielded a number of important variables for analysis. In particular, potential dependent variables include case outcome (i.e., who wins/loses at trial/mediation), case disposition (i.e., settled, mediated, trial), and case processing time. Important independent variables include type of litigant (i.e., organization or individual), case participants (i.e., repeat player or not), case type (i.e., tort, contract, asset forfeiture), type of court (i.e., state or superior), and mediated or not.

The qualitative portion of the study consisted of elite interviews with eighteen court actors and direct observation of mediation (see Appendix B for a sample interview protocol). Interview subjects were identified from the quantitative portion of the research. Names of individuals (repeat and some non-repeat players) who work in the system were drawn from case files and included judges (4), non-mediator attorneys (5), mediator attorneys (4), non-attorney mediators (4), and court administrative personnel (3) (e.g., mediation coordinator, court clerk, and the Ninth District Court Administrator). Some subjects were identified by asking previously interviewed court actors who else should be interviewed. Interviews with system elites were designed to assess their work, the civil justice system, their role in that system, and their assessment of ADR.[22] The interviews were open-ended, taped, and approximately one hour in length.

The interview phase of the research also drew on the criminal court literature to make comparisons with civil justice. As such, interviews provided answers to the following questions: how do civil justice and mediation work? Are there civil court work groups? If so, can they be characterized as consensual or conflictual? Are there existing local norms in the civil justice system, and have they changed over time? Did institutional change affect workgroups and norms?

In this study, civil cases are compared before and after the 1992 implementation of the ADR program. Additionally, the coding of mediated cases allows for a comparison of mediated and non-mediated cases. Finally, interviews with key players in the Mountain County system and mediation program will provide important qualitative data on civil justice, mediation, and the impact of mediation as an institutional change.[23]

Since this book employs quantitative and qualitative data, there will be a variety of methods of analyses employed. I will discuss these methods more specifically in the following chapters. In general, I discuss the quantitative results in the form of descriptive statistics in Chapter Three and Four; difference of means and time series are reported in Chapter Five; and qualitative results are in Chapter Six.

Chapters Three and Four provide an overview of what civil justice looks like in Mountain County. A description of the civil system and the process of mediation are presented using descriptive statistics drawn from general civil and mediated cases. For each of the mediated and non-mediated cases, the actors, case types, procedures, and disposition rates are also reported.

Chapter Five continues the exploration of civil justice and mediation by examining caseloads, disposition, and pace of litigation over time. A preliminary test of the effect of mediation on civil justice is explored in a time series analysis and through difference of means comparison before and after mediation.

In Chapter Six, in-depth interviews with court actors and mediators are reported in order to provide qualitative evidence. Here, attention is directed to the opinions of judges, attorneys, court staff and mediators (with and without law backgrounds) and how they view both civil justice and mediation.

Finally, in Chapter Seven, the question of how an institutional change affects an existing political system is revisited by summarizing the results of this study. Has mediation provided more organizational structure to loosely coupled civil courts? What happened when a new process was added to an existing "web" of institutions? How did actors adapt or change with respect to the change? How did the institutional change affect court processing and/or outcomes?

CHAPTER 3
Civil Justice in Mountain County

To study the effect of court-annexed mediation on civil courts, one must first provide a profile or "snapshot" of that system. Since little empirical work exists on civil courts, much of what we know about them is dispersed among specific studies on the work of civil court actors, civil litigation trends, and studies of specific litigation types. Few, however, offer a comprehensive profile of court functions, case procedures, and outcomes.

In particular, trends of case filing, civil procedure, and case disposal can help to gain an understanding of the administration of justice. For example, filing trends have been explored in other studies as a means of determining if a litigation "crisis" exists (see Eaton and Talarico, 1996). An analysis of similar trends in this study provides a mechanism to explore how civil justice works and what effects current reforms may have had. Mediation, remember, is often advanced as a way to ease caseload pressure and improve workload patterns for courts.

This chapter consists of a profile of 1400 civil cases filed in Mountain County, Georgia. As noted earlier, this data set consists of samples of 200 cases per year (100 Superior court; 100 State court) from 1989 to 1995. For each set of cases, data will be presented on caseloads (i.e., number of case filings per year and case types), civil court actors (i.e., litigants, judges, attorneys), and case procedures and outcomes (i.e., number of procedural actions, case disposition time, and disposition type). Remedies of cases are described to the extent that related data were available, along with any appellate actions taken on these cases. This profile sets the stage for the profile and analyses of the effect of mediation on civil court systems, topics of later chapters.

Mountain County, Georgia is located in the northeastern portion of the state and is to Atlanta. Because of its close proximity to Atlanta, Mountain County and its county seat have undergone significant growth and population changes. As of 1995, the county had a population of about 95,000.

The Mountain County civil court system is divided (like other state courts in Georgia) into Georgia State courts and Georgia Superior courts. Each of these has the distinction of being a trial court of general jurisdiction with one difference, domestic cases can only be filed in Superior courts. All other civil case types may be filed in either State or Superior courts with the potential for "forum shopping" by attorneys. Additionally, cases can be referred to mediation from either branch of the court system. An examination of caseloads provides a portrait of the civil work of the court system and includes case filing trends and types of cases filed in each court.

FILING TRENDS

Overall, civil case filing trends in Mountain County steadily increased from 1989 to 1995 in both Superior and State courts (see Table 3-1). From 1989 to 1995, Superior court case filings increased from 2417 to 2807 while State court cases increased dramatically from 546 to 1325. However, when examined over time and between years, the overall increase is not so prominent. In fact, in some years caseloads actually decreased (Superior court in 1991, 1994, 1995; State court in 1993).

While some have argued that civil litigation rates have increased at alarming rates throughout the country (see Olson, 1991), the data from Mountain County do not seem to provide evidence for this conclusion. There are increases, to be sure, but decreases as well![24] When one considers that Mountain County is growing in terms of both population and economy because of the expansion of the Atlanta metropolitan area, the findings seem less like a "crisis." This suggests that Galanter (1983, 1986) was right when he argued that caseload increases may be explained by population growth rather than people suing at alarming rates.

What do civil court filings look like in Mountain County's State and Superior courts? In the combined caseloads of State and Superior courts, it is clear that contract/commercial disputes (47.5%) and domestic cases (32.9%) dominate civil business in Mountain County (see Table 3-2). Throughout the ten-year period, torts constituted only about 10% of the

Civil Justice in Mountain County

overall civil caseload, with a smaller percentage of real property cases (5.9%) and those related to government benefits (1.6%). These results mirror other studies (DeFrances et al., 1995; Eaton and Talarico, 1996; Smith et al., 1995).

Differences in caseloads emerge when filings are divided by type of court (see Table 3-2). Some of the differences are clearly institutional, as domestic cases dominate civil litigation in Superior court (65%), followed by contract/commercial (12%), real property (9.2%), and torts (8.5%).

State court caseloads in 1989-1995 indicate that the vast majority of cases are contract/commercial (84%). These include the bulk of debt collection and wage garnishment cases. The remaining cases include torts (11.6%) and some property actions (2.4%). Only four domestic cases were filed in State courts over the seven-year period.

Initial observations, then, confirm that domestic cases are, by rule, filed in Superior court and that debt collection cases, by routine, are filed in State court (Table 3-3). Also, a slightly higher percentage of tort cases was filed in State court. This may be a function of forum shopping, type of case, or dollar limits.

What changes have occurred in these Mountain County case filings over time? In aggregate, both contract and domestic case filings seem to have increased over time (Table 3-3). Tort, real property, and government benefits cases fluctuated, but generally decreased over the time period. In Superior court, case filing fluctuated, with increases overall in domestic and contract cases (Table 3-4) and wild fluctuations in tort and contract filings. In State court, contracts increased from 1989-1995 while real property, government benefits, and domestic cases dropped steadily over time (Table 3-5).

In State court, tort filing patterns were quite interesting. Filing rates remained fairly consistent (above 10%) with the exception of slight dips in 1991 and 1992 (7.3% and 9% respectively). As noted earlier, a higher number and percentage of cases were filed in State court rather than Superior. When tort filings in Superior court are low, tort filings in State court are quite high (e.g., 1993: 3% Superior; 13.3% State), suggesting some variation of "forum shopping." The reverse pattern, however, is not as dramatic. When tort filings are low in State court, Superior tort filings are only slightly higher (e.g., 1991: 7.3% State; 8.9% Superior).

Case filing trend patterns in Mountain County are largely explained by institutional features of the court system. Domestic cases are almost exclusively filed in Superior court by rule. Although no formal rule exists, State courts are dominated by contract/commercial cases and focus on debt collection and wage garnishment. This results in an equitable share of case workload between the two courts.

Table 3-6 presents data on civil case filings within sub-categories for a more refined profile of filing rates. Among tort cases, the overwhelming majority of case filings are auto accident cases (62.1% total). As suggested earlier, more auto tort cases are filed in State court (67.4%) than in Superior court (54.7%). It may be, then, that State court handles more routine torts than Superior court. Note, however, that a larger percentage of medical malpractice cases are filed in Superior court along with other professional malpractice claims, combination cases, and other cases (e.g., fraud, dog bite). Interestingly, a higher percentage of product liability and premise liability cases were filed in State court.

In the category of contract/commercial cases, a large majority of cases consisted of debt collection that involved overdue accounts (58.1% total). In the second largest category, wage garnishments make up another 35% of contract/commercial cases. The remaining cases constitute less than 10% of the total contract/commercial cases and consist of contract fraud, poor workmanship, unspecified breaches of contract, and others. Overall, both debt collection and wage garnishment cases were filed in State court more often than Superior court, with the higher stakes cases (i.e., contract breaches, poor workmanship, and commercial fraud) filed in Superior.

Real property cases varied widely in filing patterns, but constituted a very small percentage of the overall civil caseload. The largest category (33.3%) featured combinations or other property cases (i.e., injunctions, declaratory actions, and various types of takings, evictions, and repossessions). A large portion of real property cases were drug asset forfeiture cases (22%) followed by repossessions (20%) and takings (12.3% govt.; 10% utility). A much smaller percentage focused on zoning or eviction cases (less than 2% overall). When examined by court type, there are important differences. Most real property cases are filed in Superior court. All asset forfeiture, zoning, and most taking cases were also filed in Superior court. In State court, the overwhelming majority of cases were repossessions, combinations, and evictions. Real property cases in State and Superior courts were small in number, however, so the findings here may not illustrate consequential court variation.

Among domestic cases, most are "deadbeat daddy" or child support contempt cases (48.7% total). Divorces constitute 37% of all domestic cases. "Support" cases are filed by the primary care giver with some by the local District Attorney on behalf of welfare recipients. A number of others involved URESA cases, which target out-of-state parents in arrears on support payments. While not indicated in Table 3-6, most divorce cases are routine and uncontested. The remaining domestic cases focus on divorce decree modifications for child support, visitation, or alimony (about 4%); custody modification (2%); and family violence act, combinations, or other domestic types (all less than 5% each). Since domestic case filings are almost always filed in Superior court, only 5 cases in the sample of State court filings were domestic (mainly child support contempt garnishments).

A final case category centered on government benefit and business regulation cases. Only 23 government benefit and no business regulation cases were identified in the sample of general civil cases. Of the former, almost all were filed in Superior court and dealt with welfare fraud cases (e.g., food stamp fraud). There were only two cases (8.7%) of workers compensation claims, litigation generally filed in federal district courts.

When examining the general civil caseload within sub-categories, we find that most tort cases are routine auto cases and that product liability and malpractice cases are generally rare. These data support suggestions by recent studies that tort reforms may be poorly aimed at a relatively small number of cases (see Eaton and Talarico, 1996; Eisenberg and Henderson, 1992). Additionally, we find that State court seems to process the more routine torts (i.e., auto), contract/commercial (i.e., debt collection and garnishments), and real property (i.e., repossessions). However, Superior court has its share of routine cases with respect to the domestic filing rule. Again, differences in case filing trends seem to reflect institutional factors.

LITIGANTS

As presented in Tables 3-7 and 3-8, the litigants in the Mountain County civil system look much like those in other civil settings. The prevailing civil case involves a single plaintiff versus a single defendant (see Table 3-7). Almost 75% of cases involved one plaintiff and about 65% a single defendant. A modest number of cases included two plaintiffs (17.3%) or defendants (26%). Cases with three or more litigants on either side were rare (less than 10% in each category). These results support the conclusion that general civil litigation is fairly simple with respect to participation of litigants. It is possible that this is also a function of the location of Mountain County.

"Litigant type" is also relatively unsurprising. Table 3-8 breaks down litigant type for plaintiff and defendant for the first four litigants listed in a case. For the most part, individual plaintiffs are suing individual defendants. The first listed plaintiff was most often an individual (33.3%), followed by government agencies (20.7%), bank or financial institutions (16.4%), hospital/medical (13.8%), other business (12.9%), and insurance (2.8%). The second, third, and fourth plaintiffs listed in cases were overwhelmingly individuals (over 85%). The large number of government plaintiffs is a function of the domestic suits filed by the Georgia Department of Human Resources on behalf of welfare recipients. In these case types, state government is an important "repeat player," one with possible advantages over individual defendants.

The first defendant listed is almost always an individual citizen (90.5%) followed distantly by "other businesses" (6.9%). The second, third, and fourth listed defendants, however, differ much more by type. When a second defendant is listed, that defendant is likely to be a business (43%) or an individual (37.1%). Third and fourth defendants are also most likely to be individuals or businesses. The fact that the second-listed defendant is more often a business may be due to plaintiffs suing an individual coupled with a business (e.g., wage garnishment cases).

Civil caseloads, then, seem to be driven by individual litigants opposing each other for economic aid or recovery. However, the State of Georgia is a "repeat player" especially by virtue of its filing on behalf of individual plaintiffs in welfare disputes.[25] The fact that the state is more involved in civil litigation than originally thought may serve as the basis for the kind of organization in civil systems that was previously only found in criminal courts.

ATTORNEYS

Economic factors seem to play a very large role in the number and types of representation in civil justice. Since most civil cases involve the transfer of wealth in suits ranging from torts to debt collection, the ability to hire attorneys to negotiate the process is important in these transfers.

The conventional profile of attorney participation in civil cases is that the defendant and plaintiff are each represented by a single attorney. This generally holds in Mountain County, where the vast majority of plaintiffs are represented by a single attorney (79.4%), although a plurality of defendants represent themselves (38.1%). Interestingly, no attorney was used for a sizeable proportion (36.7%). In these instances, it seemed that the defendant did not answer the complaint or that service of the defendant was not completed.

Also of interest is that approximately 6% of the plaintiffs filed *pro se*. A closer inspection of these cases indicated that almost all were routine divorce cases filed in the courthouse by the plaintiff and defendant. The data in Table 3-9 also establish that cases with more than two attorneys on either side are fairly rare (less than 15%).

These data indicate that civil litigants employ a single attorney for most cases. However, for some litigants, the expense of an attorney may be a luxury that they cannot afford, or the case itself may be so simple as to not require the skill of an attorney.

What types of attorneys generally participate in this variety of cases? The results presented in Table 3-10 generally confirm what was noted initially. On the plaintiff side, the most common attorney is one in private practice or a member of a firm. As for defendants, most either represented themselves or did not answer the case. The second highest category of defendant representation was by attorneys in private practice. Interestingly, a significant proportion of plaintiff attorneys (first listed) were government attorneys (21%), but government represented defendants much less often (less than 1%). Finally, in cases where more than one attorney was employed, the attorney was most often in private practice.

What do the data on attorney participation say about civil justice in Mountain County? First, the bulk of civil and domestic suits in Mountain County consist of a plaintiff who is represented by an attorney. However, the defendant either litigates *pro se*, does not answer the complaint, or later defaults. In essence, this challenges the prevailing wisdom that most civil cases include attorney representation for both defendants and plaintiffs. It would be interesting to know if this was true of larger, urban jurisdictions as well.

Additionally, a fairly large amount of participation by the government occurs on the plaintiff side, but not the defendant. This should not be surprising when considering that a fairly large number of plaintiffs are government agencies acting to retrieve checks from "deadbeat daddies" or trying to capture the assets of drug offenders. The consistent entry of governments into the civil law realm may indicate that government attorneys in these cases have "repeat player" advantages over defendants who are often represented pro se and are typically "one shotters" (Galanter, 1974).

The surprisingly large percentage of pro se representation in Mountain County courts was striking and interesting. The type of case or case complexity, however, may explain this phenomenon. As noted, many of the pro se cases for plaintiffs and defendants were simple, non-contested, divorce actions or other cases that were defaulted on by defendants (e.g., routine debt collection cases or wage garnishment actions). More complex cases with higher stakes and complex legal issues were more likely to fit the prevailing model of litigation where both parties are represented by private attorneys. In these cases, plaintiffs were more likely to find an attorney to take the case on contingency because of financial incentives. Higher stakes cases, then, provide higher potential gains for plaintiffs and losses for defendants. Finally, complex cases also offered more in the way of civil procedures such as motions and hearings that require familiarity with the legal process.

Unlike the right to counsel extended to criminal defendants by the Sixth Amendment of the U.S. Constitution,"there is no comparable right to legal assistance for indigent parties in civil cases" (Smith, 1991: 43). Economics, then, are an important factor for those seeking civil justice and those defending claims. An economic calculus potentially exists for litigants choosing whether to seek representation. For plaintiffs, when the costs of hiring an attorney are weighed against the stakes of the case, it may be a better use of time to act *pro se*. For instance, in a simple divorce filing or wage garnishment action, the expense of an attorney to the defendant might outweigh the costs of defending ones self (e.g., little at stake or to lose, few costs in time of learning and performing the legal procedures for the case).[26] The amount of pro se representation in small claims or magistrate courts is just such an example. For defendants who have outstanding debt and poor credit ratings, the cost of hiring an attorney may be astronomical and the choice of acting pro se becomes, in effect, the only option.

Pro se representation in a few areas (e.g., "deadbeat daddies") represents potential policy problems where governments have established institutions to represent economically disadvantaged plaintiffs. The institutionalization of this process seems to present advantages for plaintiffs who are represented by "repeat players," especially if the defendant is unrepresented. One example of this is the efforts of the Georgia Department of Human Resources to represent welfare recipients in the collection of outstanding child support payments. Another is the effort by states to track down child support contempts against out-of-state defendants (URESA cases). The movement of government into the arena of civil court systems on behalf of plaintiffs is an interesting institutional change in itself and certainly merits further study.

LOCAL LEGAL CULTURE

One additional aspect about attorney participation in civil cases is the role of local legal culture and context. While this study does not offer a comparison of different jurisdictions, there is still something to be said about the culture of civil justice in a single court system. A description of "repeat player" activity, for instance, provides a source of data for future comparisons.

Among plaintiff attorneys in the general civil sample, the vast majority of those identified were "single shotters" (87.8%). In categories measuring the number of appearances per attorney identified, only 8% appeared in 2 to 4 cases. Appearances in more than four cases were even rarer. Two government attorneys accounted for over 100 appearances (116 and 149 each) by representing welfare mothers in child support recovery cases. The trends for defense attorneys were similar to plaintiffs. Overall, defense attorneys were "single shot" players (about 85%) but, the percentage of repeat appearances was slightly higher than plaintiff attorneys.

Many attorneys, however, handle both defense and plaintiff litigation. Landon (1990) discusses how many attorneys in small towns are constrained by economics and must often represent plaintiffs or defendants. One might expect that attorneys from a jurisdiction the size of Mountain County might follow this pattern. The final column of Table 3-11 takes this into account by examining the total attorney appearances regardless of representation type.

As a percentage of the total attorneys in the dataset, "repeat players" remained few in number when we include appearances by counsel for both plaintiffs and defendants. Attorneys with 2-4 appearances accounted for 7.9% of the total attorneys in the dataset. Attorneys with more than 5 appearances in the dataset were again quite rare.

In total, the data indicate that "repeat" player status is fairly rare. Among attorney types, defense attorneys are more apt to be "repeat players" than plaintiff attorneys. One might have thought, in a jurisdiction the size of Mountain County, that a relatively small number of attorneys would be representing a large number of litigants. However, the close proximity of the Atlanta metropolitan area provides a source of attorneys who enter the system and dilute the presence of local "repeat players." In Tables 3-12 and 3-13, the participation of "locals," "outsiders," "pro se," and the types of opposing relationships among these attorneys are described.[27] As a whole, a plurality of attorneys was local (Table 3-12: 48.3% local vs. 42.7% outsider). Plaintiff attorneys were slightly more likely to be "outsiders" while a large majority of defense attorneys were "locals."[28]

Some factors might explain the difference in "local/outsider" participation among Mountain County civil attorneys. First, the "local/outsider" differences between plaintiff and defense attorneys do not take into account "pro se" representation. Most "pro se" defendants and plaintiffs are "locals" litigating in routine cases (e.g., divorce, debt collection). When "pro se" representation was included in the "local" category, both plaintiffs and defendants were more likely to be locals. Second, plaintiffs in many case types are wealthier than defendants (e.g., debt collection) or the costs of litigation are decreased by contingent fee representation (see Kritzer and Pickerill, 1996). Plaintiffs, then, may have the ability to hire more expensive attorneys from larger law firms outside the jurisdiction (e.g., Atlanta) while defendants are left "pro se" or with lower cost local attorneys.

Table 3-13 presents a profile of opposing attorney relationships by jurisdiction. The results indicate that the most common pairing in Mountain County cases is the "local" attorney facing a "pro se" plaintiff or defendant (about 34%). These pairings accounted for about one-third of the cases. "Pro se" defendants or plaintiffs who were opposed by an attorney from "outside" of Mountain County made up about 21% of the pairings. "Pro se" plaintiffs faced "pro se" defendants in less than 10% of the cases (e.g., uncontested divorces).

When two attorneys faced each other, the expectation was that they would be "local." Surprisingly, a slightly larger percentage of "local" attorneys faced "outsiders" (16.1% vs. 15.3% "local/local"). "Outsiders" faced "outsiders" in only 5% of the cases examined. The slightly larger percentage of "locals" facing "outsiders" could be due to the relatively close proximity of the Atlanta metropolitan area.

What do these preliminary results say about the roles of attorneys in civil justice? First, a very large portion of civil cases in Mountain County

Civil Justice in Mountain County 57

involves plaintiffs or defendants who are unrepresented. This may be, in part, a function of the economic status of the individual in the suit coupled with the complexity of the case type. Non-contested divorces, for example, involve simpler procedural actions than a "soft tissue" tort action. These simple suits might allow individuals to represent themselves cheaply.

The possibility of distinct local legal cultures may exist due to the large presence of "local" attorneys who presumably know each other well and interact. Variations in context, then, might affect case processing (e.g., by speeding disposition time and increasing settlements). However, the percentage of "repeat players" identified in the sample was quite low due, in part, to the entry of a large percentage of "outsiders". One other confounding result, namely high *pro se* representation, suggests that the type of cohesiveness among criminal system actors is not present in civil systems (see Kritzer and Zemans, 1993).

Despite this, it will be interesting to see if "local" or "repeat" attorneys have more success in civil litigation procedure and outcomes. These results might confirm that local legal culture matters in civil systems even though it is not as institutionalized. Additionally, particular attorney pairings might help explain differences in civil justice success. Attorneys who have experience with system norms and who have consistent working relationships with opposing attorneys might cooperate for mutual benefits.

JUDGES

In criminal court systems, judges play a very significant role in the disposal of cases, namely, that of sentencing. Previous research indicates that most civil and domestic cases settle before reaching trial. In some respects, then, judges may have less influence in civil cases than they do in criminal cases (e.g., their roles in plea bargaining and sentencing). However, judges do manage civil caseloads by enforcing pretrial procedures and ruling on motions made by attorneys (see Kritzer, 1990).

For each case, data on case assignment were coded and are reported in the following section.[29] Cases in Mountain County are assigned to judges by the Clerk of Court's office when cases are initially filed by litigants. From inquiries made to the Clerk's staff, it was learned that cases are assigned to judges in a systematic fashion. When a case is filed, it is placed on the docket of the particular court and assignment is based on the alphabetical order of the plaintiffs last name. One portion of the alphabet is assigned to a single judge, another part to a second, and so on. Afterwards, the calendar is set by the judge assigned to the case.[30]

Once a case is assigned to a judge by the Clerk's office, it generally remains with the same judge throughout the process. The only exceptions to this rule are in cases where a judge may recuse him/herself from a case, when litigants request a temporary hearing (which are held on a rotating basis by the three Superior court judges, one retired Superior court judge, and the State court judge), and/or when a scheduling conflict occurs in pretrial matters.

In the time period of this study, the State court had one full-time judge and one part-time judge; the Superior court was staffed with three full-time judges. One change in staff occurred in 1993 when one Superior court judge was appointed to the Georgia Court of Appeals and was replaced by the local district attorney, who was appointed by the governor.[31] From the sample of cases from 1989-1995, what was judge assignment like in Mountain County?

Based on the case assignment rules of Mountain County, judges should handle relatively equal proportions of cases. One expectation is that most of the cases would be handled by the three full-time Superior court judges and the one full-time State court judge. The data here only indicate the judge to which the case was originally assigned and do not capture cases where judges filled in during the pre-trial process or heard motions when a regular judge was absent. Consequently, the data under-represent the amount of participation of part-time judges, retired senior judges, or others outside the system.

Table 3-14 presents the number of cases assigned to particular judges of both courts. In State court, the single, full-time judge was assigned all of the cases sampled in the first three years (1989-1991). Beginning in 1992, a very small percentage of the cases was directly assigned to a part-time judge (less than 10%).[32] The addition of a part-time State court judge reflects the increase in State court business and a possible need for more help with increasing caseloads (particularly when considering the criminal work State court preforms).

In Superior court cases, three full-time judges participated in Mountain County over the period examined. Since cases were assigned by the last name of the plaintiff, the caseloads for the judges were remarkably uniform. In the sample, each judge generally took about one third of the cases, with some variation (see Table 3-14). A transition year appeared in 1993, when a new judge was appointed to the bench in replacement of a judge who was elevated to the Georgia Court of Appeals. The former Superior court judge continued to take a very small number of cases for the next two years (8 and 3 respectively), while the new judge took over the remaining caseload. One retired judge formally took part in a limited number of cases over the time period (less than 10 a year).

One interesting finding with respect to judge participation is the relationship to the overall caseload trends reported earlier. While the county's civil caseload is growing, the number of judges has been the same in the period of the study.[33] The only exception is the appointment of a part-time judge in State court. Caseload trends may reflect a need for more judges statewide. In 1999, the Judicial Council of Georgia recommended and received eight new judgeships statewide based on caseload trends, including filings, weighted caseloads, open cases, population, and days of assistance of senior judges. The Council suggested that those circuits with the most need were recommended for additional judicial seats. There was no suggestion as to whether the number of judges added were enough to deal with the realities of caseload increases.

While there is no evidence to declare a crisis in the courts, evidence of the use of retired and part-time judges, the implementation of a Tuesday "temporary hearing day," and the institutionalization of mediation reflect that caseload increases may be taking a toll on the work of the court system. Mountain County judges may have seen the need for these institutional reforms as a means of curbing caseloads or heading off future problems with increases. Alternatively, if a caseload crisis does not exist in the court system, then there may be other reasons for the adoption of these reforms. With mediation, for instance, co-option may have been a motivation.

CIVIL PROCEDURE

Civil procedure, in general, begins with a complaint by the plaintiff, service of the defendant with the complaint by law enforcement, an answer by the defendant, pre-trial procedures (e.g., hearings, motions, discovery, subpoenas) and a disposition of case settlement, dismissal, or a trial by jury or the judge (bench). In the cases examined here, particular attention was paid to each of these steps for civil cases. What does information from Mountain County cases tell us about procedures in civil court cases?

Case procedures were coded as "events" in a case's "life."[34] The amount of formal pretrial actions or events filed and heard in civil cases is few (see Table 3-15). Pretrial actions or case filings included continuances, leaves of absence, motions (e.g., compel, dismiss, etc.), and discovery. The number of pretrial actions filed in civil cases averaged a bit less than one per case and ranged from 0 to 32. In a large majority of cases, no pretrial actions were filed with the Clerk's office (72.6%). Pretrial hearings were even fewer in number, ranging from 0 to 5 per case and averaging closer to zero than one per case (see Table 3-15). Most pretrial hearings were formal hearings on summary judgment or evidence (e.g., motion to compel discovery). Overall, these results suggest that most general civil cases are very routine or involve much more consensual behavior among litigants and attorneys than expected (i.e., few actions are formally filed and were likely negotiated without conflict).

Post-trial actions in Mountain County civil court cases were even rarer than pretrial actions (see Table 3-16). Less than three percent of the cases had post-trial motions, and less than one percent of the cases had post-trial hearings present in case files. This is not surprising because most cases end with pre-trial disposal. For the most part, post-trial actions were motions either for new trial or to compel post-trial discovery to collect judgements from nefarious litigants.

Interviews with attorneys revealed that most court actions are discussed informally with opposing attorneys over the phone. Those actions, then, that are filed might indicate the most contentious of cases where attempts to negotiate informally do not bear fruit.

CASE DISPOSITION

The final portion of the work of Mountain County civil justice is that of case disposal. Two aspects are highlighted in this regard: case processing speed and case resolution. Previous studies have shown that trial rates are very low and that settlement is the overwhelming norm for civil case disposition. For example, an examination of Georgia tort cases found that approximately 6% of cases are disposed of in jury or bench trials (Eaton and Talarico, 1996). Settlements, dismissals, summary judgments, and transfers made up the rest of case disposal.

Civil Justice in Mountain County 61

What does case disposition look like in the sample of Mountain County cases? Table 3-17 presents data on case disposition by case type. As expected, jury and bench trials are a rare phenomenon, accounting for less than 6% of the sample. The highest percentage of jury trials existed in combination cases (13%), tort cases (9.3%), and to a lesser degree real property cases (3.7%). Only one domestic and six contract cases were disposed of by a jury. The variation in jury trials seems to be a function of case complexity since the routine cases of divorce, contract, and debt collection were much less likely to be formally tried. Bench trials were also rare (about 3.5%). However, some variation existed by case type. A larger percentage of total domestic (6.1%) and real property (8.6%) cases were disposed of by bench trial than in other case types.[35]

The largest proportion of cases was settled before or after trial by attorneys and clients (36%).[36] Of case types, more torts (63.6%) were settled, followed by combination cases (47.8%), contracts (46%), and property cases (about 25%). A modest proportion of domestic cases was settled in this manner (17%).

Other forms of settlement considered separately here are consent agreements and decrees. Consent agreements are final judgments of a court that are entered by agreement of the parties and that do not apply to other persons. Consent agreements made up a very large proportion of total case disposal (22.6%), with the largest case type being domestic (51.5%). Most domestic consent agreements resulted primarily from a state rule that case settlements involving children must be approved by a judge. Domestic agreements involving children are titled "Consent Order and Decree of Divorce" and are signed by the judge. Consent agreements were rarely used in other types of cases, in part because the cases were settled privately between attorneys. However, a large percentage of government benefits (86%) and a modest percentage of property cases (20%) were settled in this manner. When combining private case settlements with consent decrees, related negotiations constitute the largest method of cases disposal for civil cases (about 59%).

In addition to their involvement in trials, judges play a formal role in other pretrial rulings (Kritzer, 1990). Some examples include ruling on motions for dismissal, summary judgment, and default rulings. Additionally, judges make pretrial orders in many domestic cases, can dispose of cases by granting transfers to other jurisdictions and can dismiss cases for a "lack of prosecution" (i.e., in cases where no action is taken after a period of time).

In total, pre-trial dispositions by judges accounted for a little over one-third of civil cases. These percentages are enlarged by the impact of cases that were ruled in default because a defendant did not answer or appear for court (18%) and by pre-trial orders in domestic cases (10%). The largest percentage of default actions occurred in contract debt collection cases and property actions such as asset forfeiture for drugs. These findings are important because when defendants do not appear, there is a potential loss of court time and resources. The remaining cases disposed of by judges in pre-trial actions were relatively few in number. For instance, summary judgments accounted for a smaller percentage of cases than jury trials. Finally, a small percentage of cases were either pending or transferred to another jurisdiction (less than 2%).

Not surprisingly, from the data we learn that most cases settle before trial and that trials (jury and bench) are quite rare. It should not, however, be assumed that judges do not participate often in civil case work. Almost one-third of the case dispositions involved pre-trial orders, ruling on motions, defaults, and summary judgments. In each of these areas, a judge takes at least some court time to analyze and rule on a case. In addition, consent agreements (while like settlements) involve the approval of judges.

Because most cases are settled, few outcomes of civil litigation are found in case files. Additionally, in many domestic cases it is difficult to assess who wins and who loses. For example, does a father who gains custody but has to pay alimony win or lose? In the very small proportion of civil cases that went to trial, only 75 of 1403 cases were decided by a judge in favor of a party.

Despite the lack of information on who wins and who loses, case disposition type and speed tell us a great deal about the administration of justice and what one might expect of the civil system. Case processing speed, measured from date of filing to date of disposal, is one factor of central concern to litigants and attorneys. For litigants, the speed at which a case proceeds impacts the redistribution of wealth at stake in many cases and also impacts families (e.g., custody battles). For court actors such as attorneys and judges, processing speed or delay determines the amount of cases that a system handles and attorney workload (e.g., brokering justice for clients).

Case processing time for general civil cases is examined over time (see Table 3-18) and by case type (see Table 3-19). Interestingly, when we examine average case speed over time, it appears that case processing time has decreased dramatically (Table 3-18). In 1989, case processing time averaged 225 days from complaint to disposition. From 1990 to 1991, case processing time increased to 323 and 301, respectively. However, with 1992, case processing time began to decrease with a low of 163 for 1995.

Of particular interest to this study is the fact that the increase in case processing speed coincides with the implementation of the 1992 Mountain County mediation pilot program. Additional decreases in processing time also occurred after the Ninth District Dispute Resolution Program began in 1993. While these results are preliminary, it may be that court-annexed mediation has diverted cases and has allowed attorneys and judges more time to spend on those that remain in the formal system.

One factor that correlates with case processing speed is case type (Table 3-19). Domestic, government benefit, and "other" cases are processed at a higher speed than torts, contracts, and property cases. For example, tort cases were disposed of in an average 340 days while domestic cases took approximately 156. These results are not surprising given that many domestic cases involve non-contested actions where cases are filed and disposed of in a plenary fashion. In government benefits cases, the actions can be even more routine as a government officer processes the case, achieves an agreement with the defendant, and later files the case for approval as a consent decree (e.g., food stamp fraud cases).

On the other hand, torts, contract, and property cases are probably more complex and require more civil procedures that inevitably slow the process (e.g., motions and discovery). For example, in contract cases, wage garnishments are common and take longer to process. In these cases, disposition does not formally occur until the money is paid or the case is dismissed for want of prosecution.

SUMMARY OF CIVIL JUSTICE IN MOUNTAIN COUNTY

The aforementioned profile of general civil cases serves as the basis of several preliminary conclusions. First, civil justice in Mountain County is a routine and increasingly dominant part of the court system. Civil case filings have increased over the time period of the study, but most of the cases are routine (e.g., divorce, debt collection). Furthermore, most cases involve an individual suing another individual, and most defendants represent themselves. When attorneys are involved, there is usually only one on each side. Both pro se representation and single attorney representation indicate that cases are not that complex.

Interestingly, the pro se phenomenon is larger than originally thought and is potentially a problem for both courts and litigants. In most of these cases, it may be that defendants cannot afford attorneys and are left, as a consequence, at a disadvantage. For courts, pro se cases take more resources as judges are obliged to insure that the procedural requirements of the law are followed and that pro se litigants are not at a severe disadvantage in the case. Interestingly, mediation, as originally conceived, could potentially encourage pro se representation, especially as it is viewed as informal.

The pattern of repeat player attorneys and "locals" versus "outsiders" suggests that local legal culture might affect civil justice. A plurality of attorneys are "locals," with a higher percentage for the defense than the plaintiff. If repeat players and/or locals have advantages over other attorneys, local legal culture becomes very important. More consensual attorney relationships and repeat player knowledge could lead to higher settlement rates and speedier dispositions.

As actors in the process, judges seemed at the outset to have a less important role in civil justice than attorneys. However, it is possible that judges have a rather large role in case processing and even disposition by ruling on motions and holding pretrial hearings. Information on pre-trial actions, however, did not bear this out entirely. For the most part, motions and pre-trial hearings were fairly rare in general civil cases. Case disposition type provided further evidence of judicial roles in civil cases. Even though most cases settle and trials were rare, a fairly large percentage of cases consisted of judicially disposed pre-trial orders, defaults, dismissals, summary judgements, or transfers. This suggests that the role of judges in civil litigation needs to be studied further.

In this chapter, I have focused on what civil justice looks like in Mountain County. The addition of mediation has, of course, added a new component to the civil justice system with the adoption of a formal procedure to divert cases for settlement. In the next chapter, I provide a similar profile of civil cases that were referred to mediation. In this profile, general civil cases will be compared with the data from mediation cases for a preliminary comparison.

TABLE 3-1

Mountain County Civil Court Filings 1989-1995: State and Superior courts*

Year	Superior Filings	State Filings
1989	2417	546
1990	3083	840
1991	2896	904
1992	3025	994
1993	3083	887
1994	3028	972
1995	2807	1325
Totals	*n = 20,341*	*n = 6468*

*Note: Data from State Court obtained from docket records. Superior Court data from the Ninth Judicial District Court Administrator's Office.

TABLE 3-2

Mountain County Case Types: Aggregate 1989-1995*

Case Type	Total (Freq/%)		Superior Ct.		State Ct.	
Tort	140	10.0%	60	8.5%	80	11.6%
Contract/ Commercial	664	47.5%	85	12.1%	580	83.8%
Real Prop.	81	5.9%	65	9.2%	16	2.4%
Domestic	462	32.9%	455	64.7%	4	0.6%
Govt. Benef.	22	1.6%	22	3.1%	0	0.0%
Other	5	.4%	4	0.6%	1	0.1%
Combo.	23	1.7%	12	1.7%	11	1.6%
Totals	1397	100%	703	100%	692	100%

* Based on a sample of 200 cases per year (100 each court).

TABLE 3-3

Mountain County Civil Case Filing Trends:
Total Civil Docket*

Case Type	1989	1990	1991	1992	1993	1994	1995	(n)
Tort	14.1%	11.6%	8.0%	9.0%	8.0%	11.4%	7.9%	141
Contr/Comm.	43.7	45.2	48.7	46.2	51.8	46.5	50.5	664
Real Prop.	9.5	6.0	5.6	4.5	5.5	4.0	5.4	81
Domestic	29.1	33.7	36.5	33.7	32.7	32.7	33.2	462
Govt. Ben.	3.0	2.0	0.5	2.1	0.5	2.0	1.0	22
Other	0.0	0.5	0.0	1.0	0.5	0.5	0.0	5
Combo.	0.5	1.1	0.5	3.5	1.0	3.0	2.0	23

n = 1421

* Random sample of 200 cases a year by court type.

TABLE 3-4

Mountain County Civil Case Filing Trends: Superior court*

Case Type	1989	1990	1991	1992	1993	1994	1995	(n)
Tort	15.2%	8.2%	8.9%	9.1%	3.0%	10.8%	4.9%	60
Contr/Comm.	8.1	10.2	11.9	7.1	22.8	9.8	14.6	85
Real Prop.	13.1	9.2	7.9	9.1	7.9	7.8	9.7	65
Domestic	56.6	67.3	70.3	66.7	63.4	63.7	65.0	455
Govt. Ben.	6.1	4.1	1.0	4.0	1.0	3.9	1.9	22
Other	0.0	1.0	0.0	2.0	0.0	1.0	0.0	4
Combo.	1.0	0.0	0.0	2.0	2.0	2.9	3.9	12
	100%	100%	100%	100%	100%	100%	100%	n=703

* Base on sample of 200 civil cases a year (100 each court).

TABLE 3-5

Mountain County Civil Case Filing Trends:
State Court*

Case Type	1989	1990	1991	1992	1993	1994	1995	(n)
Tort	13.0%	14.9%	7.3%	9.0%	13.3%	12.2%	11.1%	80
Contr/Comm.	79.0	79.2	85.7	85.0	81.6	83.7	87.9	657
Real Prop.	6.0	3.0	3.1	0.0	3.1	0.0	1.0	16
Domestic	2.0	1.0	1.0	1.0	1.0	1.0	0.0	7
Govt. Ben.	0.0	0.0	0.0	0.0	0.0	0.0	0.0	0
Other	0.0	0.0	0.0	0.0	1.0	0.0	0.0	1
Combo.	0.0	2.0	1.0	5.0	0.0	3.1	0.0	11
	100%	100%	100%	100%	100%	100%	100%	n=772

* Based on a sample of 200 cases a year (100 each court).

TABLE 3-6

Mountain County Case Filings, 1989-1995: Case Types Within Case Categories, State and Superior courts*

Case Category/ Case Type	Total %	(n)	State %	(n)	Superior %	(n)
Torts						
Auto	62.1%	(95)	67.4%	(60)	54.7%	(35)
Med. Mal.	5.2	(8)	4.5	(4)	6.3	(4)
Premise Liab.	7.2	(11)	7.9	(7)	6.3	(4)
Product Liab.	1.3	(2)	2.2	(2)	0.0	(2)
Oth. Prof. Mal.	2.6	(4)	1.1	(1)	4.7	(3)
Combination 1-5	0.7	(1)	0.0	(0)	1.6	(1)
Other	2.3	(32)	2.1	(15)	2.4	(17)
Contract/Commercial						
Debt Collection	58.1%	(364)	60.5%	(320)	45.3%	(43)
Wage Garnishment	35.0	(219)	35.3	(187)	32.6	(31)
Fraud;Contr/Comm.	3.0	(19)	2.3	(12)	7.4	(7)
Poor Workmanship	1.3	(8)	.9	(5)	3.2	(3)
Unspec. Breach	2.2	(14)	.8	(4)	10.5	(10)
Other	.3	(2)	.2	(1)	1.1	(1)
Real Property						
Govt. Land Taking	12.3	(10)	5.3	(1)	14.5	(9)
Util. Land Taking	9.9	(8)	0.0	(0)	12.9	(8)
Repossession	19.8	(16)	57.9	(11)	8.1	(9)
Prop. Eviction	1.2	(1)	5.3	(1)	0.0	(0)
Asset Forf. (Drugs)	22.2	(18)	0.0	(0)	29.0	(18)
Zoning	1.2	(1)	0.0	(0)	1.6	(1)
Other	33.3	(27)	31.6	(6)	33.9	(21)

TABLE 3-6 (Cont.)

Mountain County Case Filings, 1989-1995: Case Types Within Case Categories, State and Superior courts*

Case Category/ Case Type	Total %	(n)	State %	(n)	Superior %	(n)
Domestic						
Divorce	37.2	(172)	0.0	(0)	37.6	(172)
Mod.Div/Sup/Vis	3.7	(17)	0.0	(0)	3.7	(17)
Mod. of Cust.	2.2	(10)	0.0	(0)	2.2	(10)
Ch. Supp. Contempt	48.7	(225)	60.0	(3)	48.6	(222)
Family Viol. Act	1.3	(6)	0.0	(0)	1.3	(6)
Combination 1-5	2.2	(10)	0.0	(0)	2.2	(10)
Other	4.8	(22)	40.0	(2)	4.4	(20)
Govt. Benefits						
Welfare Fraud	82.6%	(19)	0.0%	(0)	86.4%	(19)
Workers Comp.	8.7	(2)	0.0	(0)	9.1	(2)
Other	8.7	(2)	100.0	(1)	4.5	(1)
Business Reg.						
Any Business Reg.	0.0	(0)	0.0	(0)	0.0	(0)
	n = 1345		n = 643		n = 706	

* Based on a sample of 200 cases a year (100 each court).

TABLE 3-7

Number of Litigants in the Mountain County Civil System: 1989-1995*

Number of Litigants	Plaintiffs	Defendants
Cases w/ 1	74.7% (1040)	64.9% (899)
Cases w/ 2	17.3 (240)	26.0 (361)
Cases w/ 3	4.8 (67)	4.0 (56)
Cases w/ 4	1.4 (19)	1.7 (24)
Cases w/ 5	1.0 (14)	.9 (12)
Cases w/ 6 or More Lits.	.8 (10)	2.5 (32)
Average	*1.4 Litigants*	*1.7 Litigants*
Total	*100% (1390)*	*100% (1384)*

*Data based on a sample of 200 cases per year (100 per court).

TABLE 3-8

**Litigant Type Mountain County Civil Cases:
First Four Litigants***

Litigant Type	Lit. 1	Lit. 2	Lit. 3	Lit. 4
Plaintiff				
Individual	33.4%	85.9%	95.7%	91.4%
	(461)	(294)	(91)	(32)
Insurance	2.8%	0.6%	2.1%	2.9%
	(39)	(2)	(2)	(1)
Bank/Financial	16.4%	0.3%	0.0%	0.0%
	(226)	(1)	(0)	(0)
Hospital/Medical	13.8%	1.5%	0.0%	0.0%
	(191)	(5)	(0)	(0)
Other Business	12.9%	4.4%	1.1%	5.7%
	(178)	(15)	(1)	(2)
Govt. Agency	20.7%	7.3%	1.1%	0.0%
	(285)	(25)	(1)	(0)
Totals	100%	100%	100%	100%
	(1380)	(342)	(95)	(35)

TABLE 3-8 (Cont.)

Litigant Type Mountain County Civil Cases:
First Four Litigants*

Litigant Type	Lit. 1	Lit. 2	Lit. 3	Lit. 4
Defendants				
Individual	90.5%	37.1%	47.3%	61.0%
	(1258)	(182)	(59)	(39)
Insurance	0.6%	2.2%	4.0%	3.1%
	(8)	(11)	(5)	(2)
Bank/Financial	0.6%	10.0%	16.7%	7.8%
	(8)	(49)	(21)	(5)
Hospital/Medical	0.4%	4.5%	0.8%	3.1%
	(5)	(22)	(1)	(2)
Other Business	6.9%	43.4%	28.0%	17.2%
	(96)	(212)	(35)	(11)
Govt. Agency	1.0%	2.8%	3.2%	7.8%
	(14)	(14)	(4)	(5)
Totals	*100%*	*100%*	*100%*	*100%*
	(1389)	*(490)*	*(125)*	*(64)*

* Based on a sample of 200 cases per year (100 per court).

Table 3-9

Number of Attorneys in Mountain County Civil Litigation:
Plaintiff and Defendant Representation

Number of Attorneys	Plaintiff %	(n)	Defendant %	(n)
One	79.4%	(1114)	17.2%	(242)
Two	11.3%	(159)	5.4%	(76)
Three	2.0%	(28)	1.6%	(22)
Four	0.6%	(8)	0.7%	(10)
Five	0.1%	(2)	0.1%	(1)
Six or More	0.0%	(0)	0.2%	(3)
Pro Se	6.4%	(90)	38.1%	(534)
Missing*	0.1%	(2)	36.7%	(515)
Total	100%	(1403)	100%	(1403)

*Note: Cases in this category included no answer by defendant or lack of service of the defendant resulting in a default judgement.

TABLE 3-10

Type of Plaintiff and Defendant Attorney:
Mountain County General Civil

Attorney Type (First Four Listed)	Plaintiff %	(n)	Defendant %	(n)
First Attorney Listed				
Pro Se Attorney	6.6%	(93)	38.3%	(538)
Private Attorney	71.3%	(999)	24.0%	(337)
Government Attorney	21.0%	(295)	0.4%	(6)
In House Attorney	0.4%	(2)	0.1%	(2)
Other	0.0%	(0)	0.1%	(1)
Missing*	0.7%	(10)	37.0%	(519)
Totals	100%	(1403)	100%	(1403)

TABLE 3-10 (Cont.)

**Type of Plaintiff and Defendant Attorney:
Mountain County General Civil**

Attorney Type (First Four Listed)	Plaintiff %	(n)	Defendant %	(n)
Second Attorney Listed				
Pro Se Attorney	0.2%	(3)	0.7%	(10)
Private Attorney	11.6%	(163)	7.0%	(98)
Government Attorney	2.6%	(37)	0.4%	(6)
In House Attorney	0.0%	(0)	0.0%	(0)
Other	0.0%	(0)	0.0%	(0)
Missing*	85.6%	(1200)	91.9%	(1289)
Totals	100%	(1403)	100%	(1403)
Third Attorney Listed				
Pro Se Attorney	0.0%	(0)	0.1%	(1)
Private Attorney	2.1%	(30)	2.1%	(30)
Government Attorney	0.5%	(7)	0.0%	(0)
In House Attorney	0.0%	(0)	0.0%	(0)
Other	0.0%	(0)	0.0%	(0)
Missing*	97.4%	(1365)	97.8%	(1372)
Totals	100%	(1403)	100%	(1403)

TABLE 3-10 (Cont.)

**Type of Plaintiff and Defendant Attorney:
Mountain County General Civil**

Attorney Type (First Four Listed)	Plaintiff %	(n)	Defendant %	(n)
Fourth Attorney Listed				
Pro Se Attorney	0.0%	(0)	0.1%	(1)
Private Attorney	0.5%	(7)	1.0%	(14)
Government Attorney	0.2%	(3)	0.0%	(0)
In House Attorney	0.0%	(0)	0.0%	(0)
Other	0.0%	(0)	0.0%	(0)
Missing*	99.3%	(1393)	98.9%	(1388)
Totals	*100%*	*(1403)*	*100%*	*(1403)*

* Note that Missing cases refers to where no attorney was present in the file. In the "fist attorney listed" reasons include no answer or no service of defendant. Thereafter, denotes no additional attorneys listed.

Table 3-11

**"Single Shot" and "Repeat Player" Attorneys:
Percentages of Plaintiff, Defendant and Total Attorneys***

Appearances	Plaintiff	Defendant	Total
"One Shotters"	87.8% (1056)	84.7% (276)	87.2% (1270)
2 - 4 Apps.	8.0% (95)	10.4% (34)	7.9% (115)
5 - 10 Apps.	2.7% (32)	4.0% (13)	2.9% (43)
11 - 19 Apps.	1.2% (15)	0.9% (3)	1.7% (25)

Table 3-11 (con't)

Appearances	Plaintiff	Defendant	Total
20 or More	0.3% (4)	0.0% (0)	0.3% (5)
Totals	100% (1202)	100% (326)	100% (1458)

* Based on a sample of 200 cases per year stratified by type of court (1403 total).

Table 3-12

Attorney Location: "Locals" and "Outsiders" to the Mountain County Civil System*

Attorney Location	Totals	Plaintiff	Defendant
"Locals"	48.3% (805)	43.1% (564)	67.5% (239)
"Outsiders"	42.7% (711)	48.3% (633)	22.0% (78)

Table 3-12 (Cont.)

Attorney Location: "Locals" and "Outsiders" to the Mountain County Civil System*

Attorney Location	Totals	Plaintiff	Defendant
"Unknown"	9.0% (150)	8.6% (113)	10.5% (37)
Totals	100% (1664)	100% (1310)	100% (354)

* Excludes pro se and other cases with no attorney (e.g. defaults). Attorneys coded "local" if from Mountain County, else coded "outsider".

Civil Justice in Mountain County

Table 3-13

Attorney/Opponent Pairings:
Who Opposes Who in Mountain County Civil Court Cases?

Attorney/Opponent Pairing	Frequency
Attorney Versus Attorney Pairings	
"Local versus Local"	15.3% (123)
"Local versus Outsider"	16.1% (129)
"Outsider versus Outsider"	5.2% (42)
Pro Se Pairings	
"Local versus Pro Se"	33.7% (271)
"Outsider versus Pro Se"	21.2% (170)
"Pro Se versus Pro Se"	8.5% (68)
Total Cases*	*100% (803)*

* 600 cases produced missing data because an attorney faced no attorney or defendant (e.g. lack service) or info. on office location was unknown.

Table 3-14
Participation of Judges in Mountain County Civil Cases*

Judge/ Ct. Type	1989	1990	# of Cases per Year 1991 1992 1993			1994	1995	Totals
State court Cases								
Fulltime	101	98	96	97	98	103	106	699
Parttime	0	0	0	5	4	0	3	12
Superior court Cases								
Ftime A	29	29	35	30	28	39	21	211
Ftime B	27	25	29	20	8	3	0	112
Ftime C	30	40	30	36	27	25	34	222
Ftime D	0	0	0	2	28	27	28	85
Retired	5	2	2	7	2	2	7	27
Other	2	0	1	1	0	2	3	9

Table 3-15

**Pre-Trial Actions in Mountain County Civil Cases
1989-1995**

Total #	#Actions	#Hearings
"None"	72.7% (1019)	88.5% (1242)
"One"	14.5% (203)	8.6% (121)
"Two"	4.6% (64)	2.4% (33)
"Three"	2.2% (31)	0.3% (4)
"Four"	1.6% (22)	0.1% (1)
"Five +"	4.5% (63)	0.1% (2)
Average per Case	.78	.15
Range	0-32	0-5

Pretrial Actions included continuances, discovery attempts (depositions), leaves of absences, and motions (compel, dismiss, etc.). Number of actions ranged from none to 32. Pretrial hearings included hearings on motions or other formal hearing before a judge. Did not include routine temporary hearings in divorce proceedings (i.e. separation agreements).

Table 3-16

**Post-Trial Actions in Mountain County Civil Cases
1989-1995**

Total #	# Actions		# Hearings	
"None"	97.3%	(1365)	99.1%	(1390)
"One"	1.7%	(24)	0.8%	(11)
"Two"	0.6%	(9)	0.1%	(1)
"Three"	0.2%	(3)	0.0%	(0)
"Four"	0.1%	(2)	0.0%	(0)
"Five"	0.0%	(0)	0.0%	(0)
Average Per Case	.04		.01	
Range	0-4		0-2	

Post-trial actions and hearings include motions to reconsider, motions to compel post-trial discovery, etc.

Table 3-17

**Case Disposition Types in Mountain County, 1989-95:
by Case Types**

Disposition	Tort	Contract	Property	Domestic
Trials				
Jury	9.3% (13)	0.9% (6)	3.7% (3)	0.2% (1)
Bench	2.9% (4)	1.1% (7)	8.6% (7)	6.1% (28)
Settlements				
Pre/Post Trial	63.6% (89)	46.0% (303)	24.7% (20)	16.9% (78)
Consent Decree	4.3% (6)	5.3% (35)	19.8% (16)	1.5% (238)
Pretrial (Judge)				
Summary Judge.	2.9% (4)	2.0% (13)	2.5% (2)	0.0% (0)
Pretrial Order	0.0% (0)	0.4% (2)	2.5% (2)	10.4% (48)
Default	5.0% (7)	29.9% (198)	21.0% (17)	6.1% (28)
Dis. Lack Pros.	5.7% (8)	10.1% (67)	3.7% (3)	4.1% (19)
Other Dismissal	1.4% (2)	1.7% (11)	11.1% (9)	2.8% (13)
Others				
Transfer	2.9% (4)	0.3% (2)	0.0% (0)	1.5% (7)
Pending	2.1% (3)	2.7% (18)	2.5% (2)	0.4% (2)
Totals	*10.0% (140)*	*47.5% (663)*	*5.8% (81)*	*33.1% (462)*

Table 3-17 (Cont.)

Case Disposition Type in Mountain County, 1989-95:
by Case Types

Disposition	Govt. Bfts.	Other	Combo.	Totals
Trials				
Jury	0.0% (0)	0.0% (0)	13.0% (3)	1.9% (26)
Bench	0.0% (0)	20.0% (1)	8.7% (2)	3.5% (49)
Settlements				
Pre/Post Trial	4.5% (1)	20.0% (1)	47.8% (11)	36.0% (503)
Consent Agrmnt.	86.4%(19)	0.0% (0)	4.3% (1)	22.6% (315)
Pre-trial (Judge Ordered)				
Summary Judge.	0.0% (0)	0.0% (0)	4.3% (1)	1.4% (20)
Pre-trial Order	4.5% (1)	0.0% (0)	0.0% (0)	3.7% (52)
Default	0.0% (0)	0.0% (0)	4.3% (1)	18.0% (251)
Dis. Lack Serv.	0.0% (0)	0.0% (0)	8.7% (2)	7.1% (99)
Other Dismiss	4.5% (1)	60.0%(3)	4.3% (1)	2.9% (40)
Others				
Transfer	0.0% (0)	0.0% (0)	0.0% (0)	0.0% (0)
Pending	0.0% (0)	0.0% (0)	4.3% (1)	1.9% (26)
Totals	1.6% (22)	0.4% (5)	1.6% (23)	100% (1396)

Table 3-18

Average Case Processing Time in Mountain County Civil Cases: Time Trends, 1989-95

Year	Average Days to Disposition	(n)
1989	225 Days	(198)
1990	323 Days	(199)
1991	301 Days	(195)
1992	242 Days	(200)
1993	214 Days	(200)
1994	218 Days	(192)
1995	163 Days	(186)

Note: Measured from complaint date to disposition.

Table 3-19

Average Case Processing Times in Mountain County, 1989-1995: By Case Types

Case Type	Average Days to Disposition	(n)
Tort	340 Days	(135)
Contract	279 Days	(644)
Real Property	247 Days	(80)

Table 3-19 (Cont.)

Average Case Processing Times in Mountain County, 1989-1995: By Case Types

Case Type	Average Days to Disposition	(n)
Domestic	156 Days	(456)
Govt. Benefits	151 Days	(22)
Other	115 Days	(5)
Combination	410 Days	(22)

* Days calculated from complaint date to disposition.

CHAPTER 4
Civil Mediation In Mountain County

What does mediation look like in Mountain County? Here I provide a statistical profile of caseloads, actors, procedures, and dispositions of cases that were referred to mediation by Mountain County judges since it began in early 1992 until 1995. These cases were identified and located at the Ninth Administrative Judicial District's Office of Dispute Resolution. After coding relevant information from the mediated case files (see Appendix A for codesheet), the case numbers were tracked through the Mountain County system and the full case file was examined in the Clerk of Courts office. The mediated case data include information similar to the general civil cases profiled earlier (e.g., time from mediation to disposal; actor participation in mediation; number and length of mediation sessions).

CASELOAD PATTERNS

How many and what types of cases were referred to mediation by Mountain County judges? Answering this question is somewhat complicated because of the time between the original filing date and the eventual referral to mediation. This examination of mediated caseloads, then, includes those that were filed formally prior to the start of the mediation program in 1992.

Over 600 cases were referred to the Ninth District Office of Dispute Resolution from case filings in Mountain County between 1990 and 1995. Table 4-1 indicates that of the cases filed in this time period, referrals to mediation increased dramatically after the pilot program ended in 1992 and reached a peak of 216 cases in 1994. The mediated caseload then dropped slightly in 1995 to 169 cases. The drop in referrals to mediation is not surprising considering the decline in overall civil filings in Mountain County Superior courts in 1994 and 1995 (see Table 3-1).[37]

In general, mediated cases filed in Mountain County courts (1990-1995) were referred from the Superior and not the State court (see Table 4-1). No cases were referred by State court judges in 1991 or 1992, and thereafter only 47 of the total 627 cases (7.5%) examined were referred by State court.

One possible explanation for low State court referrals is the type of cases. Some cases simply might not be appropriate for mediation or may be viewed that way by the judge. As explained earlier, State courts in Georgia do not handle domestic disputes, with the bulk of their civil caseloads consisting of simple debt collection and wage garnishment.

In the aggregate, the overwhelming majority of cases referred to mediation were contested domestic disputes such as divorces and modifications of divorce agreements (see Table 4-2), issues of exclusive Superior court jurisdiction. Of the remaining cases, torts constituted about 15% of the mediated cases, followed by contract/commercial cases (about 10%) and a mix of combination, real property, and others that made up less than 5%.

When divided by court type, we see that domestic cases make up the overwhelming majority of Superior court referrals. Torts (about 12%) and contract/commercial (about 7%) make up the largest portions of others. Of the 47 cases referred to mediation by State courts, a slight majority (53.2%) were tort cases, with the remaining either contract/commercial (42.6%) or combinations (4.2%).

When examined over time, the types of cases remain constant as a whole (see Table 4-3). Domestic cases make up the largest proportion of case filings throughout the period of the study (ranging from 58% to 100%). Torts and contract/commercial cases made up the largest remaining proportions.

One thing that can be said about mediation referrals is that the percentage of cases is much smaller than expected (see Table 4-4). One possible explanation is the focus on divorce and specifically those that are contested, especially as the latter make up a low percentage of Mountain County cases as a whole. Additionally, State courts referred a very low percentage of their caseloads. It may be that State court cases are not well suited to mediation or that State court judges may have reservations as to the appropriateness and or effectiveness of that alternative.

REFERRAL PATTERNS

When examining mediated case type by subcategory, we gain a better understanding of the types of cases judges generally refer to the program (Table 4-5). Similar to general civil caseloads, the largest proportion of tort cases referred to mediation were auto collisions (about 61%). The remaining types of mediated torts were those in an "other" category (about 23%). "Other" cases included fraud, conversion, and torts such as dog bites. Premise liability cases represented about 9% of tort cases in the mediated sample. When compared to the general civil variety (see Table 3-6), mediated torts are of similar type.

Contract/commercial cases were rarely referred to mediation (Table 4-5). Of these, the largest percentage was debt collection cases (about 38%). A sizeable percentage of "poor workmanship" contract breaches was also referred to mediation (23%). Contract fraud and other contract breaches made up only 9% of the contract/commercial cases referred. Mediated contract cases do not include wage garnishments, but rather a higher percentage of contract breaches and frauds.

Very few real property cases were referred to mediation in Mountain County (Table 4-5). Of these, there was one land condemnation and eleven property disputes that did not fit the coding scheme. For example, a 1993 action involved a property boundary dispute between neighbors that was appealed from Magistrate Court.

The most common type of domestic case referrals was contested divorce (about 58%). Divorce modifications (e.g., increase in child support or change in the visitation schedule) made up approximately 19% of these referrals. A final domestic referral of some significance was the "deadbeat daddy" case (i.e., a contempt of child support payment). About 17% of these cases were referred to mediation by Mountain County judges. Custody changes, family violence, or related combinations represented less than 7% of domestic case referrals as a whole.

Although the mediation referrals parallel the general civil caseload, differences emerge when case categories are examined. A larger proportion of mediated domestic cases consisted of divorce actions, and fewer were "deadbeat daddy" cases than in the general civil caseload. Similarly, a smaller percentage of debt collection cases was referred to mediation than found in general caseloads, while there was a larger proportion of contract/commercial fraud cases sent to mediation.

It should not be assumed that the most routine types of cases are referred to mediation by judges. Fewer procedural or administrative types of cases (e.g., wage garnishments, "deadbeat daddy" cases, and property condemnations) were referred to mediation. These cases generally included ongoing attempts to collect money or property rather than actual dispute settlement. Most cases referred to mediation, on the other hand, were contested divorce cases in which there was an obvious dispute.[38] A look at the types of actors involved in mediated cases might shed more light on this process.

MEDIATION PARTICIPANTS

The participation of various actors in mediated cases is more complicated than in general civil cases. Since mediation adds an additional process or stage to traditional civil procedure, there are theoretically more opportunities for individuals to participate. Litigants and attorneys may participate in a case prior to referral (e.g., in filing and discovery), during mediation itself, and after mediation if issues remain unresolved. Judges may participate in cases in customary fashion (e.g., pre-trial hearings and motions, trial procedure, judgment), but also have the additional option of referring a case to mediation. Finally, mediation involves the additional participation of varied staff in scheduling and the actual mediator who presides.

In the profile of general civil cases, we learned that most cases involved a dispute between a single plaintiff and defendant (see Table 3-7). Mediated caseloads were even more likely to have single litigants, with nearly 90% of the cases involving a single plaintiff or defendant (Table 4-6). Only 8% of the cases involved two plaintiffs, and two defendants were only found in 9% of the cases.

When a single litigant is involved in a mediated case, nearly 94% are individuals as opposed to business or governments (see Table 4-7). Second, third, and fourth litigants are also more likely to be individuals. The second largest litigant category was a business other than financial, insurance, or medical (less than 5% of mediated cases). In general, there is little difference between the plaintiff and defendant litigant type.

As noted, a significant number of individuals were not represented by counsel in general civil litigation. Additionally, in many civil cases (particularly debt collections), the defendant was either not represented at

Civil Mediation In Mountain County

all or was found in default. Thus, representation of litigants in general civil cases was not constant across all categories.

What does attorney participation look like in cases referred to mediation? One potential difference that surfaced is that mediation adds an additional process to general civil procedure. Attorneys, then, may participate in the early portion of a case prior to mediation referral. However, after referral to mediation, an attorney may also spend time preparing clients for mediation and may even represent them in the mediation itself. Mediation, then, has the potential to expand the participation of attorneys in civil cases.

Like the general civil cases described earlier, a single plaintiff attorney generally faced a single defense attorney in mediated cases (see Table 4-8). However, unlike the general civil variety, a higher percentage of litigants in mediated cases was represented by an attorney (96% of plaintiffs and over 90% of defendants). This may be because mediated cases were more likely to be contested. Overall, very few mediated cases included more than one attorney on either side. Only about 15% of plaintiffs or defendants hired more than one attorney in cases that were referred to mediation.

The type of attorney employed in mediated cases was also similar to the general civil variety. In each instance where attorneys were employed by a plaintiff or defendant, they generally were classified as private practitioners (see Table 4-9). This held for 96% of plaintiffs and almost 90% of defense attorneys. The second largest category of attorney type was *pro se* (less than 10%), followed distantly by governmental attorneys (less than 1%).

Higher private attorney participation in mediated cases may reflect the fact that litigants are not as financially strained in mediated cases or, alternatively, that more is at stake in these disputes. In general civil cases, the proportion of *pro se* litigants was higher because these cases were more routine (e.g., uncontested divorces) or there was a substantial financial pressure for the litigant (e.g., debt collection).

Mediated cases often consisted of contested divorces or tort and contract cases where more was at stake financially for disputants. If there is more to win (or lose) for litigants and the dispute is contested, it makes some sense to employ a private attorney. It may be that even with financial pressure, mediated cases represent instances where the dispute is important enough to seek legal advice, but where a low-cost solution (such as mediation) might be acceptable to both parties.

Finally, and of some surprise, was the low participation rate (less than 10%) of attorneys in mediation sessions (Table 4-10). In almost 70% of the mediated cases examined, no attorney showed up with his/her clients. If one attorney decided to show up for mediation, then it was likely that the opposing attorney would show up also (in 6% of cases). Only one attorney was present in about 3% of mediated cases.[39]

Earlier, it was hypothesized that mediation might actually boost the participation of attorneys in civil cases. The extraordinarily low participation rates of attorneys in mediation sessions, however, does not support related claims. However, the data do not capture preparation and counsel prior to mediation. It may also be the case that a mediation referral stimulates opposing attorneys to talk about the case earlier in the process. Participation rates, if not communication itself, then, may still be boosted by the presence of mediation.

I suggested before that attorneys may find it in their interest to attend and insure a "fair", legal agreement for their clients. Additionally, attendance may boost billable hours. Of course, flat fee payments may have already been arranged. In this arrangement, attending a mediation may require more time and result in a lower hourly fee. Data presented in Table 4-10 seem to bear this out, as few attorneys attended at all, and when they did attend, counsel was present for both sides. Finally, it is possible that mediation gives attorneys the opportunity to settle cases more quickly and to boost overall profits by quickly processing flat fee cases and reserving time for more lucrative cases. If a case can be settled in mediation, both the client and attorney are saved time and money.

LEGAL CULTURE AND MEDIATION

Previously I emphasized that Mountain County attorneys were mainly "one shotters" with a "local" plaintiff attorney paired against an "outsider" defendant attorney in most situations. Attention was also directed to the large number of pro se litigants and the close proximity of Atlanta that complicated attorney relationships. It appeared that the same attorneys did not come into contact with sufficient regularity for attorneys to form close ties or "workgroups" such as those found in criminal courts (e.g., Flemming, Nardulli, and Eisenstein, 1992).

Closer attorney relationships, however, might be established if lawyers have more opportunities to work together in mediated cases. Mediation might provide a local, civil "culture" as plea bargaining does in criminal justice. As an institutional change, then, mediation may serve as the focal point of legal culture not previously found in civil courts.

We can learn more about attorneys and mediation by comparing the "repeat player" data with the similar data reported earlier in general civil cases. In other words, do the same attorneys participate in mediation (i.e., "repeat players")? Are local attorneys more likely to participate in mediated cases? What is the most consistent opposing attorney relationship in mediated cases (e.g., "local" v. "local")?

Overall, attorneys in mediated cases were much more likely to be "repeat players" than attorneys in general civil cases (compare Table 3-11 and Table 4-11).[40] "One shotters" constituted the dominant category in mediated cases, but the percentages there were lower than in general civil cases. For example, the total percentage of "one-shotters" in mediated cases was about 62% as compared with 85% of general civil cases.

Of the "repeat players" in the general civil system, about 8% had from two to four case appearances as compared with about 24% for mediated cases. The remaining "repeat player" categories (e.g., "5-10" case appearances) also had higher percentages in mediated than general civil cases. It should also be noted that, like general civil cases, defendant attorneys were slightly more likely to be "repeat players" than plaintiff attorneys.

When compared with the general civil profile presented earlier, these data raise questions about why mediated cases are more likely to include repeat attorney participation. One possibility is that certain attorneys find it beneficial to mediate disputes and so persuade the judge to refer the case. It may also be the case that judges who support the program are more likely to refer cases to attorneys who support and have experience with mediation. Finally, attorneys who consistently participate (willing or not) in mediation may be more likely to face the same attorneys in litigation or the attorneys who participate as mediators. More contact between attorneys who participate in the Mountain County system, finally, may foster closer ties among attorneys or makeshift "workgroups" that are less cohesive than the criminal variety, but still have the capacity to speed the processing of cases in the civil system.

When compared with the results of general civil cases in Mountain County (see Table 3-12), mediated cases were much more likely to have "local" attorneys (see Table 4-12). Over 70% of defense and plaintiff attorneys in mediated cases were locals versus the approximately 50% in the general civil arena. Also, there was little difference between plaintiff and defendant attorneys. In general civil cases, defense attorneys were much more likely to be "outsiders." However, in mediated cases, plaintiff and defense attorneys were locals in about 73% of the cases (respectively), and plaintiff attorneys were slightly more likely to be "outsiders." Since most mediated cases were domestic, individual litigants may have felt more comfortable with local attorneys.

A final area of interest is "who opposes whom" when attorneys get involved in mediation (Table 4-13). In general civil cases (see Table 3-13), the largest proportion of cases consisted of a "local" or "outsider" attorney paired against a pro se litigant (33.7% and 21.2% respectively). One might argue that in these cases the deck is "stacked" unfairly against litigants who cannot afford representation. With mediation, pro se litigants were infrequently matched with an attorney (less than 10% of cases).

Evidence of attorney participation in mediated cases, then, is mixed. Litigants are more likely to be represented by attorneys in cases referred to mediation, but, interestingly, the attorneys rarely participate in the mediation itself. Additionally, "local" attorneys are more likely to participate in mediated cases and are more likely to face each other. Even though attorneys do not participate in mediation sessions, it is possible that mediation provides a mechanism for increasing contact between attorneys. "Local" attorneys who are apt to know each other participate in most cases referred to mediation. It may be the case that attorneys who know each other prepare their clients for mediation prior to the session, discuss the case by phone, and use the opportunity for mediation to settle or iron out issues.

When a case is referred to mediation, attorneys who know each other might use the opportunity to their mutual advantage by satisfying clients and by processing cases more quickly. Mediation, then, encourages attorneys to interact more often and earlier to settle cases that could end up in trial or that could carry costly and time consuming motions and discovery. Such a "legal culture" of cooperation, spurred by mediation, may be similar to the concept of "legal culture" found in criminal trial courts where "workgroups" form around plea bargaining.

JUDGES AND MEDIATION

As noted, judges play significant roles in civil court cases, even though the majority of such cases settle before trial. Rulings on motions, discovery, pre-trial orders, and settlement conferences all involved judges and generally set the boundaries for a case or even its disposition. Mediation also gives judges power as "gatekeepers." In this capacity, the judge has the power to refer a particular civil case to mediation.[41]

The referral patterns for particular judges in Mountain County are reported in Table 4-14. All of the judges who work in the Mountain County State and Superior courts have referred cases to mediation. A limited number of cases, in fact, were even referred by the part-time judge in State court and the retired or substitute judges in Mountain County. In this respect, then, Mountain County judges seemed to support mediation by participating in case referral.

One question of interest is whether particular judges are more likely to refer cases to mediation than others? As indicated in Table 4-14, a very small percentage of mediated cases were referred by State court judges, with some referrals by the part-time State court judge. As noted, the low rate of State court referrals is not surprising given that all domestic cases are filed in Superior court.

In Superior court, three full-time judges were responsible for most of the case referrals. Judge "A" referred more cases than any other judge in the system and referred over 50 per year since 1992. Judge "C" was responsible for the second largest number of referrals, and his participation has increased over the short time period. Judge "B" (who was replaced by Judge "D" in 1993) had a very high level of referrals. However, his referrals per year decreased, albeit slightly, over the time period. It should also be noted that a retired judge and other substitute judges had been known to refer cases from time to time to the Ninth District Office of Dispute Resolution.

Judges from Superior court, then, participated in the mediation program at a modest referral rate of 30-60 cases a year. The participation of State court judges was considerably below that of Superior courts, but case type may play a large role. Despite the consistent level of participation by Mountain County judges, it is still the case that less than 10% of total civil caseloads is referred to mediation. Although further research will have to explore this, it may be that the Ninth District Program has all the cases it can handle given limited resources and its service to 15 counties in Georgia. Alternatively, the local legal culture may be making use of the program for aims other than efficiency (e.g., co-option, self-interest). This point, then, has serious ramifications for the success of the court-annexed ADR. If judges are not referring enough

96 Alternative Dispute Resolution

cases to the program, the ability for the program to meet the stated efficiency goals will be compromised.

CIVIL PROCEDURE AND MEDIATION

The procedure and disposition of mediated cases generally conform to what we know from the literature. In general civil litigation, most cases are settled prior to trial, although some types of settlement include agreements between participants that require judicial participation (e.g., consent agreements and decrees). Additionally, a fairly large proportion of cases was disposed of by judges through default procedures and motions such as summary judgment and dismissal.

Mediated cases go through similar case events as do general civil cases (i.e., filing, answer, discovery, motions, etc.). In fact, mediation can be construed as yet another case "event." The process of mediation is set out in the following section and highlights an important question. How do hearings and motions in mediated cases compare with those in general civil? The answer to this question provides one aspect by which to evaluate the effectiveness of mediation. The number of hearings and motions is commonly used to operationalize court workload (see Clarke et al., 1995). Proponents of mediation argue that court workload decreases when mediation is attached to court systems. This profile of mediated case procedures provides an opportunity for a preliminary comparison with general civil cases.

Advocates have argued that mediation and other forms of ADR save court resources and speed the administration of justice (see Harrington and Merry, 1988; Hermann, 1993). Previous studies have found that ADR has decreased the level of court workloads as measured by hearings and motions filed before the court (Kobbervig, 1991; McEwen, 1991).

Pretrial actions and hearings found in mediated civil case files are reported in Table 4-15. On average, Mountain County mediated cases had an average of 2.66 pretrial actions (0-32 range) and less than one (.22) pretrial hearing per case.[42] About 32% of mediated cases included no pretrial actions and 85% included no pretrial hearings.

Comparisons with general civil cases yield interesting results (compare Table 3-15 and 4-15). Mediated cases had over three times as many pre-trial actions per case as general civil (2.66 vs. .78). In addition, there were more pre-trial hearings in mediated cases than in the general civil variety (.22 versus .15). This pattern suggests that mediated cases are complex and therefore more time-consuming than general civil cases. However, these results do not control for type of case or for complexity. A large proportion of general civil cases included very routine debt collection and uncontested divorce cases that, as noted, do not typically feature many pretrial actions. One additional possibility is that cases that do not settle in mediation may have more pre-trial actions and hearings that skew the averages. In any case, the data presented show that mediated cases carry higher workloads, but they are still low overall.

Post-trial actions and hearings in mediated cases were very few in number (Table 4-16). Over 95% of mediated cases had no post-trial actions while almost 98% had no post-trial hearings. There is little difference between mediated and general civil cases in this regard. Mediated cases had only slightly higher numbers of post-trial actions (.05 versus .04 per case). There was also virtually no difference in post-trial hearings (.02 mediated versus .01 general civil per case).

CASE DISPOSITION AND MEDIATION

In this section, we come to the final portion of the profile of Mountain County mediated cases, case disposal. ADR is frequently advanced as a way to increase settlement rates and to speed case dispositions. It is assumed that cases will settle in mediation or at least earlier than in general civil cases.

As noted earlier, it is quite rare for civil cases to proceed from filing to trial. Most cases in Georgia civil courts and around the nation are disposed prior to trial (Eaton and Talarico, 1996; DeFrances et al., 1995). Proponents of ADR in Georgia argue that by annexing mediation and trial courts, settlement rates will increase and trials will decrease (Supreme Court of Georgia, 1993). Assessing the disposition types of mediated cases, then, tells us something about whether this assumption has some validity.

Table 4-17 presents dispositions in Mountain County mediated cases by major case type. In general, trials were a bit more common in mediated cases than in general civil. In mediated cases, 11.2% were disposed of by bench or jury trial as opposed to only 5.4% in the general civil profile. The fact that trials, as a whole, were more common in mediated cases is quite interesting and contrary to the claims of ADR supporters. One possibility, again, is that mediated cases consist of the more difficult or complex cases as compared with the more routine variety in general civil litigation. When we examine trial rates by case type, we find some ancillary support for this argument, as torts made up the largest percentage of jury trials (20 out of 37). Bench trials, however, were more common in mediated domestic cases (30 out of 33 cases). It is possible that these are contested cases that involve difficult issues such as child custody or domestic violence.

Almost 34% of mediated cases were settled in the mediation session itself. When combined with other forms of pre-trial settlements, this constitutes 68% of mediated cases, a higher percentage than the 59% of general civil cases. A larger percentage of general civil cases was actually disposed of before trial, but these required the direct action of a judge (33.1% general civil vs. 20.2% mediated).

Overall, the highest trial rates occurred in mediated tort cases (about 23%). In domestic cases (the bulk of mediated cases), however, less than 10% of cases proceeded to trial from mediation. Furthermore, there were larger settlement rates in other case types. One reason is that 23% of domestic cases were disposed of by a pre-trial order. Here, a case is disposed of before trial, but with some time and action by a judge in the form of a "decree of divorce." These actions are similar to consent decrees except that not all of the issues are agreed to by the litigants and a formal ruling is made by the judge (much as in a motion).

Domestic cases have the highest rate of disposal by mediation (37%). Combinations/others cases (33%) and real property cases (27%) were the next highest case categories disposed of by mediation. Finally, contracts and torts were the least likely to reach agreement in mediation (20%).

Based on these comparisons, we can conclude, albeit cautiously, that while a higher percentage of mediated cases go to trial, a larger percentage are disposed of without pre-trial judge action. It may be that courts work more efficiently with mediation because judges are spared many pre-trial actions. A final place to examine efficiency is by comparing the case disposal time of mediated and general civil cases.

When viewing Table 4-18, we see that the disposition time for mediated cases has decreased over the time period of the program. On average, mediated cases were disposed of 307 days from filing. However, over time disposition decreased from a high of 517 in 1991 to a low of 227 days in 1995. In interviews, judges confirmed that, early in the program, they referred some of the older, pending cases to see if mediators could do something prior to actual trial. In other words, some of the first cases referred to mediation may have been in the system for quite some time before the judge referred them to mediation.

One could also argue that the large number of uncontested divorces and debt collection cases in the general civil sample skew comparisons with the mediated variety. Since mediated cases are typically contested divorces, then, controlling for case type is important. As a preliminary attempt at a more viable comparison, Tables 3-19 and 4-19 show case disposal time by case type.

Among mediated cases, domestic cases were disposed of faster than the other varieties (about 250 days from filing until disposal). The second fastest disposition time for mediated cases was real property disputes at about 364 days. Contract/commercial, torts, and combination/other cases all took longer with averages of over 400 days.

When comparing disposal time by case type with the general civil sample, we find interesting results. Despite the claims of mediation supporters that case disposition times would decrease under ADR, the only mediated case type that was resolved more quickly was combination/other cases. Finally, the domestic variety of general civil cases was processed faster (156 days) than those mediated (250 days).

Some qualifications need to be restated. For instance, general civil domestic cases include uncontested divorces. If we take other variables into consideration (e.g., case complexity), it may be that mediated cases are actually processed faster. The stage when a case is actually referred to the program is also important. Also, it may be that adding ADR does not actually speed the disposal of cases, but adds time to the process by including another "hurdle" (see MacCoun et. al., 1992).

In measuring case disposal from filing to disposition, several scholars have emphasized that case processing measures are problematic (see Hanson and Keilitz, 1991). For example, some cases are not referred to mediation until very late, while others might be referred shortly after filing. Hanson and Keilitz (1991) found that cases in Fulton County referred to arbitration were processed more quickly when the "clock" was started at referral time. Additionally, mediation referrals did not slow the processing of cases not referred into the program. Cases might be viewed as speedier in disposition, then, if time is measured from referral to mediation to ultimate disposal. These differences will be further explored in later chapters.

SUMMARY OF MEDIATION IN MOUNTAIN COUNTY

This chapter profiled mediated cases and provided some interesting preliminary comparisons of general civil cases and those referred to mediation. Overall, most mediated cases were contested domestic cases. The fact that mediated cases were generally domestic made many comparisons difficult. Case processing speed and the number of pretrial actions, for instance, were actually greater than those reported in general civil cases. These differences may not be so surprising if one takes into account the fact that many of domestic cases in the general civil cases are filed uncontested (see Chapter 3).

On the whole, the mediation program seems to have expanded its case referrals from Mountain County over time, but the percentage of the total county caseload that is referred remains quite small at less than 10%. It would be interesting to know why judges do not refer more cases to the program or what factors lead them to refer some rather than others. I suggested earlier that the program may be backed up with cases given that it handles 15 counties in the Ninth District. However, it may be that other motivations are leading to poor use of the program. For example, the local legal culture may have adopted the program to co-opt community mediation. Mediation may also be selectively employed for the self-interested motivations of court actors (e.g., to free up time for other cases) and not the "public good" of court efficiency.

Civil actors on the whole are similar in mediated cases as in general civil, especially to the degree that single plaintiffs are facing single defendants. This was even more pronounced in mediated cases, in part because of the large number of pro se cases filed in Mountain County civil courts. Interestingly, pro se representation was less frequent in mediated civil cases than in the general civil variety (reported in Chapter 3). The participation of judges in Mountain County mediation was higher than originally anticipated, with a few judges referring more cases than others. With regard to pre-trial participation, judges had more case involvement in mediated than in general civil cases.

Interestingly, and potentially important, was the participation of attorneys in mediated cases. Attorneys who handled cases referred to mediation were more likely to be "repeat players" and "local" than those participating in general civil cases. Judges in Mountain County may feel more comfortable referring cases to "local" attorneys who are familiar with the program. Surprisingly, though, attorneys rarely participated in the actual mediation session.

Despite this, mediation has the potential for forming court workgroups that had previously existed only in criminal courts. Mediation provides an arena that could establish closer working relationships among civil attorneys and provide for bargaining opportunities, much as plea bargaining does in criminal courts. Mediation, as an institutional change, serves to encourage attorneys to interact earlier and more often than in traditional civil litigation.

Case processing speed was also reported as a measure of court efficiency. Interestingly, the length of time to dispose of a case decreased over time and this decrease centered around the time of mediation implementation in 1992. Referring cases to mediation, then, could be saving time for judges and lawyers to devote to other cases.

Finally, mediation does not seem to affect trial rates. However, a larger number of cases that are referred to mediation do settle. These seemingly diverging results may simply reflect that a smaller percentage of general civil cases are disposed of by direct judge action (such as motions to dismiss and default judgements). In this respect at least, mediation seems to free judges and attorneys to work on other civil cases in the system.

While the data here are only preliminary, the results are exciting and encourage further examination of mediated cases and comparisons with general civil cases. In chapter 5, I will offer more definitive comparisons of mediated and general civil cases and in Chapter 6, I analyze the perspectives of system actors.

Table 4-1

**Yearly Case Referrals to Mediation by Court:
1990-1995 Filings**

Year	Superior court	State court	Totals
1991*	3	0	3 (0.5%)
1992	43	0	43 (6.9%)
1993	148	14	162 (25.9%)
1994	185	20	205 (32.7%)
1995	159	10	169 (27.0%)
1996**	42	3	45 (7.2%)
Total	*580 (92.5%)*	*47 (7.5%)*	*627 (100%)*

* 1991 Represents early cases in the Pilot project.
** 1996 Cases filed in 1995, but referred in 1996. Does not include cases filed and referred in 1996.

Table 4-2

Mediated Case Types (1990-1995 Filings)*

Case Type	Superior	State	Total (Freq/%)
Tort	68 (11.7%)	25 (53.2%)	93 (14.8%)
Contract/ Commercial	40 (6.9%)	20 (42.6%)	60 (9.6%)
Real Prop.	12 (2.0%)	0 (0.0%)	12 (1.9%)
Domestic	446 (77.0%)	0 (0.0%)	446 (71.1%)

Mediated Case Types (1990-1995 Filings)*

Case Type	Superior	State	Total (Freq/%)
Other	1 (0.2%)	0 (0.0%)	1 (0.2%)
Combo.	13 (2.2%)	2 (4.2%)	15 (2.4%)
Totals	*580 (100%)*	*47 (100%)*	*627 (100%)*

*Cases actually referred to mediation from 1991 - 1996.

Table 4-3

Mediated Case Referral Trends:
Aggregate 1991 - 1996*

Case Type	1991	1992	1993	1994	1995	1996	Totals
Tort	0%	13.7%	25.6%	13.2%	14.2%	20.0%	n=93
Contract/ Commercial	0%	12.4%	14.0%	9.3%	5.3%	11.1%	n=59
Real Prop.	0%	2.5%	2.3%	1.0%	2.4%	2.2%	n=12
Domestic	100%	70.8%	58.1%	73.2%	74.0%	64.4%	n=446
Other	0%	0%	0%	0%	0.6%	0%	n=1
Combo(Above)	0%	0.6%	0%	3.4%	3.6%	2.2%	n=15
Totals	100% (4)	100% (161)	100% (43)	100% (205)	100% (169)	100% (45)	n=627

- *Note: Cases filed in the years of 1990-1995.*

Table 4-4

Percentage of General Civil Caseloads Referred to Mediation: 1991-1995*

Mediated/Gen. Civil	1991	1992	1993	1994	1995	Totals
Superior courts						
Mediated	3	43	148	185	159	538
Gen. Civil	2896	3025	3083	3028	2807	14839
% Referred to Med.	*0.1%*	*1.4%*	*4.8%*	*6%*	*6%*	*3.6%*
State courts						
Mediated	0	0	14	20	10	44
Gen. Civil	904	994	887	972	1325	5082
% Referred to Med.	*0.0%*	*0.0%*	*1.5%*	*2.0%*	*0.7%*	*0.8%*

*Note: The mediated cases above are those referred in that year. They do not reflect that some may have been filed in a previous year.

Table 4-5

Mediated Case Referral Types within Sub-categories:
Aggregate 1991-1996

Case Category/ Case Type	Frequency	Percentage
Torts		
Auto	57	61.3%
Medical Mal.	3	3.2%
Premise Liab.	8	8.6%
Product Liab.	1	1.1%
Other Prof. Mal.	1	1.1%
Combo.	1	1.1%
Other/Unknown	22	23.7%
Total	*93*	*100.0%*
Contract/Commercial		
Debt Collection	23	38.3%
Garnishment of Wages	0	0.0%
Contract/Comm. Fraud	5	8.3%
Poor Workman./Breach	14	23.3%
Breach Contract (Unspec.)	9	15.0%
Unknown Type	9	15.0%
Total	*60*	*100.0%*
Real Property		
Condemnation of Land	1	8.3%
Other	9	75.0%
Unknown	2	16.7%
Total	*12*	*100.0%*

Table 4-5 (con't)

Domestic

Divorce	257	57.6%
Mod. of Div./Supp./Visit	83	18.6%
Mod. Change of Custody	4	0.9%
"Deadbeat Dad"/Contempt	75	16.8%
Family Violence	5	1.1%
Combo.	9	2.0%
Other/Unknown	13	2.9%
Total	*446*	*100.0%*
Grand Total	*627*	*100.0%*

Table 4-6

Number of Litigants in Mountain County Mediated Cases: Filed 1991-1996*

# of Litigants	Plaintiffs	Defendants
Cases w/ 1	562 (89.7%)	553 (88.2%)
Cases w/ 2	56 (8.9%)	47 (7.5%)
Cases w/ 3	6 (1.0%)	17 (2.7%)
Cases w/ 4 Or More	3 (0.6%)	10 (1.7%)
Average	*1.16 per case*	*1.2 per case*
Totals	*627 (100%)*	*627 (100%)*

* Cases actually filed from 1990 - 1995.

Table 4-7

**Types of Litigants in Mediated Cases:
Referred 1991-1996***

Litigant Type	Lit1	lit2	lit3
Plaintiffs			
Individual	599 (95.5%)	61 (89.7%)	9 (81.8%)
Insurance	4 (0.6%)	1 (1.5%)	1 (9.1%)
Bank/Financial	7 (1.1%)	1 (1.5%)	0 (0.0%)
Hospital/Medical	0 (0.0%)	0 (0.0%)	0 (0.0%)
Other Business	15 (2.4%)	5 (7.4%)	1 (9.1%)
Government Agency	2 (0.3%	0 (0.0%)	0 (0.0%)
Totals	*627 (100%)*	*68 (100%)*	*11 (100%)*
Defendants			
Individual	586 (93.4%)	48 (62.3%)	16 (55.2%)
Insurance	1 (0.2%)	3 (3.9%)	3 (10.3%)
Bank/Financial	1 (0.2%)	0 (0.0%)	2 (6.9%)
Hospital/Medical	2 (0.3%)	1 (1.3%)	1 (3.4%)
Other Business	34 (5.4%)	25 (32.5%)	6 (20.7%)
Government Agency	3 (0.5%)	0 (0.0%)	1 (3.4%)

Table 4-7 (con't)

Types of Litigants in Mediated Cases:
Referred 1991-1996*

Litigant Type	Lit1	lit2	lit3
Totals	627 (100%)	77 (100%)	29 (100%)

* Note: Based on cases filed in Hall Co. Courts 1990-1995.

Table 4-8

Number of Attorneys in Mediated Cases:
Plaintiff and Defendant Representation

# of Attorneys	Plaintiffs % (n)	Defendants % (n)
"One"	81.5% (511)	72.6% (455)
"Two"	13.2% (83)	12.6% (79)
"Three"	1.8% (11)	3.5% (22)
"Four"	0.3% (2)	1.0% (6)
"Five"	0.0% (0)	0.2% (1)
"Six"	0.0% (0)	0.3% (2)
Pro Se	3.2% (20)	9.9% (62)
Totals	100.0% (627)	100.0% (627)

Table 4-9

Type of Plaintiff and Defendant Attorney:
Mountain County Mediated Cases

Attorney Type (First Four listed)	Plaintiff % (n)	Defendant % (n)
First Attorney Listed		
Pro Se	3.5% (22)	10.1% (63)
Private	95.9% (601)	89.5% (561)
Legal Aid	0.2% (1)	0.0% (0)
Government	0.2% (1)	0.3% (2)
In House Attorney	0.0% (0)	0.0% (0)
Other	0.0% (0)	0.0% (0)
Missing*	0.3% (2)	0.2% (1)
Totals	*100% (627)*	*100% (627)*
Second Attorney Listed		
Pro Se	0.0% (0)	0.0% (0)
Private	12.8% (80)	15.2% (95)
Legal Aid	0.0% (0)	0.0% (0)
Government	0.0% (0)	0.3% (2)
In House Attorney	0.0% (0)	0.0% (0)
Other	0.0% (0)	0.0% (0)
Missing*	87.2% (547)	84.5% (530)
Total	*100% (627)*	*100% (627)*

Table 4-9 (Cont.)

**Type of Plaintiff and Defendant Attorney:
Mountain County Mediated Cases**

Attorney Type (First Four listed)	Plaintiff % (n)	Defendant % (n)
Third Attorney Listed		
Pro Se	0.0% (0)	0.0% (0)
Private	2.1% (13)	3.7% (23)
Legal Aid	0.0% (0)	0.0% (0)
Government	0.0% (0)	0.2% (1)
In House Attorney	0.0% (0)	0.0% (0)
Other	0.0% (0)	0.0% (0)
Missing*	97.9% (614)	96.2% (603)
Total	*100% (627)*	*100% (627)*

* Missing cases in "first attorney listed" represents cases with no attorney found. Missing cases in other attorneys listed include cases where there was no attorney listed because only one was present in the case.

Table 4-10

Attorney Participation in Mediation Sessions

Attorney Present	Percentage	(n)
No Attorney Present	70.1%	(436)
Plaintiff Att. Only	1.8%	(11)
Defendant Att. Only	1.6%	(10)
Both Atts. Present	6.0%	(37)
Unknown/Missing*	20.5%	(127)
Totals	*100%*	*627*

* Missing/Unknown cases represent those where no record of attorney presence or absence was noted in the mediated case file. No attorney Present represented that no attorney was listed on records as having participated.

Table 4-11

**"Single Shot" and "Repeat Player" Attorneys:
Mediated Cases**

Appearances	Total	Plaintiff	Defendant
"One Shotters"	61.8% (196)	65.9% (141)	55.8% (141)
2-4 Appearances	23.7% (75)	22.4% (48)	31.2% (57)
5-10 Appearances	8.2% (26)	7.9% (17)	9.8% (18)
11-19 Appearances	3.8% (12)	1.9% (4)	2.7% (5)
20 or More	2.5% (8)	1.9% (4)	0.5% (1)
Totals	100% (317)	100% (214)	100% (183)

* Note that figures above do not include attorneys who where missing from the file or cases with no attorney listed (e.g. pro se).

Table 4-12

Attorney Location: "Locals" and "Outsiders" to Mountain County Mediated Cases*

Attorney Location	Totals	Plaintiff	Defendant
"Locals"	73.1% (860)	72.4% (441)	73.8% (419)
"Outsiders"	20.1% (236)	23.0% (140)	16.9% (96)
"Unknown"	6.8% (81)	4.6% (28)	9.3% (53)
Totals	*100% (1177)*	*100% (609)*	*100% (568)*

* Excludes pro se and other cases with no attorney (e.g. defaults). Attorneys coded "local" if office in Mountain County, else coded "outsider".

Table 4-13

Attorney/Opponent Pairings: Who Opposes Who in Mountain County Mediated Cases?

Attorney/Opponent Pairing	Frequency
Attorney versus Attorney Pairings	
"Local versus Local"	57.2% (320)
"Local versus Outsider"	25.2% (141)
"Outsider versus Outsider"	6.4% (36)
Pro Se Pairings	
"Local versus Pro Se"	7.3% (41)

Table 4-13 (con't)

Attorney/Opponent Pairing	Frequency
"Outsider versus Pro Se"	2.1% (12)
"Pro Se versus Pro Se"	1.6% (9)
Total Cases*	100% (559)

* 68 cases produced missing data because information on attorney office could not be found in the record.

Table 4-14

Participation of Judges in Mediated Cases:
Who Refers Cases?*

Judge/ Ct. Type	# of Mediated Referred Per Year					
	1991	1992	1993	1994	1995	Totals
State court Cases						
Fulltime	1	12	12	8	7	40
Parttime	0	1	2	2	2	7
Superior court Cases						
Ftime A	7	28	65	50	54	204
Ftime B	7	14	1	0	0	22
Ftime C	13	33	33	51	50	180

Table 4-14 (con't)

Judge/ Ct. Type	# of Mediated Referred Per Year					
	1991	1992	1993	1994	1995	Totals
Ftime D	0	4	55	42	37	138
Retired	0	3	2	2	1	8
Other	2	1	6	5	2	16

* Note that judges names were not reported as a condition of anonymity for interview reported later.

Table 4-15

Pre-Trial Actions in Mountain County Mediated Cases
Referred 1991-1996

Total #	# Actions	# Hearings*
"None"	31.6% (198)	85.5% (536)
"One"	20.3% (127)	10.5% (66)
"Two"	15.5% (97)	2.6% (16)
"Three"	11.0% (69)	0.8% (5)
"Four"	4.2% (26)	0.2% (1)

Civil Mediation In Mountain County

Table 4-15 (con't)

Total #	# Actions	# Hearings*
"Five +"	17.4% (109)	0.6% (3)
Average Per Case	2.66	.22
Range	0-49	0-9

Pretrial actions included continuances, discovery attempts (depositions), leaves of absences, and motions (compel, dismiss, etc. Pretrial hearings included hearings on motions or other formal hearings before a judge.

* Note: Unlike general civil cases, domestic cases hear DID include routine temporary hearings that occurred commonly in divorce cases. Comparisons with general civil cases are invalid until corrected.

Table 4-16

Types of Post-Trial Actions in Mountain County Mediated Cases
Cases Referred 1991-1996

Total #	# Actions	# Hearings
"None"	95.8% (600)	97.9% (614)
"One"	3.5% (22)	1.9% (12)
"Two"	0.5% (3)	0.2% (1)
"Three"	0.0% (0)	0.0% (0)

Table 4-16 (con't)

Total #	# Actions	# Hearings
"Four"	0.2% (1)	0.0% (0)
"Five"	0.0% (0)	0.0% (0)
Average Per Case	.05	.02
Range	0-4	0-2

Post-trial actions and hearings include motions to reconsider, motions to compel post-trial discovery, motion for new trials, etc.

Table 4-17

Mediated Case Disposition Types:
by Major Case Types

Disposition	Tort	Contract	Property	Domestic
Trials				
Jury	21.7% (20)	10.3% (6)	0.0% (0)	2.3% (10)
Bench	1.1% (1)	1.7% (1)	9.1% (1)	6.8% (30)
Settlements				
Mediated Sett.	20.7% (19)	20.7% (16)	27.5% (3)	37.6% (167)
Pre/Post Trial	53.4% (49)	43.1% (25)	36.4% (4)	2.5% (11)
Consent Decree	0.0% (0)	10.3% (6)	18.2% (2)	24.3% (108)
Pretrial (Judge)				
Summary Judge.	0.0% (0)	3.4% (2)	0.0% (0)	0.0% (0)

Table 4-17 (con't)

Disposition	Tort	Contract	Property	Domestic
Pretrial Order	0.0% (0)	0.0% (0)	0.0% (0)	23.2% (103)
Default	0.0% (0)	1.7% (1)	0.0% (0)	1.1% (5)
Dis. Lack Pros	2.2% (2)	6.9% (4)	0.0% (0)	1.4% (6)
Other Dismiss	0.0% (0)	0.0% (0)	0.0% (0)	0.0% (0)
Others Transfer	0.0% (0)	0.0% (0)	0.0% (0)	0.0% (0)
Pending	1.1% (1)	1.7% (1)	0.0% (0)	0.9% (4)
Totals	*100% (92)*	*100% (58)*	*100% (11)*	*100% (444)*

	Tort	Contract	Property	Domestic
Trials Jury		6.7% (1)		5.9% (37)
Bench		0.0% (0)		5.3% (33)
Settlements Mediated Agree.		33.3% (5)		33.7% (210)
Pre/Post Trial		33.3% (5)		15.1% (94)
Consent Agree.		6.7% (1)		18.7% (117)
Pre-Trial (Judge Ordered) Summary Judge.		0.0% (0)		0.3% (2)
Pre-Trial Order		0.0% (0)		16.6% (103)

Table 4-17 (con't)

Disposition	Tort	Contract	Property	Domestic
Default		0.0% (0)		1.0% (6)
Dis. Lack Pros.		6.7% (1)		2.0% (13)
Other Dismiss		13.3% (2)		0.3% (2)
Others				
Transfer		0.0% (0)		0.0% (0)
Pending		6.7% (1)		1.1% (7)
Totals		100% (16)		100% (621)

Table 4-18

**Average Case Processing Time:
Mountain County Mediated by Year Filed**

Year	Time from Filing to Disposition	(n)
1990	1208 days	n = 3
1991	517 days	n = 30
1992	452 days	n = 97
1993	300 days	n = 173
1994	244 days	n = 154
1995	227 days	n = 150
Totals	*307 days*	*n = 607*

* Missing cases include those that are pending or where dates were missing.

Table 4-19

**Average Case Processing Time:
Mountain County Mediated by Major Case Type**

Case Type	Time from Filing to Disposition	(n)
Tort	447 days	n = 88
Contract/Commercial	498 days	n = 56
Real Property	365 days	n = 12
Domestic	250 days	n = 437
Combination/Others	406 days	n = 14
Totals	*307 days*	*n = 607*

* Note that missing cases include those that are pending or where dates were missing.

CHAPTER 5
The Impact of Mediation On Case Processing In Mountain County

The data presented in Chapters 3 and 4 offer descriptive profiles of civil justice and mediation in Mountain County. Preliminary analyses of these data yielded very interesting and contrasting patterns about the effect that mediation had on the general civil system. On one hand, the mediation program did not seem to speed up case disposition, decrease trial rates, or limit pretrial filings and actions as compared to the general civil case sample. On the other hand, mediated cases had higher settlement rates than general civil cases, and were less likely to be disposed of by direct judge action in pretrial processes. Most important was a decrease in case processing time among the general civil cases shortly after program implementation. It may be, then, that referring cases to mediation speeds up case processing overall.

The comparison of mediated and general civil cases, however, is more complicated than one might expect. The above results, for example, do not take into account the type and/or complexity of cases referred to mediation. This is important, as mediated cases are significantly different from the average civil case.

In this chapter, I provide the first of two answers to the question: how has mediation affected civil litigation in Mountain County? Using quantitative evidence culled from case records, I take a closer look at the effects of mediation on civil justice in Mountain County by controlling for some factors that may contribute to case efficiency variation. I also assess the effects of mediation on civil justice over time. These data are presented in a simple interrupted time series analysis--three years before and after the mediation program began in 1992. Later, in Chapter 6, I will provide a more qualitative answer to the same question.

SUMMARY OF PERTINENT RESERACH

Social scientific studies of mediation as it affects civil court systems are rare, as Keilitz (1994) has noted. Most studies of mediation provide in-house assessments of programs that emphasize impact. According to Harrington (1982; 1985), these studies detail attention to the effect mediation has had on both courts and clients. In the following section, I follow Harrington's assessment of the social scientific literature on mediation (1982, 1985) by providing an overview of what we know about the effects of mediation on civil courts.

There are some studies that have assessed the impact of mediation on civil and domestic cases in civil courts. These studies have primarily addressed the "effects on pace, litigation costs, court workload, trial rates, [and] settlement rates" (National Center for State Courts, 1994). In general, these studies yield mixed results as to the effect of mediation.

Studies of the effects of mediation on criminal and civil cases generally have found little impact on court workload. On the criminal side, Harrington specifically notes that criminal court mediation does not reduce court congestion or delay (1982: 176). Similarly, studies of mediation in domestic and civil cases have also found little impact on the overall workload of courts (Pearson, 1994: 61). In this regard, note that research on the Neighborhood Justice Centers emphasizes that the number of cases referred to mediation is too small to impact court workloads (Harrington, 1982; Ray, 1981).

This said, researchers argue that mediation removes the most difficult and time consuming contested cases that courts must handle (Pearson, 1994; Fix and Harter, 1992; McIssac, 1981). By removing these particular cases, Fix and Harter argue that the impact of mediation is felt by judges and court personnel (1992; see Pearson, 1994).

The evidence on how domestic mediation affects court resources is more mixed, however, when we examine repeat appearances in the justice system and what happens to cases that do not settle in mediation. In one study, researchers found that post-divorce appearances in courts may actually increase as a result of mediation (Keilitz et al., 1992).

Cases that do not reach agreement in mediation might increase costs for courts. In their study of the Washington, D.C. Multidoor Courthouse, Fix and Harter (1992) found that these cases use up considerable legal system resources. Cases proceed from court to mediation, receive resources from the mediation program, and then return to the court system for more legal intervention. When one includes the additional resources of the mediation program (e.g., mediator time and administrative costs), these cases may cost more than the average civil or domestic case.

One additional way to measure the effect of mediation on court workload is to examine the number of formal actions taken in a case. For instance, do mediated cases have fewer motion or discovery attempts than non-mediated cases? Two studies of mediation in non-domestic civil cases reported that the number of motions and hearings decreased overall (Kobbervig, 1991; McEwen, 1991). For example, in McEwen's study of ADR in two Maine counties, fewer hearings were held in mediated cases (30%) versus the control group cases (54%). However, in their study of North Carolina civil mediation, Clarke and his colleagues (1995) found that mediated cases did not reduce court workload as measured by the average number of motions and pretrial orders. However, several judges reported that mediation did free up time by settling cases earlier in the process (vii). Many of these cases might normally have proceeded to the trial date and taken up scheduled court time--only to "settle on the courthouse steps."

In addition to scrutinizing caseloads and pretrial actions, studies commonly compare litigation time for mediated and general civil cases. As reported in the study by Clarke et al. (1995: iv), judges argued that mediated cases settled earlier, thereby saving court time and resources. Studies of non-domestic civil cases, however, have produced mixed results on case processing speed (Schultz, 1990; Kobbervig, 1991; McEwen, 1991; Clarke et al., 1995).

In his study of Florida, Schultz (1990) found that mediated cases were processed faster than non-mediated cases from mediation referral to disposition date. However, when processing speed was measured from filing to disposition, general civil cases were processed faster than mediated cases (in part, because "older" cases were referred to mediation). In McEwen's (1991) study of New Jersey, those cases that were successfully settled in mediation were processed faster than non-mediated cases. However, these effects were muted when cases that did not settle during mediation were later sent back into the system. Kobbervig (1991) also found limited time savings in cases mediated in Minnesota. These mediated cases were processed at the same speed or slower than those that were arbitrated or those that were disposed of in the court system (1991). In North Carolina, though, processing speed was significantly slower than cases in a control group. However, the researchers reported that a significant proportion of cases referred were settled prior to mediation, thus speeding disposition for a subset of cases (Clarke et al., 1995). The data on domestic cases also yield mixed results (1994). Some studies conclude that settlements are quickly reached in mediated cases as compared to cases that are litigated. In both the Charlottesville, Virginia and Denver, Colorado studies, cases that settled in mediation yielded time savings (Emery and Wyer, 1987; Pearson, 1981, respectively). However, in the Denver study, cases that did not settle in mediation moved slower because they were processed in mediation and then sent back to the courts (Pearson, 1981). Finally, in a study by the National Center for State Courts, case processing speed was inconsistent among four jurisdictions in Florida, Nevada, New Mexico, and North Carolina (Keilitz, 1992). In its explanation, NCSC attributes the observed differences to the complexity of case processing patterns by courts and local legal culture (Keilitz, et al., 1992; See Pearson, 1994).

Proponents of mediation hypothesize that mediation refers cases out of adversarial court systems and into a process that promotes consensus and agreement. Cases, then, should be more likely to settle. Studies of non-domestic civil cases were directed to this proposition. In studies of Florida, Maine, and Minnesota programs, mediated cases had only slightly higher settlement rates than the general civil variety (McEwen, 1991; Schultz, 1990). Even though cases may not settle during mediation, they may be more likely to settle soon afterwards through negotiation. McEwen (1991) raises the possibility that mediation may increase settlement overall by putting some of the issues in a case to rest by "getting parties talking" prior to trial (see also Keilitz, 1994). Additionally, Clarke et al. (1995) argue that some cases might settle shortly after referral but before the mediation for similar reasons.

Evaluations of settlement rates in family disputes seem to show more mediation effects than in general civil litigation. According to Pearson, across studies "settlements stand in the 50-75 percent range" (1994: 60-61). For example, settlement rates in the Denver program were 60 percent (Pearson, 1981), while the court-annexed program in Charlottesville yielded an even higher rate of 75 percent (Emery and Wyer, 1987).

Like research on settlement rates, studies of general civil trial rates offer mixed evidence. In Maine, McEwen (1991) reported evidence that ADR decreased trial rates (10% in assigned ADR cases, 2% in voluntary ADR cases) over those not mediated (13%). In the Minnesota program, the experimental group cases had slightly higher trial rates (Kobbervig,

1991). More recent evidence from North Carolina, however, establishes the contrary (Clarke et al. 1995). Neither settlement rates nor trial rates were significantly affected by the mediation of civil cases (35-37).

All of these studies suggest that mediation provides "spillover" effects that are sometimes difficult to measure (Pearson, 1994). One very old legal adage is that cases tend to "settle on the courthouse steps" and right before trial. One "spillover" effect of mediation is that cases may settle shortly after a failed mediation. Mediation, for instance, might resolve some of the issues in a case and lead to a quicker settlement. In Denver, Pearson (1981) found that a majority of cases that failed in mediation settled later, with only 20% of the remaining cases disposed of by judicial action (see Pearson, 1994).

Mediation is also argued to cause cases to settle after referral but prior to mediation. Some argue that by referring a case to mediation, attorneys consult with their clients (and each other) to plan for the mediation session. By getting people "talking" earlier in the process, parties may settle a case rather than proceed to mediation. For trial courts, such a pattern would prove valuable by speeding caseflow. Two studies have found evidence that significant proportions of cases settle between referral and the actual mediation (Kressel et al., 1991; Keilitz et al., 1992; See Pearson, 1994). For instance, Kressel and colleagues (1991) found that about 17% of custody/visitation disputes referred to mediation reached agreement prior to mediation.

A final impact that mediation may have on civil court systems is the stimulation of different types of agreements and remedies. Proponents argue that mediation provides an arena that focuses on the development of consensus, even a different institutional process for resolving disputes. The differing rules and norms in mediation should stimulate different actor behavior and different outcomes, patterns consistent with theories of new institutionalism.

Mediation proponents such as Keating and Love (1998), for example, argue that the decision in mediation is made by the parties and that they participate to persuade each other, not the mediator. The role of the mediator in mediation, then, is to facilitate discussion, to bring out the emotions underlying the dispute, and to facilitate listening. While the issues in adjudication are limited to legal issues, those in mediation are limited only to what the parties decide to discuss. Finally, remedies in mediation are considered to be beneficial to both sides as the process is collaborative and cooperative.

In general, most research finds that mediated outcomes are likely to be different from those of the formal justice system (i.e., negotiation and adjudication). McEwen (1992) emphasizes that

> [mediated] outcomes may include greater specification of settlement terms, non-monetary arrangements, and/or detailed conditions for implementation of the agreement. Like negotiation, mediation often--but not always--leads to somewhat lower monetary settlements than might be awarded after trial (155-156).

However, Pearson's (1993: 66-68) survey of the research on family mediation indicates that many of these studies are imperfect at best and that the results are mixed. Some studies identified substantial mediation agreements (Richardson, 1988) while others reveal the opposite (Ray, 1988; Pearson, 1993: 66-68). Most, however, find that outcomes resemble each other in many ways. For example, joint parenting arrangements seem to be the dominant form of custody in both mediated and adversarial agreements (Dusquesnal, 1991; Pearson, 1991; Kelly, 1990; see Pearson, 1993). Despite these arrangements, Maccoby and Mnookin (1992) emphasize that the primary custodial parent is still the mother, regardless of forum. Visitation arrangements, property division, and alimony awards also appear to be similar in both mediated and non-mediated forums (Pearson, 1993: 68). Finally, as to amounts offered in divorce orders, one study in Delaware found that child support order levels are lower in mediation (see Pearson and Theonnes, 1985), while a recent comparison in Georgia found that mediated agreements closely approximated court guidelines (see Bohmer and Ray, 1992).

One area where mediation does seem to make a difference in child support is in benefits and extension of coverage. Mediated agreements seem more likely to extend coverage past the age of 18 and were more likely to include college expenses, insurance, and other medical expenses (Kelly, 1990; Pearson, 1991; see Pearson, 1993).

Despite the differences between mediated and non-mediated case outcomes, others suggest that there are remarkable similarities. Pearson (1993: 67), for example, argues that other institutional factors, like state child support guidelines, may be responsible for the consistency in the outcomes of family law forums. This suggests that institutional change does produce alterations in the behavior of system actors but that the behavior may lead to unintended outcomes. This is consistent with the theories of new institutionalists (see March and Olsen, 1989; Smith, 1988), as well as the work of policy implementation scholars of the "bottom up" school (see Mazmanian and Sabatier, 1989 or Goggin et al., 1990). In this chapter, I will highlight the changes that have been produced by mediation in the civil justice process of Mountain County, Georgia. My primary focus here is on civil procedure and the disposal patterns of mediated and general civil cases. Because of the problems inherent in identifying, investigating, and comparing outcomes of civil cases, this chapter does not provide an assessment of the outcomes of the systems.

DATA AND METHODS

As noted earlier, the data in this chapter focus on the impact of mediation on case processing in Mountain County. Building on Chapters 3 and 4, this effort offers more refined comparisons of mediated and non-mediated cases before and after the implementation of the program. To understand the potential changes highlighted previously, this portion of the study looks at mediated and non-mediated cases by addressing the issues of case type and complexity. By using more refined comparisons, key case processing variables are examined before and after program implementation.

The methods of data analysis include simple descriptive statistics, comparisons of means, and time series. As to caseloads and workloads, controls are included for case type and time, while court workload measures consist of pretrial actions and motions. Additionally and for a more refined comparison, uncontested cases are removed from the general civil sample.[43]

The results that follow consist of the percentage of settlements in mediation versus the number of partial agreements and non-agreements. Data are also included on how quickly cases are mediated, on agreements made in follow-up mediation, and when in the case process mediation cases are disposed of.

Next, comparisons of mediated and general civil case dispositions are provided by case type and whether the case was contested. A time series is also used to examine whether the intervention point of the mediation program marks decreased settlement and trial rates.

Finally, data related to litigation time for mediated and general civil cases are presented. These address four questions: What is the average pace of litigation when measured from filing versus referral dates? How do mediated and general civil case processing speeds compare for aggregate, domestic, torts, and "contested" case levels? What are the rates (in days) for cases that settle in mediation and those that do not? Finally, does pace of litigation improve before and after mediation?

IMPACT OF MEDIATION ON CASELOADS

With the start of the mediation program in 1992 as an interruption point, did the mediation program in Mountain County significantly impact Mountain County civil court caseloads and workloads? For the period of this study (1989-1995), Mountain County Superior court caseloads ranged from 2417 in 1989 to a high of 3083 in 1993. As a whole, the trend indicates that caseloads were rising slightly over the period. Also, State court filings ranged from a low of 546 in 1989 with a steady increase to 1325 in 1995 (Table 3-1). In the study's time period, then, Mountain County general civil caseloads rose steadily.

By comparing the number of cases referred to mediation from Mountain County civil courts, the impact of mediation on the overall caseload appears negligible (see Table 4-1). The largest number of Superior court cases referred out of the system was 185 in 1994. Overall, though, the referral of civil cases from Superior court increased dramatically from 43 in 1992 to the mid-to-high 100s in 1993-1995. In State court, even though the caseloads rose a great deal, only 14, 20, and 10 cases were referred to mediation during 1993-1995.

Despite the fact that a larger number of civil cases was referred by the Mountain County Superior court, the data support assertions by Harrington (1995) that the extremely small proportion of cases referred can have only a minimal impact on civil court case processing. For example, in Figure 5-1, time series presentation of the percentage of Mountain County civil caseloads referred to mediation indicates that the total percentage of cases referred from Superior courts steadily increased from 1991 to 1995. However, that percentage reaches only 6% by 1995. State court judges referred even smaller percentages of cases (approaching only 2% in 1994).

The conclusion that effects on caseloads are negligible, however, may be somewhat misleading. Some cases that are filed in court systems are, in fact, not eligible for mediation. For example, many of the cases in the Mountain County system may not have been answered by defendants or the case was so simple as to not warrant mediation (e.g., uncontested divorce filings). Other cases may not be referred to mediation because a judge views them as inappropriate (e.g., a debt collection case where the amount is undisputed and garnishment proceedings are established). It is possible, then, that mediation does have an impact on court systems in certain case types where mediation is most often employed (i.e., domestic relations). Additionally, it is possible that the types of cases that are mediated are the types of cases that take up more court resources and time (e.g., contested divorces and child support actions). Thus, by removing even a small number of these cases, the courts may be free to place effort in other areas (e.g., criminal cases).

IMPACT OF MEDIATION ON COURT WORKLOAD

Although mediation may not have a substantial effect on overall caseloads, it is possible that it leads to increasing settlements, decreasing litigation time, and decreasing the workload of judges and other court officials. There are, however, real difficulties in finding information on how much time a judge or attorney spends on a case (Clarke et al., 1995). One way that scholars have attempted to measure pretrial workload is simply to count the number of motions and other pretrial actions found in case files and compare mediated and general civil cases along these lines.

Chapters 3 and 4 indicated that mediated cases took up more court time as measured by the number of pretrial actions and hearings. These results, however, are based on aggregate case figures and do not control for the types of cases most likely to be sent to mediation. Additionally, the general civil cases included uncontested actions that were usually filed with the clerk's office in a rather routine fashion. These cases may have distorted any comparisons.

For finer comparisons, a variety of case types was analyzed. These included domestic only, divorce only, torts, automobile torts, and all "contested" cases. Controlling for these case types provides a more accurate means to compare mediated and general civil cases. Additionally, since mediated cases are likely to be contested cases, contested general civil cases were separated for similar analysis. What do the measures of court workload look like, then, when controlled for these case types and complexity?

In "all domestic cases" and "divorce cases only," there were mixed results. On average, there were more pretrial hearings in general civil cases. However, there were more pretrial actions in mediated cases (see Table 5-1). Even so, the differences may be considered minimal because the median number of pretrial hearings for each was zero. The median number of pretrial actions was also zero for general civil and only one for mediated cases.[44]

In all tort cases, there were more pretrial hearings and total actions in mediated cases, with a median of 4 total actions in mediated cases as compared with 1 in general civil cases. For automobile torts, results were also mixed, with the number of pretrial hearings nearly indistinguishable. However, mediated cases had slightly more total pretrial actions.

When comparing mediated cases to those formally answered or contested by defendants, the results show some effects of mediation. Total pretrial actions were slightly higher than in contested general civil cases. Of further interest is that contested general civil cases, as predicted, had slightly more pretrial hearings. The differences are probably insignificant, though, given that the means were very similar and the medians both zero.

As a whole, the results are mixed. When viewing the results in the aggregate, as in Chapter 4, we find that mediated cases do not reduce court workload. In both the measures of pretrial hearings and total pretrial actions, the averages were higher for mediated cases. However, more refined comparisons that control for case type and complexity show some effect for mediation.

One possible explanation for this is that mediated cases are the more difficult cases in the court system and would entail more work in any case. Judges may refer cases to mediation that would be most likely to expend court resources with the hopes that they would settle and save future court time. This parallels Clarke et al.'s (1995: vii, 37) suggestion that senior judges think that mediation saves court resources by getting cases to settle earlier in the process rather than settling at the "courthouse door" before a scheduled trial.

Despite the aforementioned results, it is necessary to consider some measurement problems. First, the number of pretrial actions does not include the actual referral of cases to mediation. Mediated case actions,

The Impact of Mediation

then, are slightly underestimated. This suggests that mediation may present an additional step in the civil process that actually provides more work for courts.

Second, the measurement of hearings and motions can be viewed as imperfect given that the data were culled from case files. Even though this is a commonly used data source (see Clarke et al., 1995), an interview with one Mountain County attorney revealed that many motions and case actions take place and are never formally filed with court clerks. Thus, the total number of actions may be under-represented as well.

IMPACT OF MEDIATION ON CASE DISPOSITIONS

Mediated and general civil cases have been argued to have different disposal patterns. In general, proponents of mediation argue that settlement rates are higher in mediation and that trial rates are lower. In order to assess the impact of mediation on settlement and trial rates, it is necessary to understand disposition patterns for mediated caseloads. How are mediated caseloads disposed of, and where in the process of a case's "life" are they disposed?

Table 5-2 provides a profile of whether a case reached agreement if referred to mediation. In the 621 cases referred to mediation, 35.3% reached a full agreement in the mediation itself.[45] In a slightly lower percentage of cases (34.9%), no agreement was reached by disputants. However, claims that mediation often resolves some issues even if the case does not settle have some support here. About 13% of all mediated cases reached a partial agreement where some issues were left to adjudication or formal settlement. Finally, in about 17% of cases referred to mediation, no mediation occurred. These cases included those where a party in the case did not show up or where a case may have been settled between referral and the mediation.

In Table 5-2, the amount of time it takes for a case to be mediated is reported. The average mediation lasted approximately 2 1/3 hours and ranged from no time to 14 total hours--including additional mediation sessions. Some mediation, then, is repeated when a settlement cannot be reached or a partial settlement is made. In the vast majority of cases (93.9%), however, there is only one mediation effort, whether the parties settle or not. Only 34 of the cases (5.5%) had an additional mediation session, three with three additional attempts and one case with four mediation efforts. In these cases, parties reached agreement later in 20 cases and remained at impasse in 16.

As to settlement and disposal, where in the "life" of a case are mediated cases disposed of? About 10% of the cases referred to mediation actually settled before the mediation session date, suggesting that mediation may get disputants and their attorneys "talking" and may lead to quicker settlement of cases. In about 35% of cases, as mentioned earlier, parties reached full agreement in the mediation session itself. The largest proportion of mediated cases actually settled after mediation but prior to the trial date. This finding suggests that mediation might lead to partial agreements or avenues in which a case can settle before trial. Most cases settle anyway so the results may not be so surprising unless the cases actually settled earlier than general civil cases or would not have settled save for mediation. Finally, in 69 cases (about 11%) the parties did not settle and the case was eventually disposed of at trial.

Because mediated cases may inherently differ from the average civil case, comparison of mediated and general civil cases should control for case type. How do mediated case dispositions compare with general civil cases of similar variety?

In an earlier section on court workloads, the most accurate and interesting comparisons were in the areas of domestic and other contested civil cases. The "domestic" category is the modal case type referred to mediation, while the "contested" measure allows us to control (in an imperfect way) for the most complex of general civil cases. In Tables 5-3 and 5-4, a summary comparison of mediated and general civil cases along these two dimensions (leaving out comparisons of divorce, tort, and auto cases analyzed above) is provided.

Comparisons of mediated and contested general civil sample produce remarkably similar results (see Table 5-3) along four categories: trials, settlements, judge ordered dismissals, and others. When comparing this more refined general civil sample of contested cases, we find similar trial rates (slightly lower at 9.9% than 11.2%). However, mediated cases had higher settlement rates than general civil cases, largely because of the fairly high percentage of cases that are disposed of by pre-trial judge action. In the contested sample, however, we find that settlements in mediated cases were only slightly higher (67.5% v. 63.9%). Also of interest is the fact that a similar percentage of mediated cases and general civil cases was disposed of by pretrial judge action (20.2% v. 19.1%).

When comparing cases of a similar nature and complexity (here contested cases), the results differ from the aggregate comparisons presented in earlier chapters. These data prompted questions on whether mediation made a real difference in case disposition. Here, it appears that contested general civil cases have slightly lower to similar settlement rates and slightly lower trial rates.

As to case type, most mediated cases fall in the domestic variety. Comparing general domestic cases with mediated domestic cases is also necessary to control for case type. How do dispositions differ on this dimension? Interestingly, the efficiency goals of mediation proponents do not seem to be met in the general area of domestic relations (see Table 5-4). Mediated domestic cases had a higher percentage of trials (9.1% v. 5.5%), a lower percentage of settlements (64.3% v. 68.5%), and a higher proportion of cases disposed by judges in a pretrial setting (25.9% v. 24%). The comparisons in Table 5-4 are significant with a the chi-square figure of 467.814 ($x < .001$).

When controlling for case type and complexity, mediation does not seem to impact court efficiency. For the most part, trial rates are indistinguishable or higher in mediated cases, and settlement rates are mixed. Additionally, a fair proportion of mediated cases (as in general civil) have disposition types that involve pretrial actions by judges.

Does this completely eliminate the possibility that mediation impacts disposition? When viewing the data on mediation agreement rates discussed above, it is clear that a large proportion of cases do not settle in mediation. Some of the research reviewed earlier indicates that cases that do not settle in mediation, however, may be quite contentious and lead to trial or require judge-aided disposal. However, a fair proportion of cases involved partial agreements, which may lead to a later settlement and even speed the settlement. Finally, these data are not compared over time, before and after mediation intervention. As it stands, the general civil case sample includes cases that existed before the program was in effect. The next section, then, examines settlement and trial rates for mediated and general civil cases in a time series.

What do dispositions look like for mediated and general civil cases over time? Trial and settlement rates for aggregate, mediated, and general civil caseloads are analyzed in Figures 2 and 3. As explained earlier, 1992 should be viewed as the point of program intervention, so general civil cases will be analyzed before and after mediation, and mediated cases will be assessed only during the latter.[46]

In Figures 2 and 3, aggregate caseloads are compared for trial and settlement rates over time. On each graph, trial and settlement rates are compared for all cases (labelled aggregate), general civil, and mediated caseloads. The aggregate trend in Figure 2 is not clear as to whether trial rates are affected by mediation. Trial rates were fairly low between the years of 1989-1991 (range between 5% and 8.5%), but early in the program years (1992-1993) trial rates actually increased to around ten percent. Thereafter, there was a sharp drop in trial rates (1994 to 3.7%) and then a subsequent increase to 6% in 1995. Figure 2, provides a separate trend analysis for mediated and general civil cases.

Interestingly, trial rates in general civil cases decreased after mediation started in 1992, with drops after the early mediation years of 1992 and 1993. It may be that removing mediated cases from the system led to lower overall trial rates because the more difficult, contested cases were referred to mediation. The total number of trial cases, however, is quite small, so it is difficult to draw firm conclusions.

The trend in Figure 2 lends some support to the above claim as it seems that trial rates for the mediation cases were high early in the program history. However, in 1994 and 1995 the trial rates for mediated cases also decreased. When compared with the trial rates for general civil cases, though, it is clear that more mediated cases proceeded to trial than general civil (11.4% total versus 5% total).

Figure 3 displays settlement rates for all cases. Taking mediated and general civil cases together, we find that settlement rates after mediation increased in comparison to before mediation (from the mid-50% range to the low to mid-60% range). Again, this may simply reflect that mediated cases are included in the sample of general civil cases. The comparison of mediated and general civil cases in Figure 3 lends additional support for this as mediated cases had higher settlement rates than general civil cases over time. Interestingly, settlements in general civil cases increased as well, with the exception of 1995.[47] It is possible that settlements are on the rise in Mountain County in general, but it is also possible that by removing cases from the system through mediation, time is freed for case settlement or removal by pretrial judicial orders. As before, Figure 3A presents data on the number of cases settled before and after mediation.

In summary, this analysis indicates that mediation may have impacted case processing in Mountain County. Trial rates in mediated cases are higher than in the general civil sample, but this may simply reflect the fact that mediation pulls the more difficult cases out of the civil system. Settlement rates in mediation are, after all, higher than in general civil cases over time.

One final way to measure the impact of mediation on civil courts is to analyze the pace of litigation. Are mediated cases processed faster than general civil cases? Does mediation free up the time of judges and attorneys for other cases?

IMPACT OF MEDIATION ON LITIGATION TIME

Does mediation affect the pace of litigation? Previous research has found that mediation seems to increase the pace of litigation or decrease delay (Clarke et al., 1995; Kobbervig, 1991; McEwen, 1991; Schultz, 1990). However, there are some caveats. Measurement of mediation from referral date to disposition often shows an increase in speed because cases are sometimes referred even years after the filing date (Schultz, 1990). However, some comparisons of mediated and general civil cases based on filing to disposition also found positive results for mediation. Mediated cases that do not settle, however, have often been found to stay in the civil process longer (McEwen, 1991).

In Table 5-5, the average pace of litigation for all mediated and all general civil cases is compared. These aggregate statistics suggest that mediated cases are actually processed more slowly than general civil cases. When pace of litigation is measured from filing to disposition, mediated cases are disposed of in about 307 days as opposed to 239 in general civil cases.

One problem with this measurement of time is that it is very conservative. For instance, it is possible (and even probable) that some cases referred to mediation are older cases that were filed as many as two years earlier. There is, then, a lag time between the filing of a case and the time a judge considers it and makes the decision to refer to mediation. It may be appropriate, then, to measure the pace of litigation from referral to disposal (see Schultz, 1990). When pace of litigation is measured in this fashion, mediated cases are processed over three months faster than general civil cases (see Table 5-5: 135 days versus 239).[48]

Using the more conservative measure of litigation pace, how do mediated and general civil cases of various types differ? As in the section on settlement and trial rates, the cases are compared along case type with attention to domestic, divorce, tort, auto, and contested claims (see Table 5-5). Interestingly, when controlling for the four major case types that are mediated (domestic, divorce, tort, and auto), general civil cases process more quickly than mediated ones. These results seem to call the arguments of ADR proponents into question. However, they do not take into account that the mediated cases could have been years old when referred or that some of the general civil cases are uncontested.

When looking at the 399 "contested" general civil cases for a more accurate comparison, the results suggest that mediation has a positive effect. Contested general civil cases process almost two months slower (360.5 days) than mediated cases (307.4 days).

The results presented in Table 5-5, then, are mixed. On the whole, mediated cases process more slowly than general civil cases when time is measured conservatively from filing date to disposition date. Mediated cases, however, do process more quickly when the measurement of pace begins with the referral and not the actual filing date. It is important to note, however, that mediated cases are different from the average civil case in the Mountain County system. When controlling for case type, mediated cases still process more slowly then general civil cases with the important exception of contested cases.

Previous research tells us that cases that settle in the mediation process faster than cases that settle through traditional negotiation (McEwen, 1991). It is difficult, however, to compare processing speed of mediated and general civil cases by disposition type. Still it is possible to compare mediated and general civil cases that are formally tried. Additionally, it is possible to compare those mediated and general civil cases that settle before trial. Related analysis starts with the average disposition speed of mediated cases by stage in the civil process.

Table 5-6 reports the average litigation time (in days) for mediated cases at each disposition stage. For the most part, delay increases as a case is disposed in later stages of the civil process. For instance, in cases where an agreement is reached in mediation, the average length of litigation is 273 days as opposed to 403 days for cases that are later disposed of at trial. Unexpectedly, cases that settled between referral and eventual mediation were processed more slowly than those that settled in mediation (315 days versus 273). It is possible, though, that the sample of 62 cases is skewed by older cases that were referred long after filing.

Table 5-6 also reports a comparison of mediated and general civil litigation pace with controls for disposition type. Here, cases that went to trial are compared with those that were disposed of before trial.[49] Neither comparison yields results that support the arguments of ADR proponents. Mediated cases that went to trial were processed about two months slower (403 days versus 341 days). Similarly, mediated cases that were disposed of before trial were processed more slowly than general civil cases (again by approximately two months). In the final analysis, it may be that referring a case to mediation constitutes an additional procedural hurdle.

Neither of the comparisons discussed take into account the factor of time, nor do they assess the direct impact of mediation before and after the program. Here the pace of litigation for aggregate, mediated, and general civil cases will be analyzed using an interrupted time series. Separate time series are presented for domestic cases and mediated versus general civil contested cases.

Figure 4 provides an aggregate assessment of mediated and general civil litigation pace. Here, mediated cases seem to be consistently slower in pace than general civil cases over time. Upon closer inspection, however, these trends bear out some interesting propositions posited earlier.

First, the mediated case trend from 1989 to 1992 shows that a number of cases referred to mediation were filed prior to the program's initiation in 1992. These older cases (3 filed in 1990; 30 in 1991; and 97 in 1992) referred to mediation were processed very slowly and probably skew the comparisons presented earlier, a point argued by McEwen (1991). After 1992, mediated and general civil time figures were more similar, but mediated cases remained slightly higher.

The general civil trend after program intervention is most interesting and bears further scrutiny. Beginning in 1992, even though mediated cases processed slowly over the time period, general civil cases moved more quickly each year. Two factors may be at work here. As proposed earlier, the mediation program may be removing contentious and difficult cases from the civil system. Second, mediating these cases may have the effect of freeing resources for the remaining general civil caseloads. Both forces acting in tandem, then, show **some** indirect effect of mediation on civil case processing. One way to further test this hypothesis is to examine domestic and contested general civil pace over time as well.

The data presented in Figure 5 support the assertions presented above. Inspection of the trends before and after mediation seems consistent with the argument that case type makes a difference. Mediated domestic cases are processed more slowly over the entire period than general civil domestic cases. Additionally, it appears that general civil domestic cases moved somewhat faster after program implementation.

These findings suggest that mediation has an indirect effect on civil case processing by removing some contested cases from the system. An alternative explanation is that mediation is slower because it adds another hurdle to the civil process and, thus, more time. One problem with this comparison is, of course, that general civil domestic cases include some very routine uncontested divorce cases. These cases tend to process quickly and may, then, skew the results. A final way to test whether case type may be driving speed of disposition is to compare mediated and general civil cases that are more similar.

To conclude this analysis of litigation pace of time, then, attention is directed to contested general civil cases. By examining contested general civil cases over time, one can examine cases that were most likely to be referred to mediation. Figure 6 presents a comparison of pace of litigation in all mediated cases versus contested general civil cases. What does the pace of mediated litigation pace look like versus contested general civil cases?

The results here are most interesting and provide some support for the arguments of ADR proponents. From 1989 to 1992 mediated cases were processed more slowly than the contested sample. However, the older cases that were filed prior to the initiation of mediation skewed these results.

After program implementation in 1992, however, mediated cases were processed faster than the contested cases in every year (1993-1995). Even though general civil cases seem to process faster as a whole, comparisons of similar case types suggest that mediation has had some impact. Comparing apples to apples, then, mediation seems to have had some limited effect on the pace of litigation.

The Impact of Mediation

SUMMARY

Previous research has pointed to many areas where mediation and other forms of ADR can impact or change the nature of civil justice. This chapter focused on four major areas--caseloads, court workloads, case disposal, and pace of litigation. The comparisons of mediated and general civil cases presented in this chapter yield limited and mixed results on mediation impact. The chapter also emphasizes how difficult it is to compare mediated and general civil caseloads because of case type and complexity.

In the four impact areas explored, results point to some indirect effects for mediation. First, mediation does not seem to have had much of an impact on caseloads in Mountain County. Too few cases per year are referred from the Mountain County program to make much of a dent in the number of cases that are processed yearly. However, many cases in the system are very routine and do not take up significant court time or resources.

Mediated cases were hypothesized to remove some of the more difficult or contested cases from the system and free up court resources for other cases. Do the effects noted in this study support this proposition? Aggregate comparison of mediated and general civil cases showed that mediated cases had higher workloads. However, more refined comparisons based on case type yielded mixed results where general civil cases had a slightly higher number of pretrial hearings, but not total actions. Mediation, at best, seems to generate similar workloads as general civil in similar case types, but does not seem to impact workload overall.

Some supporters of mediation contend that mediation helps to settle cases faster and lower trial rates. These arguments found some support in this analysis. Interestingly, mediated cases exhibited higher settlement rates overall, but also had higher trial rates than general civil cases. Again, this may have something to do with the complexity and type of cases that are referred to mediation.

When controlling for case type, there was evidence that mediation has had some impact. Overall, mediated cases had higher settlement rates, but similar rates of judge-ordered case disposal and trial. Finally, and even more interesting, over time and after program implementation, general civil caseloads had slightly higher settlement rates and slightly lower trial rates. Again, this provides some support for the notion that mediation indirectly affects civil justice by removing contested cases from the system and freeing actors to work on other routine cases.

Litigation time was examined in much the same manner with similarly mixed results. In the aggregate, mediated cases actually took **longer** to process than general civil cases. These results indicate that mediation may simply add another process or "hoop" for civil litigants to "jump through". However, when controlling for case complexity and time, the results suggest more positive impact.

When controlling for different case type, there was no evidence of impact. General civil cases were processed faster in every category. However, in the comparison with "contested" cases, mediated cases processed more quickly than general civil cases.

One problem related to the difficulty of assessing impact is that a fair number of mediated cases had a large gap between filing and mediation referral. This increases the disposition time of some mediated cases even though the program had not had a chance to make a difference. Interestingly, when pace of litigation is measure from referral (instead of filing date) to disposition, mediated cases are processed more quickly.

Most interesting of all is the comparison of litigation pace for aggregate, domestic, and contested mediated and general civil cases. In each of these, the results suggested that mediation has an indirect impact. Even when mediation pace is slower over time (in aggregate and domestic cases), the pace of litigation in general civil cases speeds up. Additionally, when compared to "contested" cases, mediated cases are processed more quickly.

All of these results lead to the following conclusion. When mediated cases are compared against the average civil case, the arguments of ADR proponents do not hold water. Mediated cases do not exhibit lower workloads, do not minimize caseloads, do not process quicker, and do not have lower trial rates. However, mediated cases do have higher settlement rates overall.

When comparing mediated cases with general civil cases, however, it is important to realize that mediated cases are not necessarily "average" cases. Also, even if mediated cases do not process more quickly, we cannot conclude that there has been no impact on the civil system. When comparisons of mediated and general civil cases based on case type and pre and post program, are conducted, indirect impact is found.

The higher settlement rates of mediated cases show that an important subset of the civil case population is being removed from the system at higher rates than general civil cases. As shown in the interrupted time series trends, removing these cases may have an impact on general civil case disposition. As mentioned in the section on caseloads, it is possible that mediation is not designed in such a way that efficiency in Mountain County is maximized. The program, after all, serves up to 15 courts in Northeast Georgia. If more cases from Mountain County were handled (or referred by judges), this indirect impact may be heightened.

In many ways, the results support some of the propositions of political theorists. Many policies, when implemented, do not fulfill the goals of policymakers. Why is this? It may be that institutional changes such as mediation do not constrain actors into behaving the way reformers would want. Instead, other institutions such as the norms of traditional case settlement (or the traditional civil process) may act to suppress the changes ADR proponents hoped for. Alternatively, mediation seems to "free" judges for other case processing. In addition to the ability to rule on motions, continuances, and so on, judges can now refer particular cases out of the system. There is no way here to analyze how judges came to these decisions, but the results presented indicate that judges may be referring cases that are more complex or cases of a particular type that require substantial court resources. Judges, then, may be responding to the institutional change by referring some cases so that they can spend more time on others.

These results, however, do not control for other factors that may increase the pace of litigation or settlement rates after the program. Some other factors or institutional changes may have occurred and impacted civil case processing in Mountain County. To begin to explore this, I turn to the question of how mediation is perceived by court participants.

Table 5-1

Court Workloads of Mediated and General Civil Cases

CASE TYPES	COURT WORKLOADS					
	Pretrial Hrgs.			Pretrial Actions*		
	Mean	Median	(n)	Mean	Median	(n)
AGGREGATE						
Non-Mediated	.1389	0	(1375)	.7344	0	(1374)
Mediated	.2217	0	(627)	2.6565	0	(626)
DOMESTIC ONLY						
Non-Mediated	.2116	0	(449)	.3951	0	(448)
Mediate	.1188	0	(446)	1.6764	1	(445)
DIVORCE ONLY						
Non-Mediated	.2727	0	(165)	.1697	0	(165)
Mediated	.1051	0	(257)	1.7043	1	(257)
TORTS						
Non-Mediated	.2273	0	(132)	3.0300	1	(132)
Mediated	.3011	0	(93)	5.7634	4	(93)
TORT-AUTO						
Non-Mediated	.1573	0	(89)	2.4045	1	(89)
Mediated	.1579	0	(57)	5.3684	3	(57)
CONTESTED**						
Non-Mediated	.2926	0	(417)	1.5120	0	(416)
Mediated	.2217	0	(627)	2.6565	1	(626)

Notes:
*Documents coded as pretrial actions include pretrial motions, continuances, leaves of absence, and depositions and other discovery.
**Contested non-mediated cases were compared with all mediated cases. Contested cases were those that were formally answered by defendants.

Table 5-2

Mediation Agreements in Mountain County: 1992-1995

Part One: Was Agreement Reached in Mediation?

Agreement Type	Percentage	n
No Agreement Reached	34.7%	217
Partial Agreements	13.2%	82
Full Agreement Reached*	35.4%	219
No Mediation Occurred**	16.6%	103
TOTALS	100%	621

Notes:
* Full agreements made in mediation may have been modified thereafter by attorneys or judges in final divorce decrees.
** Cases were no mediation occurred include "no shows" and pre-mediation settlements.

Part II: Average Time of Mediation Sessions (Hours)

Mean Time of Sessions:	2.31 hours
Range of Time of Sessions:	0 to 14 hours
n	416 Cases*

Note: * Data on session time was missing in 205 cases.

Table 5-2 (con't)

Part III: Agreement Reached in Follow-up Mediation?

Agreement Reached?	Percentage	n
"NO"	2.6%	16
"Yes"	3.2%	20
Not Applicable	94.2%	585
TOTALS	100%	621

Part IV: Number of Additional Mediation Sessions

Mediation Attempts	Percentage	n
No Additional Attempts	93.8%	583
"1" Additional	5.5%	34
"2" Additional	0.0%	0
"3" Additional	0.5%	3
"4" Additional	0.2%	1
TOTALS	100%	621

Table 5-2 (con't)

Part V: When in Civil Procedure is a Mediated Case Disposed?

Position in Case Life	Percentage	n
After Referral/Before Med.	10.3%	63

Part V: When in Civil Procedure is a Mediated Case Disposed? (Cont.)

Position in Case Life	Percentage	n
During Mediation Session	35.4%	217
After Mediation/Before Trial	43.0%	263
During Trial	11.3%	69
TOTALS	100%	622

Table 5-3

A Comparison of Case Dispositions:
Mediated v. Contested Non-Mediated Cases*

Disposition Type	Mediated %	n	Contested Non-Med. %	n
Trials**	11.2%	70	9.9%	41
Settlements***	67.5%	418	63.9%	266

Table 5-3 (con't)

Disposition Type	Mediated %	n	Contested Non-Med. %	n
Judge Ordered****	20.2%	126	19.1%	85
Other Dispos.*****	1.1%	7	4.3%	18
TOTALS	100%	621	100%	416

Notes:

*Contested cases are those cases answered by defendants.

**Includes bench and jury varieties.

***Includes Pre/Post trial settlements (dismissals with and without prejudice), consent agreements, and mediated settlements (for mediated cases).

**** Includes summary judge., dismissals, pre-trial orders, and default judgements.

***** Includes transfer cases and pending cases.

Table 5-4

A Comparison of Domestic Case Dispositions:

Mediated Versus Non-Mediated Cases*

Disposition Type**	Mediated %	n	Non-Mediated %	n
Trials	9.1%	40	5.5%	25
Settlements	64.3%	286	68.5%	307
Judge Ordered	25.9%	115	24.0%	108
Other	0.7%	3	2.0%	9
TOTALS	100%	444	100%	449

Notes:

* Compares mediated domestic versus non-mediated domestic cases. Does not select out contested or non-contested.

** Disposition types are calculated in the same manner as Table 4-3. See notes in Table 4-3

Table 5-5

Average Pace of Litigation in Mountain County:
Non-Mediated and Mediated Cases by Case Type

Type Case	Ave. Pace of Litigation (Days)	n
All Non-Mediated (From Filing to Disposal)	239.4	1342
All Mediated (From Filing to Disposal)	307.4	607
Mediated-Referral* (From Referral to Disposal)	135.3	512
All Domestic		
Non-Mediated	154.9	443
Mediated	250.1	437
Divorce Only		
Non-Mediated	108.1	166
Mediated	231.5	256
Tort		
Non-Mediated	331.6	127
Mediated	447.1	88
Tort-Auto Only		
Non-Mediated	308.9	86
Mediated	416.1	57
Contested**		
Non-Mediated	360.5	399
Mediated	307.4	607

Table 5-5 (con't)

Notes:
*Time in days from case referral to disposal. Does not include periods of time prior to mediation.
**Contested cases are defined as those non-mediated cases that were formally answered by defendants (does not include default judgements, lack of service, etc.).

Table 5-6

**Pace of Litigation in Mediated and Non-Mediated Cases:
By Disposition Type and Stage**

Part I: Pace of Mediated Litigation by Disposal Stage

Mediated Case Disposal Stage	Pace (Days)	n
After Referral, but b/f Med.	315.1	62
During Mediation	273.1	213
After Med., but b/f Trial	309.3	257
Disposal at Trial	403.9	70

Part II: Mediated and Non-Mediated Litigation Pace by Disposition

Case Disposition Stage	Mediated	Non-Mediated
At Trial	403.9 (70)	341.1 (69)
Before Trial*	295.0 (535)	233.9 (1272)

Note:* Cases disposed of before trial include settlements as well as judge aided disposal such as summary judgements, default judgements, etc.

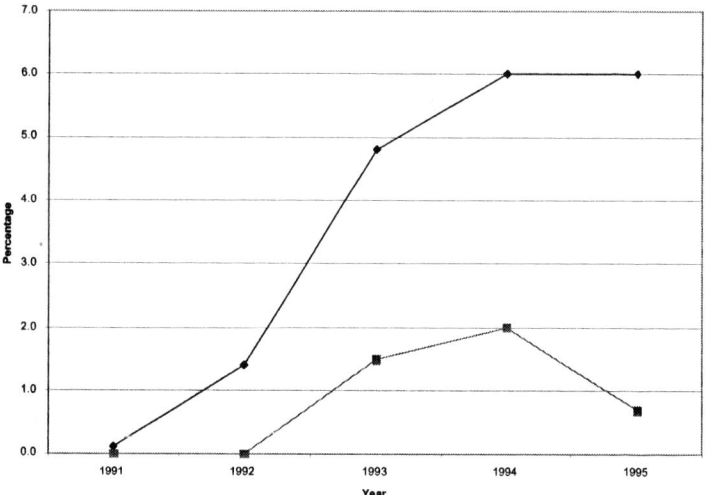

Figure 1: Percentage of General Civil Caseloads Refered to Mediation: 1991-1995

◆ Superior Courts
■ State Courts

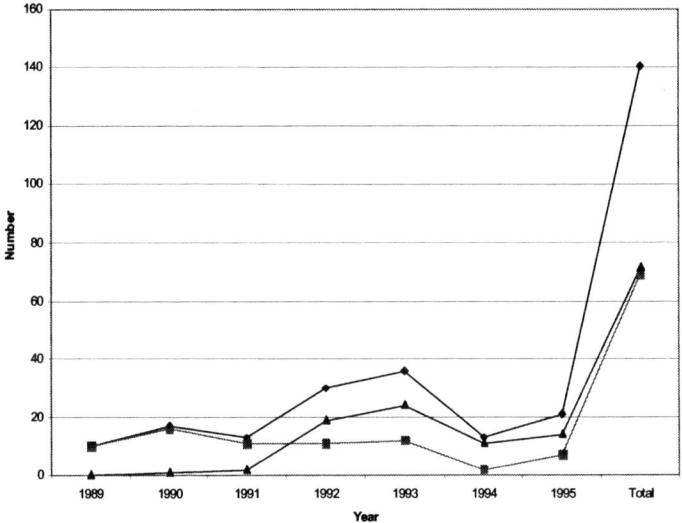

Figure 2A: Aggregate, Mediated, & Non-Mediated Trial Rates Over Time (Number)

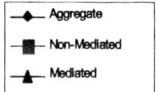

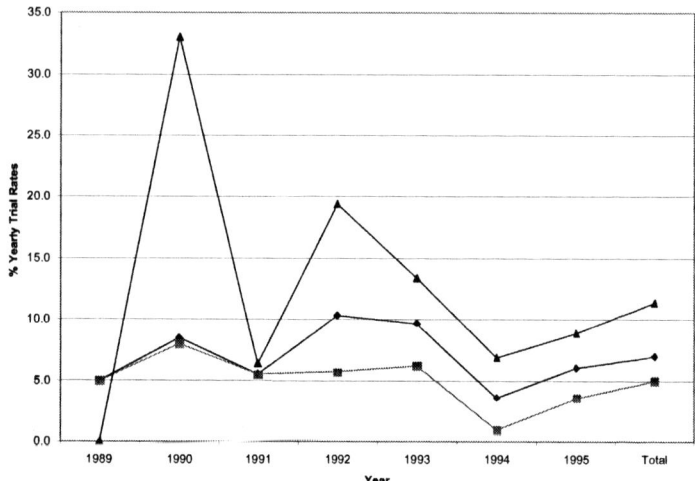

Figure 2: Aggregate, Mediated, & Non-Mediated Trial Rates Over Time

The Impact of Mediation

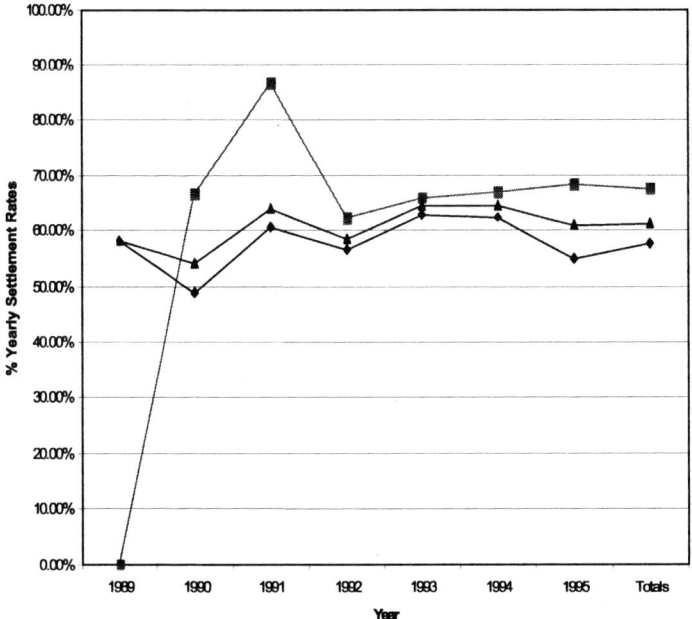

Figure 3: Aggregate, Mediated, and Non-Mediated Settlement Rates Over Time

- Non-Mediated
- Mediated
- All Cases

Alternative Dispute Resolution

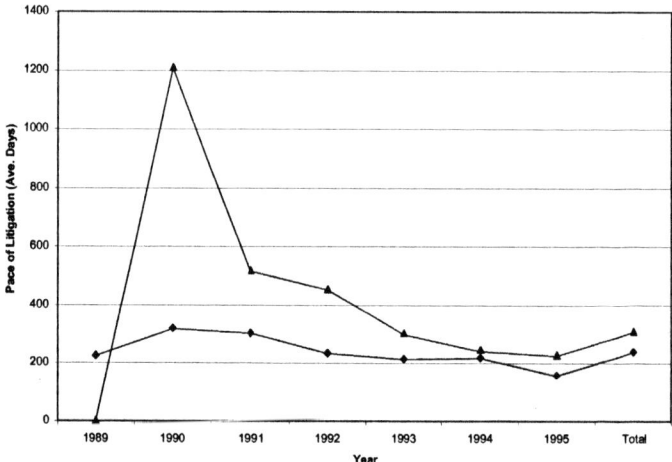

Figure 4: Aggregate Mediated and Non-Mediated Litigation Pace in Hall County: Case Filed 1989-1995

The Impact of Mediation

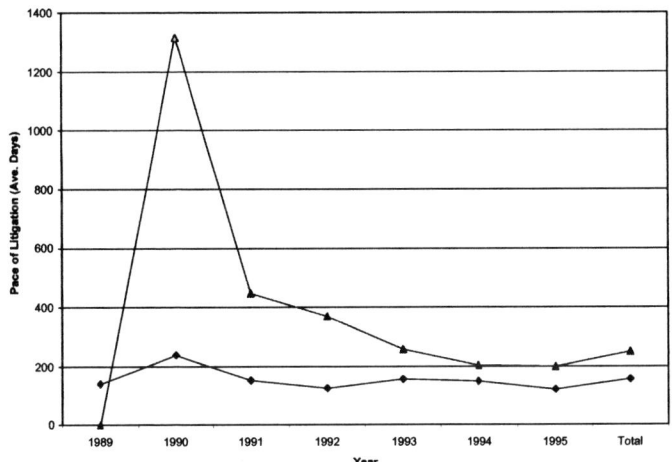

Figure 5: Domestic Mediated and Non-Mediated Litigation Pace in Hall County: Cases Filed 1989-1995

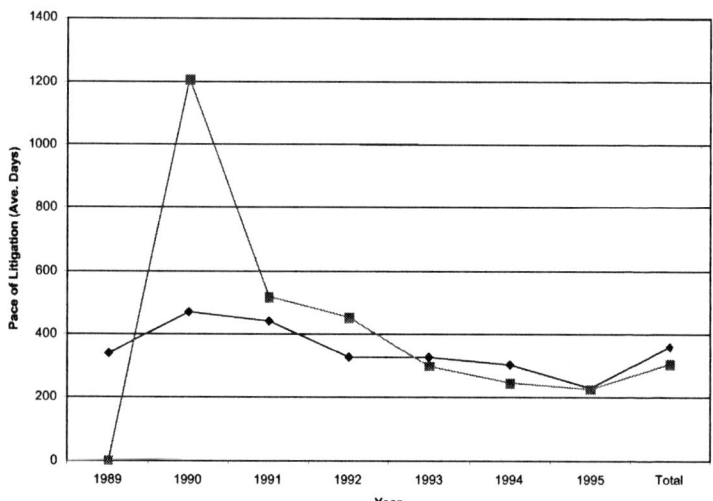

Figure 6: Mediated Versus Contested Non-Mediated Litigation Pace in Hall County: Cases Filed 1989-1995

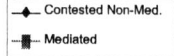

CHAPTER 6
Mediation, Civil Justice And Court Actors

In Chapters 3 and 4, I described civil justice and mediation in Mountain County and offered a preliminary analysis of their relationship. In this context, mediation in Mountain County can be viewed as a formal institutional change **inside** of the civil process that takes cases **outside** the process. Such an institutional change was hypothesized to have particular policy impacts by reformers. As explained in Chapter 5, many of the related efficiency goals were not realized or were achieved indirectly in this "annexed" system.

To complement this quantitative evidence, I conducted interviews with system participants, the results of which are presented here. In this chapter, the questions are straightforward: How do particular court actors view civil justice and the mediation program? What can we learn from court participants about mediation as an institutional change?

To begin this chapter, a supplemental literature review is included. As noted in Chapter 5, mediation has had some direct and indirect quantifiable effects. It may, however, have also affected the "craft" of civil justice as well. In the next section, then, the relevant mediation literature on satisfaction of, and costs to, participants is reviewed.

REVIEW OF PERTINENT LITERATURE

One potential effect of mediation is that the dispute resolution process takes on a less adversarial character. As a process, mediation uses a trained neutral to facilitate communication between disputants about the dispute, its origins, and potential solutions. One goal of mediation, then, is to aid the resolution of disputes by encouraging the parties to form and sign their own agreements. The responsibility is placed on the individuals (and not attorneys and judges) to work toward a consensual outcome to the dispute.

Because of this emphasis, proponents have argued that mediation yields more satisfactory agreements that remain in effect over time. Additionally, proponents suggest that the consensual nature of the process leads to higher satisfaction than that related to traditional adjudication.

Research on civil mediation shows that litigants and attorneys do find the process and the mediators to be satisfying and fair (Clarke et al., 1995: vii). It appears, however, that even though mediation is satisfying to clients, variations in satisfaction exist. These center on whether a case is actually settled, the skill of the mediator, and the time involved (Kobbervig, 1991; Schultz, 1990; Clarke et al., 1995; Fix and Harter, 1992). For the most part, mediation is viewed much more favorably if a case settles during mediation. In a Florida study, both attorneys and clients viewed the process more positively if the case settled quickly, but satisfaction did vary by mediator (Schultz, 1990).

Research conducted in the District of Columbia found that cases that were mediated and did not settle led to higher satisfaction rates than those that did not settle in traditional case negotiations with attorneys (Fix and Harter, 1992). Here, litigants also felt that the mediation process was fair and that they were able to tell their side of the story (Fix and Harter, 1992; see Keilitz, 1995). In another study, Clarke and colleagues (1995: vii) found that litigants viewed mediation conferences favorably, but that mediation did not seem to impact favorably their overall view of their cases:

> There was no significant difference in satisfaction between the Mediation group and the control group, with respect to either (1) case outcomes and procedures or (2) costs and time.

One additional risk of mediation was that plaintiffs who reached an impasse in the conference and then settled their cases later were less satisfied than those who proceeded to trial (vii).

Like research on non-domestic civil mediation, studies of family mediation overwhelmingly found that clients preferred it over adversarial proceedings (Pearson, 1995). Other studies have identified more specific examples of client satisfaction. Depner and his colleagues (1992) found that clients felt very favorable about the process and that the mediator made parents aware of community family resources. Similarly, Keilitz and colleagues (1992) found that, when compared to users of formal court processes, mediation participants felt less intimidated by their spouses and less pressure to agree to something they did not want (see Pearson, 1995).[50] Finally, Kelly (1989; 1990) found that mediation clients felt more empowered with the opportunity to have equal influence over their agreements (see Pearson, 1995).

User dissatisfaction has been identified in some studies, but generally by a minority of participants. In general, dissatisfaction was related to the feeling that the agreement had been rushed, that there had been pressure to go along with something, that the mediator was unfair, or that the process was confusing (e.g., Depner et al., 1992; Keilitz et al., 1992; Pearson, 1981; Pearson and Theonnes, 1984, 1985, 1989; Theonnes et al. 1991).

The results of research related to attorney satisfaction are somewhat different. Attorneys in the Minnesota program viewed mediation favorably, but rated the judicial process better (Kobbervig, 1991). As far as efficiency was concerned, attorneys rated the process equally with formal litigation (1991). The attitudes of attorneys in North Carolina were generally favorable (Clarke et al., 1995) as they believed that the mediators were "fair, the program reduced the likelihood of trial, and it hastened settlement" (vii). Not surprisingly, attorneys who were mediators reported higher favorability rates than those who did not mediate.

While they are not direct participants in the mediation process, judges act as "gatekeepers" for ADR systems. Judges have discretion in many pre-trial disposition procedures and later in trials, and they have even more discretion in court-annexed ADR programs. Similarly, judges in court-annexed programs most often refer cases to mediation or are left with the results of failed or partial mediated agreements when they return to the system.

One might argue that since judges refer cases to ADR systems, they might benefit from this institutional choice. In fact, in the Mountain County program, the Chief Judge of the Circuit was instrumental in its establishment. However, as noted previously, in most systems a very small percentage of civil and domestic cases are actually referred to mediation systems. Skeptics might conclude that judges merely pay "lip service" to the ADR movement but do not foster widespread use. On the other hand, mediation may only be useful in select case types that are, in fact, less numerous.

Finally, judges may vary as to what type of case is best suited to mediation. As noted in Chapter 5, it is possible that judges use court-annexed ADR for their own case processing interests. For example, judges may send routine cases to mediation, leaving them with more time to spend on politically charged issues (e.g., criminal cases).

The last major participant in mediated cases is, of course, the mediator. There have been numerous studies on the training and quality of mediators (e.g., Theonnes and Pearson, 1995; Kressel et al., 1991). Because those who train to become mediators are presumably proponents of mediation, it is not surprising that few studies examine their satisfaction with ADR programs. Of the studies discussed thus far, the North Carolina study of civil mediation provides some evidence of mediator satisfaction (Clarke et al., 1995). When assessing the attitudes of attorneys toward the program, the authors asked attorneys who were certified as mediators and those that were not. Attorney-mediators were more likely to favor the programs continuation and expansion than attorneys who were not certified.

Mediation provides a potentially cost effective process for resolving disputes. These claims have particular relevance to scholars who have argued that the adversarial nature of the civil system benefits repeat players and helps to explain why, ultimately, the "haves" prevail over the "have nots" (Galanter, 1974). If ADR proponents are correct, mediation and/or arbitration provide alternatives to courts that might even the playing field by taking away advantages that the "haves" have in courts. This, however, assumes that the playing field within mediation or arbitration is equal.[51]

For litigants, mediation and other forms of ADR offer the opportunity for cases to be settled quickly outside of the more costly, formal legal system. These include court costs and the fees associated with discovery, depositions, and other motions. Mediation, as a process, may also encourage disputants to come to agreements that would not be forged by attorneys in more legalistic settings. Since the disputants have a direct hand in making the agreement, it may also be more likely to hold up over time.

As a whole, research on mediation has confirmed that many of the cost savings alluded to by proponents are in fact enjoyed by litigants in mediation (McEwen, 1992). In a summary of the limited mediation research on cost savings, McEwen notes that:

> when litigants settle through mediation, they often save money. When mediation is another step in the litigation process, it does not increase costs substantially (1992: 155).

Additionally, McEwen emphasizes that compliance with mediated agreements "appears to be at least as high or higher than compliance with adjudicated agreements" (155).

Attorneys who represent litigants are also participants in ADR. From the research on cost savings, one might assume that attorneys who are interested in the "bottom line" might not have favorable attitudes toward mediation. Despite evidence that mediation can save clients some attorney fees, lawyers generally seem to favor its use (Clarke et al., 1995). However, these results were culled from a site where mediators were licensed attorneys and attorneys overwhelmingly participated in the sessions.

Apart from how attorneys view mediation, there has been little research on how attorneys benefit from ADR. In one study of mandatory divorce mediation in Maine, McEwen and colleagues (1993) reported that participating attorneys supported the program and identified several benefits to lawyers. These included preparation for negotiations and trial, a way to involve and better serve clients, and better management of cases (1993; see Pearson, 1993).

In the literature review provided here, I examined social science evidence related to mediation. Generally, the clients of mediation are more satisfied than those in traditional litigation. Attorneys also appeared to have favorable views of mediation, but still rate it lower than adjudication. However, attorneys who were trained as mediators typically rated mediation higher than attorneys who were not trained. Finally, some studies have found that mediation provides cost savings to the clients that agreements typically "hold up" over time.

Much of the evidence presented above is based on limited inquiry by scholars. Few studies have examined how judges, court staff, and attorneys view mediation. Finally, very little work has been done on the perceptions of court actors on the changes that ADR has brought to their court systems. These issues are examined in the portion of the research reported next.

DATA AND METHODS

The data presented in this chapter are based on interviews with civil court actors in Mountain County. These included judges, attorneys, mediators, and court staff.

To select subjects, I interviewed judges in the Mountain County system to gain their impressions of civil justice and mediation. In Mountain County, there were three full-time Superior court judges and one retired judge who regularly participated in mediation. Due to the time constraints of the judges, I was only able to interview the Chief Judge and the retired Superior court judge. Mountain County State court had one full-time judge and a single part-time judge. I was able to interview these for a total of four judges.

Two of these judges were male (the Chief and the retired Superior court Judge) and two were female (the State Court judge and part-time State Court Judge). The backgrounds of the four judges were generally similar. Each had previously practiced as an attorney in Mountainville, with one working primarily on the civil side.[52] Two of the four judges received their bachelor's degree in Georgia state or private colleges. The other two jurists received their undergraduate degrees out of state.[53] Three of the four attended law school at state-supported law schools (e.g., University of Georgia, Georgia State University), while one graduated from the University of Chicago.

Since attorneys are considered among the most important actors in the civil justice system, I interviewed those who were frequent participants. I identified these in three ways. First, I included those with frequent appearances as the primary listed defense or plaintiff attorney in actual case records. I attempted to divided the interviews equally between attorneys who were primarily defense or plaintiff representatives (some worked in both spheres). Second, I identified and separately interviewed attorneys who were also mediators in the Ninth District program. Since these attorneys wore both "hats," I could compare their answers with attorneys who were not mediators. Finally, I allowed the interviews to drive selection. Specifically, if a subject mentioned that someone was important, I would try to arrange an interview with that person. Using these methods, I interviewed seven practicing attorneys (three mediators and four non-mediators) who worked in the Mountain County system. Of the seven attorneys, six were male and one was female (an attorney/mediator). Almost all lived in Mountain County or a surrounding county. Most of the attorneys received their undergraduate and law degrees in the University System of Georgia or in a regional, private law school. Only one of the attorneys I interviewed was educated out of state. Although they were evenly split between Democrats and Republicans, all but one described him/herself as a political conservative.

Most of these attorneys worked in the civil area and handled domestic cases. In general, most could be described as general practitioners. Almost all mentioned that they worked in criminal law, but infrequently. Two attorneys directed considerable attention to domestic cases, while the others reported that they worked on torts, business law, and contracts. Only one of the attorneys acknowledged practicing primarily in a distinctive civil area (e.g., federal bankruptcy and social security claims). Finally, about half of the attorneys emphasized that they primarily represented defendants. Three, however, represented both plaintiffs and defendants, and a fourth represented mostly plaintiffs in civil and domestic cases.

I also interviewed four mediators who had worked in the program during the time of my study. These mediators were not practicing attorneys. Two of them did not have any formal legal training, while two held the J.D. degree but did not practice and were not members of the Georgia bar. Of the non-lawyers, one held an MFA in music from Julliard[54] and the other a bachelors degree. In these interviews, I generally followed the protocol for attorney-mediators (see Appendix B2), but deleted the questions specified for attorneys.

The mediators interviewed tended to be from very diverse walks of life and were evenly divided between male and female. Two of the mediators grew up and lived outside Georgia, but all had lived in the Mountain County area for at least seven years. Interestingly, the males described themselves as conservative and Republican, while the females referred to themselves as liberal or "left wing."

When asked how they decided to become mediators, three of the four mentioned seeing an ad or story in the local newspaper. Two had at least a background in law that had spurred their interest, while one of the mediators claimed that his job as a personnel director sparked his interest:

I thought well, hell, that is what I do all day long--you know--I mediate between the company and the employees and look out for what I think is the best interest of both (Mediator A).

Finally, I interviewed three administrators (excluding the Chief Judge) in the system. These included the Mountain County Clerk of Courts, the Director of the Ninth District Dispute Resolution Program, and the Ninth District Court Administrator (upon recommendation of the two above). Two of these interview subjects were male and one was female. As far as background, each of these three had lived in the local area at least two years. Two of the three held undergraduate degrees from state institutions in Georgia and one (the Ninth District Court Administrator) held a masters degree. Only one of the participants was asked about general political affiliation and claimed to be "libertarian."

As administrators, each had worked for at least five years in a court system in some capacity prior to his/her present position. One of the positions, the Clerk of Court, was elected; the others were civil service in some capacity. The mediation coordinator had a background as a mediator, had trained mediators, and had established a juvenile court mediation program in one of the counties near Atlanta.

For the most part, the questions for each class of interview subject were open-ended with the opportunity to expand or digress. In general, I asked questions about their backgrounds, work, impressions of civil justice, and assessments of mediation. I asked similar questions of attorney-mediators, with the exception of additional questions on the mediation process and mediator skill. Related protocols are included in the appendices (B1, B2, and B3).

Each of the interviews was recorded on micro-cassette and lasted approximately an hour to an hour and a half. For ease of data analysis, the interviews were then transcribed so that responses could be more easily compared.

RESULTS

This more qualitative research revealed much about civil justice, mediation, and their interaction and can be used to fill in the "voids" left from the profiles of previous chapters. In this section, I organize the interview data along three questions: (1) what does civil justice look like?

(2) what does mediation look like? and (3) how did mediation affect civil justice?

WHAT DOES CIVIL JUSTICE LOOK LIKE?

The interviews with system actors tell us much about civil justice in Mountain County and the work of civil actors. Here, I report their views on court administration, caseloads, civil procedure, case settlement, and general civil justice culture.

From interviews, it appears that the County Clerk of Court, the Ninth District Court Administrator, and judges are the primary managers of the court. Each provided most of the information on the formal administration of justice in Mountain County. In particular, they commented on budgets, caseloads, and case management.

The Ninth District Court Administrator is paid by the State of Georgia and works primarily with Superior court judges and staff from the fifteen-county area of the district. Despite his administrative responsibilities with these courts, he also works with other courts (e.g., state, juvenile, and magistrate) when the need arises. For the most part, though, Georgia State courts are administrated locally by the judge and his/her staff. A few State courts, including Hall, hired a local trial court administrator of their own.

The duties of the Ninth District Administrator include providing aid in staffing issues, purchasing, jury managing, and working as a "middleman" between the State of Georgia and the local judge. All of these duties are designed to "let the judge be on the bench managing cases." The Ninth District Administrator mentioned that he and his colleagues around the state do not typically work on individual cases or manage caseloads. Additionally, he acknowledged that he sometimes worked with attorneys on local policy issues (e.g., indigent defense, change of venues for death penalty cases).

The Clerk of Court is an elected position that is also financed by the State of Georgia. The Clerk mentioned that each of his colleagues around the state provides some administrative duties for all courts housed in the county. Some of these include keeping records of cases, wills, and deeds. Additionally, the Clerk's office collects and disburses fees and fines that are ordered by the court or the State of Georgia.

According to the Clerk of Court and the Ninth District Court Administrator, county courts in the State of Georgia are generally funded locally through county taxes. Only judicial salaries, pensions, and staff are provided by state revenues with 1 percent of that budget allocated to the courts. Other costs such as the upkeep of the office and supplies were covered by the county. The courts typically generate revenue from user fees such as filing and other court costs.

One of the reasons why courts seem to receive so little state support is the lack of political influence. Unlike executive agencies like law enforcement and corrections that are represented by the governor, the courts generally rely on the Chief Justice of the State Supreme Court when it comes to legislative lobbying. According to the Ninth District Court Administrator, the Chief Justice does not have the power to command funds from the legislature and courts are not involved in preparing the budget.

Judicial need is often established by demonstrating a workload crisis. The Mountain County Clerk of Court mentioned that the Superior court judges had been keeping a caseload count in order to request a new state-funded judgeship. As the pressure of workload is documented, courts can claim that it needs more personnel.

On the whole, most court actors (including judges and attorneys) argued that caseloads were increasing in the Mountain County system, albeit in an erratic fashion. One year criminal caseloads would be in the 4,000 range and the next in the 7,000-case range. On the civil side, the Clerk of Court emphasized that Superior court caseloads seemed to be increasing at 5 to 10 percent a year. There were, however, some declines in caseload patterns, specifically 1992 or 1993. He was not certain as to how the caseload in the State court had changed in recent years, in part because of a lack of statistical information. Furthermore, the Clerk had no explanation for the increased docket of Mountain County courts.

The Ninth District Court Administrator identified three caseload pressures: population, a litigious society, and domestic problems. He also emphasized other factors important in Mountain County (e.g., a large local bar with 150-200 attorneys) and the cultural diversity of the county.[55]

In interviews, the Ninth District Administrator stressed that judges manage civil caseloads while the district attorney manages the criminal calendars. One of the reasons, then, that civil systems may be slower is that judges often do not have sufficient aid or resources to manage case calendars, particularly in the light of caseload increases.

Interviews also suggested that Mountain County judges are responsible for the calendars of cases and making sure that cases move through the process. The judges' administrative assistant and law clerks aid this in addition to research and writing. The State Court judge specifically discussed this with respect to scheduling and maintaining court calendars:

> I think the Judge has a responsibility, not only to rule on things as they come up in the course of a case before trial, but to make sure that the case actually does proceed along some path. Lawyers may drop the ball, but the party hasn't. So somebody has got to be watching to make sure that it is moving at some point, an that's a responsibility of a judge.

Case processing, then, seems to make up a large part of a judge's work. The State Court judge further emphasized this point:

> You try to make sure the cases from 1989 are disposed of -- well, you know, making sure that you try to do some of that and spend time looking at the docket and making sure trial is all that's left...what's out there. The bulk of time is going through files.

What cases do the courts deal with most often? Interviews suggested that case work differed primarily by the type of court. The full-time State Court judge, for example, mentioned that domestic, real property, and equity cases could not be filed in the State courts. As a consequence, in State court there was less emphasis on civil justice and more emphasis on the criminal side. State court judges reported that most of their time was spent on hearings and appearances by criminal defendants. One judge stated:

> I am mostly on the bench doing sentencing, arraignments-- hearing bench trials and doing jury trials--criminal and civil.

In the civil area, then, State court deals with disputes over debt collections, contracts, and auto-related torts.

The general consensus of court actors was that the civil system was dominated by domestic disputes. The Chief Judge, for example, emphasized that the "largest block of time is on domestic, second would be criminal, and third would be general civil." Similarly, the Ninth District Court Administrator argued that much of the workload pressure in Superior court had been caused by increases in domestic litigation. Humorously, he said, "sometimes I wonder if anyone, anywhere in Georgia is NOT divorced." Also he noted, like some judges, that changes to "no fault" in divorce law brought more domestic cases to the courts. Additionally, he stated that the legal system is focusing more on domestic violence and child abuse. With agencies like welfare departments and social services requiring legal action for child support recovery and child abuse. Finally, he mentioned that once a domestic case comes into the system, it is likely that it will remain in the system or come back. For example, a divorce usually requires later modifications such as child support, visitation, or even contempt.

Attorneys, like judges, indicated that domestic cases seem to dominate the Mountain County Superior court. Many of the attorneys, in fact, admitted to spending considerable time working on these cases, although domestic litigation seemed to be fairly low on their list of case preferences. Of the attorneys with whom I spoke, most were general practitioners who worked in domestic, civil, and criminal arenas. A typical response to questions on type of work follows form one attorney:

> About a good half to 60% of what I do is family law, divorces, adoptions, child support, those kinds of things and then the rest of it is general civil litigation. We represent insurance companies.

When attorneys were more specialized, the type of expertise varied. Some defended insurance companies in torts while others represented plaintiffs in civil cases. Few of the attorneys seemed to have much criminal experience except when appointed to serve an indigent defendant. However, one attorney mentioned that he practiced civil cases for a "living" and that this then left other time for cases in which he was more interested, such as criminal.

The amount of time attorneys spent on particular segments of their job also varied. Two said they spent most of their time litigating cases, but the others said they spent considerable time on the phone, often with opposing attorneys, in depositions, negotiations, or working on discovery. One attorney who was a mediator summed up his work this way:

The most time? Probably discovery things, depositions, answering interrogatories, answering pleadings, anybody whose got a civil practice spends more time doing that than they do in court. Very few cases get tried.

While trials are important sources of a civil court's workload, nearly all of those interviewed acknowledged that pretrial procedures represent a larger portion. It is not surprising, then, that most cases settle before trial. With all of the influence that has been placed on the work of judges and administrators, the Ninth District Administrator suggested that some judges let the attorneys manage the system:

They don't schedule anything unless an attorney calls and wants to...not a lot of pressure from the judge to move the case along.

This is interesting and alludes to the importance of attorneys in civil justice that other scholars have emphasized. Lawyers have been considered the "gatekeepers" as well as the "brokers" of civil law (Kritzer, 1990, 1991; Kritzer and Pickerill, 1996). Furthermore, their work in the pretrial stages of law seems to constitute much of the work of the civil system as a whole.

Despite the fact that attorneys may "drive" the civil system, all of them emphasized the importance of judges. One attorney stated that judges encouraged settlement in civil cases by setting the rules for particular cases. A look at civil procedures and, later, case settlement provides a more complete portrait of the work of civil courts.

The procedure or "life" of most civil and domestic cases is a political process made up of rules and norms, directed by court participants. In some ways these rules are very formalistic and constrain the behavior of court actors and litigants. For example, there is a particular format by which complaints and answers must be filed in Georgia courts. There are also rules for the discovery of evidence, the taking of depositions, and the filing of motions. Many times, however, there is great discretion in the interpretation of these rules. However, there are behavioral norms that might speed or slow case processing in this environment.

Interviews of Mountain County civil actors tell us much about these subtleties of civil procedure. Most popular accounts of civil procedure emphasize its adversarial nature. Plaintiffs, defendants, and their attorneys strike at each other using the rules of civil procedure to gain advantages in trial or settlement. In this, a judge is viewed as a referee who objectively interprets the rules as they are invoked by the participants. Judges, then, stay out of the "fray", but influence play by making important decisions about these rules.

In this study, interview respondents generally emphasized a shared, cooperative, and routine method of case processing. Here, attention is directed to the important pre-trial procedures since they govern the outcome of most cases.

As mentioned earlier, cases have "lives" as they begin, exist for periods of time, and end with disposal. In the process, formal procedures such as hearings, motions, and discovery often impact the "lives" of cases. However, interview participants emphasized that these formal procedures are often avoided or supplemented by informal customs. For example, the Ninth District Court Administrator mentioned that civil justice isn't always speedy because civil actors do not always want it to be:

> What the general public doesn't always know is that sometimes attorneys don't want it [the justice system] to go fast. In general, judges try to move as rapidly as litigants want to move.

The interaction among local court actors, then, has a direct influence on the "lives" of cases and not always in a manner that one might expect. Local actors have the discretion to create new rules or norms (institutions) to govern case processing, to speed or slow it. Some of these are discussed below.

Formal procedures impact the choices of local court actors and can be said to be "real" (see Grafstein, 1992). However, even when these are imbedded in new institutions, judges, attorneys, and court staff, have some freedom to operate. For example, the Chief Superior Court Judge noted how one formal change led to alterations in his daily work:

> recent legislation that has created family violence laws that give people much easier access to the courts. We've tried a very open door policy to victims of family violence, and so basically all they have to do is show up at the courthouse, and they're given

forms to file a Petition for Family Violence Relief. They can come and see the judge, just by showing up with their petition, and I'll see them. I'll conduct an ex parte hearing and issue and Order--a temporary protective order, if appropriate. In fact, we had to counsel with the Bar about this because the Bar began to realize that pro se litigants could see a judge quicker than a lawyer...so that has added a tremendous burden in terms of wreaking havoc on our schedules.

Other formal procedures that are common to the work of court actors include motions, hearings, formal extensions of time and, of course, trials.[56] In each of these, judges and attorneys affect case disposal and speed.

While use of pretrial procedures means that judges are spending more time on cases than originally thought, the Chief Superior Court judge mentioned that these saved potential trial costs:

So we're seeing those cases twice instead of once, but we're still saving time because we are knocking out a lot of issues at the pre-trial [conference]. [The pretrial conference is] also what we use as a clearinghouse for ADR mediation.

Judges indicated that civil cases involved a lot of motions, but emphasized that most could be dealt with as paperwork--including the reading, researching, and writing of briefs. According to the State court judge, these motions were very important to the functioning of civil justice. Despite the notion that most cases settled prior to trial, then, these judges indicated that they have a direct effect on case disposal by removing cases procedurally through attorney initiated motions:

Lots of cases end with motions before they even get to trial...summary judgements, motion for judgement on the pleadings, a lot of default judgements--We have lots of folks now that are pro se, they don't even get a lawyer, and they may not understand exactly what's going on and lose before they ever go to trial (Full-time State court Judge).

Relatedly, the judges also acknowledged some control over the pace of litigation by ruling on motions. These sometimes consisted of continuances and leaves of absence. The judges interviewed indicated that leaves of absence tend to be granted to attorneys in a fairly routine manner during holidays or to attorneys from outside the district who may have to travel. Attorneys also stated that opposing attorneys typically did not object because they may need consideration later themselves.

Continuances were, however, viewed differently from leaves of absence by the State court judge. Not sure whether they were used strategically to delay a case for the purpose of reaching a settlement, she mentioned that:

> There are some attorneys that ask for continuances constantly and act like they don't want to try the case. Those are more--and sometimes they are abused, and we tend to know when that is...and try to address it when it comes up.

It is possible to infer that attorneys do use continuances as a method for delaying cases and encouraging settlement. However, the State Court judge mentioned that it just might be "laziness."

In interviews, almost all of the attorneys emphasized that most of the civil system is non-adversarial. They specifically mentioned norms of honesty, collegiality, and reciprocity. One attorney explained that discovery in civil cases is generally quite informal, in part, because of mutual trust. For example, one attorney emphasized that he would often call an attorney before filing for discovery and offer "full disclosure" if the other side agreed to the same. Those interviewed argued that being open and turning over "what you have" builds trust that is worth a great deal in speeding things along, saving clients money, and reaching settlement. Strategically withholding information or invoking "the law" to harm the other side was generally thought to impede future negotiations.

Another attorney emphasized the same thing with regard to civil depositions. Instead of following procedure and filing a formal "notice of deposition," attorneys often "call each other beforehand and decide things informally...then file the formal notice" later.

Another consensual norm among attorneys is the practice of doing "favors" for opposing attorneys. While attorneys might be viewed--as one attorney put it--as "hard-nosed" on behalf of their clients, many of those interviewed acknowledged helping the other side to further long-term interests. For example, if someone does not show up for a hearing or a meeting, "we will try to find them...not take advantage."

As a whole, the attorneys identified a reciprocity rule and emphasized that if attorneys break these norms they will not receive similar cooperation later. One attorney referred to this consensual atmosphere as the "common courtesy" norm, while others emphasized the "close knit" nature of the local bar and its interaction with the local judges. This interaction seems to promote information exchanges that have led to the development of local norms and rules that are decidedly consensual.

Interestingly, the consensual relationships between local court actors affected local rules of procedure. These locally formed institutions include pretrial conferences, "Tuesday" temporary hearings, and mediation. In pre-trial conferences and hearings, the judges typically call in the parties in contested domestic cases and encourage them to work out their differences without proceeding to trial. The retired Superior court judge also emphasized that he spent a couple days a week holding "Tuesday" temporary hearings in domestic cases. Finally, mediation, like the "Tuesday" hearings, was a creation of the local bar and bench in an effort to provide more efficient case disposition.

Regarding settlements, interview participants pointed out that they were encouraged at almost every step of a cases "life." When a case settles it clearly makes a difference as to the resources expended by courts as noted by the Assistant State Court Judge:

> A lot of times the case settles the day before a trial or the day of jury selection, and I think if you can get the attorneys focused on that case early in the process, then it saves everybody time and money...if you get to trial and they settle and you don't have another case, you've got jurors who are feeling unloved and unwanted because you brought them in and didn't even talk to them.

For their part, attorneys observed that in settlement conferences and temporary hearings, judges will point out possible trial outcomes of a case. For example, a judge might hear settlement offers by attorneys and indicate that it might be a "good deal" given what one might expect to get at trial. Each attorney, however, fell short of saying that judges pressured them to settle.

Two judges (Superior and State) were quick to emphasize the direct role that judges have in settlements. The retired Superior court judge mentioned that he had been able to convince both attorneys and clients that a case was or was not strong, thus allowing the parties to assess the costs and benefits of proceeding to trial. Additionally, this provided some indication about how the judge felt about the case.

Relatedly, the Assistant State Judge mentioned that "the judge can share with the attorneys what she has seen in the way of how juries react to these sorts of cases." The Chief Judge of Superior Court also admitted to using this approach. When asked about what keeps the civil justice system working, he referred to the jury and how he projected information to be used for settlement:

> Here it is because those common sense juries here are also extremely conservative and so, I have used our juries here to settle cases occasionally and talk with the lawyers--particularly if you get out-of-town lawyers who do not realize how conservative the juries are here. and I'll say...don't trust me, but call a local plaintiff lawyer and ask them what kind of a verdict do you expect to get in Mountain County on that?

Clearly, the "shadow" that law casts on bargaining can be cast by the judge (see Mnookin and Kornhauser, 1979). One attorney argued that all civil actors evaluate a case based on a what a jury might do with it. More specifically, he emphasized that "lawyers may disagree on what might happen [with a jury]. If they agree on it then [the case] settles." Predictions of jury verdicts can lead attorneys to settlement if their perceptions are similar, something akin to 'litigating in the shadow of informal settlement.'"[57]

Both attorneys and judges argued that formal procedures often indirectly lead to settlements, largely in the form of transaction costs on litigants and their attorneys. For instance, a judge may not agree to a continuance, and that action may stimulate attorneys to talk rather than proceed to trial:

> I think a judge can put a certain amount of pressure on folks by not giving them continuances, making them--holding their feet to the fire, sort of making them move the case along when they are

really not paying any attention to it (Assistant State Court Judge).

Similarly, rulings on motions may clear up issues or impose additional costs on one side or the other. For example, allowing additional time for discovery could impose costs on one side and initiate a move to settle the case. Additional depositions or the time it takes to answer more interrogatories could also lead a party to decide that the trial costs outweigh the potential benefits. In this vein, the retired Superior court judge specifically mentioned that an attorney's knowledge of a judge's likely ruling on evidence often sets the stage for settlement:

> A lawyer who knows the rules about what he can and cannot get in as evidence is in a much better position to negotiate a settlement than someone who is not well trained in evidence.

Finally, judges drew attention to other factors that affected case settlement in Mountain County. The Chief Judge of Superior Court mentioned that discovery led cases to settle more than most other factors. Through discovery an attorney is forced to recognize the "weaknesses in [his/her] case." Additionally, alternative dispute resolution practices such as mediation and the exploration of an early neutral evaluation program were acknowledged to stimulate settlement.

For their part, attorneys implied that the consensual nature of the civil process encouraged settlement, dispositions that were cheaper for clients than trial, and freed time that attorneys could devote to other cases. One attorney argued that it was financially better to process many cases quickly and for less money than to accumulate billable hours only to later lose the case at trial.

The consensual nature of attorney interactions alluded to earlier clearly stimulates settlements. Attorneys emphasized that the bar in Mountain County was quite cohesive, with one mentioning that along with insurance adjustors, he often worked with the same attorneys:

> In this town the bar is a pretty good tight knit bar and for some reason a lot of out of town lawyers don't practice in this area..not as much as in Atlanta or even Athens. So you get to see the same faces over and over...same lawyers because most folks try

to specialize in some area so you see the same lawyers all the time (Attorney #2).

All of this suggests the existence of local civil cultures with "going rates" for settlement, with something akin to criminal court work groups and processes. One attorney who engaged in both criminal and civil practice had a great deal to say about their differences, however, and drew attention to three. First, he argued that the role of the "state" in criminal cases is a critical difference. "In the criminal system, the state is one absolute party...In civil, you have two discrete parties." He went on to emphasize that there is not a lot of repeat process in civil courts with the exception of some companies that are constantly litigating (e.g., insurance companies). Most civil litigants have "one case going and that is it." Finally, he argued that in criminal justice, money is no real object because the state funds the prosecution and indigent defendants get publicly funded attorneys. In a civil case, money can be restrictive, especially for poor plaintiffs who have to worry about legal fees (except in contingency cases). Even those who are wealthy still balance costs rather than "wasting their money." Money, then, is a factor in determining how far a case is taken in civil justice.

Mountain County civil actors agreed that in contrast to criminal justice, no parallel structures existed in civil courts. However, all mentioned that case type, local rules, and norms provide structure for "repeat player" relationships. Although there were not distinct "repeat players" in civil cases, the State Court judge mentioned that "some attorneys have more cases than others." For example, attorneys who represented the regional hospital were consistently present in debt collections, while attorneys who defended insurance companies in automobile and other tort cases were described as "repeat players."

The local bar was also viewed to be an "informal alliance of interests" that helps to structure the interaction of court actors.

If we've got an issue that's bothering us in the domestic area, we'll just generally announce to the Domestic Relations Bar at a meeting, "We're going to be meeting on this issue." And there tends to be 15 lawyers that are going to be there that will represent the interests of the domestic bar and will be a part of developing the procedures an policies that affect their practice area just as we would in a criminal area (Chief Superior Court Judge).

Similarly, the Assistant State Court judge also emphasized how attorneys worked with judges to process cases:

> When I first came here there were local rules, and there are still local rules. We sort of make them up as we go along, depending on what the crisis is. I know there are rules about filing--there was recently some changes in the rules on domestic cases, and it all had to do with attorneys speaking to the judges and saying "This is a real problem for us."

Attorneys all concluded that Mountain County was a "closely knit" system. Each agreed that the judges worked closely with the local bar in order to fix problems in the courts and that they were able to "get in" and see judges when it was urgent. For example, attorneys called attention to a local rule that a judge would be available for temporary domestic hearings every Tuesday. This rule (worked out between the local bar and the judges) insured that attorneys and clients could see a judge for temporary hearings and get their cases under way.

The interviews with Mountain County attorneys and judges suggested that there was something similar to "going rates" based on previous jury verdicts. One attorney observed that while civil standards were not as common, they were evident in cases involving the insurance industry. Similarly, judges indicated that they may exist for civil cases when attorneys work together often and in the same case area. These typically include auto torts where insurance adjusters are involved and negotiations in domestic cases where attorneys tend to know what juries have generally offered in the past:

> The good civil attorneys in town can tell you what the best verdict you've had in a medical malpractice case in this county. They can tell you how likely you are to get damages in a soft tissue injury case. They can tell you those things and that is definitely a part of the settlement process (Chief Superior Court Judge).

One judge even noted that "I have the lawyers tell me that they know what I am going to do before I do it."

The State Court judge, however, initially disagreed that "going rates" were evident in civil cases. She mentioned that "juries are always surprising" in civil litigation and that makes it more difficult to assess a "rate." However, when asked if she felt that attorneys might have "rates" of their own, she answered "they may have, you know, especially if they do one kind of case all the time" (State Court Judge).

In some contrast, the mediation coordinator and non-attorney mediators reported that they did not often work with others in the Mountain County system. Nor did they seem to have much knowledge of the traditional civil process. Interviews with the "lay mediators" revealed that they rarely come into contact with formal civil justice before or after mediation with each emphasizing that his/her contact with the civil justice system was generally limited to the source of referral. This generally was the Ninth District Dispute Resolution Office or the local solicitor's office for criminal cases. Knowledge of the civil justice process and contact with the civil system by mediators, then, are limited to the mediation itself. More feedback or contact with other system actors might provide better integration of mediation in the system and provide a unique organizing "node" for civil justice settlements.

WHAT DOES MEDIATION LOOK LIKE?

After considering the general civil justice system, I asked each interview subject about mediation and its effects on civil justice. How and why did mediation begin in Mountain County? How was the mediation program "sold"? Finally, how did the mediation program work?

As mentioned earlier, mediation in Mountain County was primarily a "bottom-up" exercise involving private citizens, a local court administrator, the Chief Superior Court judge, and the local bar. According to the Ninth District Court Administrator, private citizens in the area had established themselves as mediators (e.g., one local psychologist), but had no way to receive cases other than advertisement. From the standpoint of the local mediators, there would be few cases without court referrals.

When citizens who were not trained in the law began to mediate disputes, however, the local court became concerned about its use and advocated some regulation (Ninth District Court Administrator). In this, the Chief Judge in Superior court was instrumental in setting up the program and he did so in part to help the surrounding counties with case processing. The Ninth District is large (covering 15 counties) and many counties did not have the money or the caseloads for their own mediation programs. So, they all combined their resources to provide mediation. Since most mediation programs receive funds from filing fees, this was the only feasible approach.

The Chief Judge proposed the program after the Georgia State Supreme Court issued rules allowing and encouraging jurisdictions to create court-connected programs. He also emphasized that the Ninth District Dispute Resolution program was a creature of both the bench and the local bar, and was created, in part, to ease tensions among attorneys about mediation:

> I've talked to a lot of judges who won't move to this [mediation] because of concerns that the Bar would revolt against it...and that's one of the reasons that when we started it, we chose to do it through a collaborative effort with the Bar, and it was a joint venture with the Bench and Bar. And so they were on board from the beginning.

Mediation was justified, primarily, but not solely, because of case management efficiency. One mediator pointed out that the State Supreme Court was also interested in making justice more satisfactory to clients throughout the districts. However, some interview subjects identified other reasons why the legal system decided to integrate ADR into the system.

One court actor argued that the legal system had co-opted mediation to make sure it could be controlled and regulated. Judges and attorneys were "worried that the movement would take over the practice of civil law and leave them with just the criminal" in the words of one respondent. More obvious self interest was also emphasized in terms of profit motive, improving the quality of work, and keeping clients happy.

Although the prospect of settling cases quickly might lead one to think that attorneys would lose money, the Chief Judge, the Ninth District Court Administrator, and some local attorneys thought that made them money. One judge noted that the attorneys were "on board" early in the program and that their reason was partially financial:

I have never heard the first complaint since we started because most attorneys charge a fee based on what they expect they are gonna have in the case. And the truth of the matter is that if they settle it through mediation, they make more money, because they get the same fee for a lot less time. And if their client's happy, they're a lot more likely to pay them than if they're unhappy...or come back for the next round.

With mediation, attorneys who charge a flat rate could process a larger number of cases faster and collect more fees. Some reported that attorneys also began to build mediation directly into their fee structure (e.g., divorce $250; divorce with mediation $400; divorce at trial $1000).

One attorney/mediator agreed about these financial motives but also stressed that mediation was a way to get rid of cases that are not interesting or problematic. Here, then, mediation is pursued to improve the quality of work:

> The advantages are the attorney can close his file and get paid. I mean that's just a blunt example, the second example would be the attorney can get rid of a dog of a case. A lot of cases look good when they come into your office and they turn sour over the course of discovery and is this the way to close it now and not keep pushing it.

Judges also appeared to have a personal interest in mediation. The Chief Judge of Superior Court discussed the benefits of mediation, including the improvement of his own workload:

> we already have more than we can do, and so if parties resolve disputes themselves, it frees up judges and systems to address those litigants who can't resolve it themselves...there are some folks who will never settle their cases, but this allows me to focus my attention and time on those cases.

Almost all of the interview participants stated that mediation was sold in Mountain County under the guise of court efficiency. A typical response about program goals came from an attorney-mediator:

> To settle the case, to keep the courts from being clogged up and to settle this stuff that can be settled...the little stuff... especially

the contract disputes...and keep it from having to go to court...to get a settlement that is workable.

The chief Superior Court judge also pointed out that mediation improves the process of justice and is not limited to improving the court system alone but also the quality of justice:

> the goals are to resolve disputes quicker and better. Quicker in that, if they settle it through mediation, that's going to be quicker than if they have to wait on a hearing and go through a hearing. Better in that, if they have reached an agreement on it, I tend to think it's going to last longer. They're gonna be less likely to be back to amend it or modify it. Better in that, they will have spent less money getting it because they haven't had to pay to litigate. Better, in that, every time you have a contested case hearing or a contested trial, we move people backwards.

The interview subjects also discussed how mediation works. According to judges, attorneys, mediators, and administrators, mediation in Mountain County begins with judicial referral in civil cases and with the solicitor or District Attorney in criminal or Victim-Offender Restitution Cases (VORPs). According to the Ninth District Dispute Resolution Coordinator, Mountain County typically refers domestic and criminal cases to the program. With the former the most common, other civil suits referred to mediation were property or contract disputes and some automobile torts.

The State Court judges did not typically refer many cases to mediation, largely because most of their cases were debt collection or wage garnishments. One judge stated that the few State court cases that were sent to mediation were:

> really messy, but they ought to settle...if it sounds like they are not all that far apart or they've got lots of players or that these complicated issues fill up the docket...or in cases where parties have an on-going relationship, used to be friends or something.

This said, the judge in question estimated that she typically referred less than 5% of her civil cases to mediation.

In addition to case type, other factors led judges to refer some cases and not others. When a case revolved around money and there was room for compromise, it was deemed appropriate for mediation. One judge also looked to the actors in the case for guidance:

> An important factor is I'm looking for lawyers who support using mediation for that case. In other words, if I say to the lawyers, "What do ya'll think...let's send this to mediation?" and I sense from one or both that they don't want this case in mediation, I'm not going to send it (Chief Superior Court Judge).

Some cases, however, were regarded as simply inappropriate for mediation, such as personal injury cases with damages attached. According to one judge, cases with "significant legal issues" would not be sent unless "I have ruled on the legal issue" first.

Mediators also agreed that domestic cases were most appropriate for mediation but offered differing opinions on other cases. One acknowledged that not all cases should be mediated while another argued that any case type was a candidate for mediation, but that some cases were better than others. For one mediator, complex cases that might really confuse a jury could benefit from mediation (e.g., business and land disputes), especially if the parties knew more about the case and were better able to deal with each other on confusing issues.

Mediators who did not practice law provided similar assessments. Some argued that domestic cases were more difficult to mediate than criminal or other civil cases because there was more "baggage" behind the dispute. In criminal cases, for example, some emphasized that people are anxious to mediate cases because there was a trial date waiting if they did not reach an agreement.

After the case is selected by the judge for mediation, a referral sheet[58] is forwarded to the Ninth District Office of Dispute Resolution.[59] Upon receipt, the Dispute Resolution coordinator sets a calendar for the mediation and assigns a state-licensed mediator from the Ninth District Program. In some cases, the judge recommends a particular mediator for the case or allows the parties to choose their own "private" mediator from outside the Ninth District Program (Ninth District Coordinator). The chief Superior Court judge, in fact, mentioned that he would by-pass the system on occasion when he felt a particular mediator was appropriate for the case:

There are some mediators that have particular success in particular areas of mediation. The one example I can best think of is the area of business dissolutions and that type of thing where there is a lot of accounting and money issues and complex business arrangements...and on occasion, I've actually called the mediator directly and said, "I want you to do this one."

Since the time of this study, the rules on mediator assignment have been modified. According to the Dispute Resolution Coordinator, in 1996, the State Supreme Court changed the rules for model programs to allow more choice to the parties in selecting a mediator.[60] Today, when a referral is received, a letter is sent to the parties and their attorneys that confirms the receipt of their case and gives them ten days to suggest a qualified mediator. If a selection is not made in that time period, then the coordinator selects the mediator from a list of those affiliated with the program.

The difference in "private" mediators and "program" mediators can be significant in terms of fee structure. If a mediator is selected from outside the program, the parties pay more per hour for the service. More than once, the program-affiliated mediators referred to their service as "cheap" or "cheaper." One attorney/mediator shed more light on the difference in fee structure between "private" and program-affiliated mediators:

> I am building up on the private side...basically if I'm doing other court appointed or through the [Ninth District] office and used to be they could ask for me if the judge was [interested] and people would ask for me just because they knew me and seen me on another one and I was getting killed on the thing because it was, as long as it was referred through our [the Ninth District Dispute Resolution Office] I've got to charge 75 bucks for two hours and, well, that won't keep the lights burning in that conference room downstairs.

This mediator went on to argue that he had decided not to become trained for "domestic" mediation because he would then have to be placed on the Ninth District list. In turn, this would mean that he would be appointed as a mediator for the numerous domestic cases in the system and at the "cheap" rate.

Fee structure is a salient issue with respect to mediation and its community-based origins. Mediation was designed to be as cheap as possible (or even free) to participants so that access to dispute resolution would be more affordable to all parties.[61] This, in fact, was one of the stated goals of the program in Mountain County (and the state of Georgia at large). Private-based mediation, however, offers fees at variable rates. The Ninth District Court Administrator, for example, mentioned a group in Georgia where retired judges mediated "large dollar" cases for profit. The State Bar of Georgia also formed an organized section on ADR and has a substantial membership that showed the interest of attorneys in this process.

One attorney/mediator, however, cautioned that private mediation is on its way, but not yet profitable by itself:

> I look at it for down the road...it doesn't [look that way] right now. It's not mine at all, but I think as you develop your skills and your reputation that I think its coming. I think its got to and so I think I would like to be on the cutting edge or, you know, out front. Like I said, now I get about what probably averages as one a month of non-court ordered and I would hope one day that it would be financially profitable.

One additional issue that came up with respect to the mediator is that of training. To be certified to receive cases from the courts, a mediator must receive basic training to mediate minor disputes, forty hours of additional training to mediate domestic cases, and additional training for specialized cases such as domestic violence. Training typically includes seminars, "role-playing," and direct observation of veteran mediators. The amount and type of training a mediator has, then, restricts the program coordinator's case assignments.

In interviews, the issue of legal training came up more than once in discussions with mediators, attorneys, and judges. In general, some attorneys argued that mediators with a law degree were more useful than so-called lay mediators with no legal training. One attorney referred to this as a flaw of the mediation program:

It's so dependent on who the mediator is. You know, if you've got a case thats got a lot of complicated division of property and its changed forms during the marriage and you get somebody that's a non-lawyer who doesn't know what the law is--it's a waste of time...and the judges know that and they try to go through the mediation office and try to assign experienced people to those kind of cases.

However, at least one attorney thought that mediators should be laypersons:

Lawyers, irrespective of how dedicated they might be,...they're lawyers and their thought processes are different from a lay person and just like I don't think lawyers ought to be on a jury...I don't think that mediators should be lawyers.

Like some of those who worried about the skill of lay mediators, this attorney also went on to argue that in some cases some legal training might be useful, especially if the agreement provides a solution that "can't be done in the confines of the law."

The Ninth District Court Administrator provided something of a middle ground on this issue. He argued that sometimes a lay mediator may have better interpersonal communication skills necessary for a successful mediation. However, he went on to say that "all things equal (and they usually aren't)," the legal training of an attorney can make for a better mediator.

The issue of mediator selection and skill, then, seemed to be quite salient in Mountain County. This general debate was well summarized by the Chief Judge when he answered a question on the major complaints of attorneys:

the third biggest complaint you'll get from some folks. Some lawyers feel that non-lawyers have no business mediating, that they need the legal training to know. Another complaint they'll make is that they don't like mediators suggesting that they have some idea of what the judge will do [at trial]...and they don't like mediators taking that role.

Despite these complaints, the Chief Judge concluded that skilled mediators do not need a knowledge of the law unless they were in a position to make a binding decision (Chief Judge of Superior court).

Once a mediator or neutral is selected, the mediator, the parties, and their attorneys schedule the mediation at their earliest convenience.[62] The schedule for mediation is often adapted to the schedule of the parties and the mediators. Some will mediate during the day, and others will practice in the evenings when they have free time. Most cases are mediated at a neutral location. In the past, a conference room in the annex of the county courthouse was used, but more recently, disputes have been mediated at the Ninth District Office of Dispute Resolution.

Most of the work of mediators is done in the mediation itself and in preparing or writing the agreement. When asked about preparation, mediators agreed that there was very little other than scheduling clients. One argued that it was better not to know the particulars of the case prior to the mediation. This mediator typically found out about the general thrust of the case (e.g., divorce with custody), but used the lack of knowledge of the facts as an opportunity to get the parties talking and "brainstorming."

Despite the arguments about which case type was more appropriate for mediation, one mediator argued that some cases were easier than others. This mediator stated that a specific type of case was not as much of a problem to mediate as a case with a single issue:

> The most difficult to mediate is where there is a single issue like "change of custody" because when you're mediating a divorce and you've got property and debt and child related things...you've got a lot of pieces on the chessboard to move around and you can have a win-win situation a lot more easily. But in a change of custody things get tough because somebody's going to end up paying child support that wasn't there before or you know my child is going to be moved around, so there is very little incentive to mediate in that situation.

Mediators also called attention to the difference between mediation and average case settlement in interviews. They emphasized that the mediator was there to build trust and get the parties talking about the dispute. One described the work of the actual mediation more specifically:

I find that when people are comfortable they will tell you everything and of course the details come out when you are talking with them separately in a [private] caucus, but I find if you set the tone right, that people for the most part want to settle their disputes. These lingering disputes are a psychological burden to them and if they can get past their anger and through these sorts of barriers that they want to settle.

More than one of the mediators (including those with law degrees) emphasized that in a mediation, parties are given more of a chance to hear each other. In similar terms, the chief Judge of Superior court described the difference between a mediation and a traditional settlement conference this way:

To me they are very different. A settlement conference to me is more...And that's more my sitting down and helping the parties evaluate where they are, the quality of their cases, the value of the cases and that type of thing. Whereas my view of mediation is, that's not the role I would try and take. I would try to help them evaluate themselves and try to find a common ground for agreement and that type of thing.

One final issue related to mediation is who participates. Although some attorneys identified financial benefits in mediation, they were rarely present during a mediation. What did the court actors in Mountain County have to say about attorney presence in mediation?

Both the Ninth District Mediation Coordinator and a number of mediators confirmed that attorneys rarely attended the mediation session. In general, opinions about the value of attorney presence in mediation varied. When asked whether attorneys were helpful or harmful, one mediator argued that she had seen both advantages and disadvantages:

I have seen having the attorneys present very helpful especially if their clients are volatile and suspicious...or feel very vulnerable...then these thing move on better if the attorney can be there to reassure them and go off and talk with them...but I have seen it where its just the opposite. [She relayed a story about an attorney who warned that the clients were volatile and they would need private caucusing, but]...she was the one who was saying its not going to be that way, we'll just go to court and she'd start to get up.

She went on to emphasize that she had seen attorneys who could be very adversarial and in the process harmful to mediation:

if I had been able to get off with the clients, I think there would not have been any problems, but the attorneys in some cases are so concerned that this other attorney not get an advantage.

Another mediator strongly encouraged attorney participation and emphasized that they were present in 80-90% of his cases:

Well I ask for it [their presence] because a lot of times they'll say I don't think I need to be present and I will say I would like for you if you could and it would be best to be present. When the attorneys are there I am more successful there's no doubt about that...all the players, all the decision makers are right there so there's no place to go.

This mediator explained that clients would be less likely to agree to a preliminary agreement on the condition that they ask their attorneys later, something that frequently jeopardized an agreement.

Despite some endorsement of attorney presence, most mediators (and this included one attorney-mediator) argued that the adversarial orientation of attorneys could damage the process of mediation. Here, attorneys were perceived as preoccupied with the rights of their clients, something that stifled the communication necessary for successful mediation.

In this section, court actors describe the origins, development, and process of mediation. The motives for the adoption of mediation, however, seem to differ somewhat from the stated goals of the program. These more individual motives for the use of mediation may alter how actors behave in the program and the program's outcomes. What, then, did court actors and mediators say about the program's impact?

HOW HAS MEDIATION IMPACTED CIVIL JUSTICE IN MOUNTAIN COUNTY?

Most of the participants thought that the mediation program was working in Mountain County and pointed to the high success rates. These rates may be inflated, as some mediators may have included cases that settle shortly after the mediation as "agreements." One attorney/mediator mentioned this specifically:

> I'd say probably 90% [of his cases reach agreements], most do...80 or 90%, and then I give myself credit for ones that settle a week later and they call me up and say because really that's what got the thing done.

Mediated cases may settle very shortly after a "failed" mediation because the parties talk before trial. Others also mentioned that mediation gets cases to settle before they reach the "courthouse steps" and even after referral but before a mediation.

The Ninth District Mediation Coordinator acknowledged that most cases settle anyway, but emphasized that mediation allows cases to settle "earlier":

> If you've had a mediation before that [referring to trial notice or calendar calls] a lot of times it does promote settlement even if it doesn't settle in the mediation.

The part-time judge of State court also emphasized this point:

> it's my observation that cases settle at trial or moments before trial. So, I guess if you're having mediation a month or two before trial, then yes, I would say mediation would be more likely to have helped the case settle earlier.

There were, however, differing perceptions as to what happened if a case did not settle in mediation. One attorney argued that mediation did not speed up the process if it was unsuccessful:

If you're talking about overall [mediation settling cases faster] because so many cases settle now than used to, I think, than, yeah, but if you are talking about does it speed up the process of getting your final hearing then I don't think so because the judges now are taking it.

These comments illustrate the difficulty of measuring the effectiveness of mediation programs. Although a case does not settle during mediation, it may still be affected by the process. While settlement as a measure of impact may artificially enhance the perceived effectiveness of the program, the speed of case disposition is also an important measure of program effectiveness used in many studies of case management and ADR (e.g., Clarke et al., 1995).

Some court actors complicated the measurement issue further by arguing that mediation prompts cases to settle **before the mediation** takes place. This brought up the issue of whether mediation might "jump start" a case as the mediation coordinator had argued. One attorney observed:

yeah definitely, if you've got lawyers that are doing their job when they see a deadline coming they try to settle the case before then so it really pushes it up further.

Another factor that was said to have an impact on mediated agreements was the point at which a case was referred. Some mediators have argued that ADR needs to get to cases earlier--that cases that are in the system too long bring "baggage" that is hard to lose or carry "costs" that make trial more attractive. Others, typically attorneys, argue that a case can be referred too early. If a case is referred before discovery, then people might not be bargaining with all of the facts. One attorney/mediator summed up this debate quite well:

I don't think anybody's figured out when to mediate yet. There's no good system that I've seen...An insurance adjuster in a big case I mediated...said you know you can mediate too late or too little, what's the point in mediating a week before trial, you've spent all the money for the most part, the only advantage is the certainty of what the settlement will be. On the other hand if you do it too early and I've seen some cases where they have done a lot of discovery on medical issues and things and they are reluctant to settle because of a lack of information.

Another mediator, however, concluded that older cases were sometimes more suited to mediation, particularly in the domestic arena:

> if the parties have been separated for months or years they may have had virtually no communication except through their lawyers or hostile phone calls or something like that they've not really sat down in a situation that was conducive to any sort of exchanges of thought. At the very least, I feel like mediation, even when you don't get an agreement, these parties may have heard the other for the first time in a long time.

Another perceived benefit of mediation is that parties are able to craft their own agreements. Therefore, some argue that they are more likely to abide by them. This would resulted in fewer contempt cases for the courts and even fewer modifications of divorce agreements such as child visitation and support. For the most part, interview participants either believed that mediated agreements held up or had "no idea." The Ninth District Court Administrator specifically emphasized that ADR agreements are generally enforced as a contract and that most agreements in the Atlanta Justice Center "held up." He attributed this to the disputants' "ownership" of the agreements.

Others, particularly mediators, had no idea what happened to a case after it was mediated. One mediator argued that it would be unlikely that she would see the same parties again because there is no guarantee that a case would be mediated a second time. Nor would she be assigned the case by the coordinator. Others noted that they did not receive any feedback whatsoever as to what happened afterward.

Apart from the more specific question on how mediation has changed the civil process, I also asked each participant if the new program changed the general civil justice environment. Most argued that court-annexed mediation has changed the system in some manner. The most typical response was that mediation changed the behavior of attorneys by changing the procedure that a case goes through. Also, some argued that these behavioral changes produced some changes in outcome.

Some argued that mediation formalized the process of civil justice, with one attorney arguing that mediation had changed the procedures dramatically:

> I think procedurally it has changes everything because you've got new deadlines things that have to be done by then and the judges expect you to come in to that pre-trial hearing and even though you know its about to be ordered to mediation they expect you to already have the case firmed up.

The fact that mediation presented new deadlines led some attorneys to argue that they were forced to begin work earlier. One attorney noted, a bit differently, that mediation was "just an extra step in the process." However, this attorney went on to say that it "forced lawyers to assess cases in hard numbers a little quicker than normal." Another, however, argued that mediation affected no real change in the system because attorneys would have discussed the case with each other anyway. Overall, though, most participants felt that mediation stimulated case discussion earlier and led to earlier settlement.

Apart from these perceived benefits, more than one participant pointed to other behavioral changes that seemed to "free" court actors in some way. A number of participants, including judges, attorneys, and attorney-mediators, mentioned that the mediation program may have improved awareness of this option and may have improved communication among attorneys. For example, the State Court judge argued that mediation provided "another avenue, another option" for addressing civil cases. Similarly, judges concluded that even if mediation had no effect on case processing speed or caseload, the program did allow them to make new decisions about how a case should be processed.

Interview respondents also argued that awareness of mediation as an alternative had increased. The mediation coordinator, for instance, noted that more parties are beginning "to ask for it." Interestingly, some judges, attorneys, and attorney-mediators noted that attorneys had begun to ask for mediation as well and even elected to use the process outside of the court system. One attorney-mediator observed that:

> I've had a couple cases where they wanted mediation right up front. I've had a couple of cases where they wanted mediation

before the suit was filed and that's really I guess that would be the ultimate thing and that's pretty rare.

Another attorney-mediator also addressed this point and pointed out that "I've seen more people just call outside the system and just say 'we've got a contract dispute, will you mediate it.'" According to the Chief Superior Court judge, clients seem to realize that they have new avenues for addressing disputes and attorneys are more involved in the process of mediation. He also argued that some attorneys have involved themselves in the process of referral by identifying potential cases for the program.

> we don't have to spend as much time looking for the cases in the general civil or domestic that need to go to mediation, the lawyers will identify them for us. They'll call us and say 'judge, would you consider sending our case to mediation?'...so, yes, the recognize it as having added a level of structure to it [civil justice].

Attorneys and their clients, then, may have benefitted from mediation.

Another interesting question is whether mediation might have prompted more interaction among attorneys. For the most part, attorneys disagreed, largely because they emphasized that they would have discussed the case anyway and because most did not attend the mediation. One mediator, however, argued that mediation may have improved communication among attorneys.

> attorneys seem to know each other better when there is mediation. They participate and they refer back to cases they've had together.

Finally, several participants emphasized that mediation had become institutionalized in Mountain County. However, turnover of civil court personnel had presented some problems in that. Of particular concern was turnover among judges in the system. Since judges are the "gateway" to mediation for most civil cases, new judges not familiar with ADR or who may be opposed to it might lead to fewer referrals. The mediation coordinator stressed this when she mentioned that turnover amounted to having to re-institutionalize the process by educating participants about ADR.

SUMMARY

In this chapter, court actors addressed how civil justice works, how mediation works, and how mediation affects civil justice. What have we learned?

First, it is clear that "norms" govern civil justice in Mountain County. In discussing how civil justice worked in Mountain County, actors noted a consensual atmosphere among participants. Interviews, then, did not exhibit the notion that justice is adversarial. Judges, court administrators, and local attorneys often worked together to process cases and efficiently manage the system. For example, both judges and attorneys encouraged settlement and found it in their interest to do so. Most interesting was the cooperation between the local bar and judges to make rules for the system (e.g., "Tuesday" hearings and the adoption of mediation). In general, these court work groups may constitute a local legal culture similar to those discovered in criminal courts.

The mediation program was a creation of the local bar, bench, and community mediators. Local mediators saw a need for more cases and turned to the courts for survival. Lawyers and judges were said to have coopted mediation in order to control and regulate its practice. Attorneys also suggested profit as a motive for mediation. The program was, however, "sold" differently to the community. In general, the stated goals were to improve court efficiency and to satisfy litigants. Participants also discussed how cases were processed in mediation.

Finally, I asked individuals about how mediation impacted the civil justice system. In general, the interviews suggested that mediation had a hidden impact on case processing. Court actors modified their behavior in response to the institutional change of mediation. Although most cases settled anyway, court actors agreed that mediation stimulated earlier settlement and that it allowed participants to resolve some of the issues before attorneys intervened. They also argued that mediation saved parties money and provided financial advantages for attorneys, prompting both clients and their attorneys, perhaps, to request mediation. Finally, it seems that cases were mediated outside of the court system, particularly by attorney-mediators. However, at the time of the study, these cases were rare. As mediation becomes institutionalized or more widely known, then, fewer disputes may make their way into the formal civil system.

In sum, interviews showed that the institution of mediation affected the environment of civil justice in Mountain County. This was evident whether the program met its goals of case efficiency or not. The interviews presented in this chapter pointed to alterations in the behavior of court actors based on this institutional change. There is, then, some hope that mediation might meet efficiency goals in the future along with the self-interested goals of court actors. At the very least, the culture of civil justice in Mountain County has changed as a result of mediation.

CHAPTER 7
Conclusion

The research reported here has provided an exploratory view of mediation and civil courts through a neo-institutional lens. The purpose of this inductive analysis was to build a foundation for deductive research by addressing several questions. What does civil justice look like? How does mediation work within a civil justice system? How has mediation affected civil justice? Using typical methods of field research, I employed a triangulated research strategy with interviews, observation, and content analysis to gather data.

The results of this study of civil justice and mediation help to lay a foundation for deductive social science by comparing general civil and mediated civil cases, by assessing the effects of mediation as a policy on civil justice, and by learning more about civil justice and mediation from civil court actors. This study provides preliminary data to construct theory on the effects of institutional change within court systems. In this final chapter, summaries of the most important findings are presented. Following this, these results are analyzed against the institutional framework that guided the study. Finally, the policy and heuristic implications are presented.

SUMMARY PROFILE OF CIVIL JUSTICE IN MOUNTAIN COUNTY

At the outset, I posed a descriptive question, namely, what do civil justice and mediation look like in Mountain County? Examining actual mediated and general civil case files, I concluded that civil justice in Mountain County was a routine, but dominant, part of the court system. In general, civil and domestic case filings increased over the study's time period, but most of these were minor lawsuits such as simple, uncontested divorces and debt collection cases. When interviewed, civil court actors such as local attorneys and judges confirmed that caseloads were increasing and that the civil portion (particularly domestic) presented a serious workload challenge to the court.

In most cases, Mountain County litigants were individuals suing other individuals. Civil and domestic cases typically were processed with few pretrial hearings and motions and ranged in litigation time from less than a month to several years. Finally, the overwhelming majority of cases were disposed of before trial. While settlement rates were high, a surprising proportion of the cases was disposed of before trial but with significant effort by the judge.

Civil litigation, in most cases, appeared to be driven by attorneys. In the majority of general civil and domestic cases analyzed, a single attorney served the litigants on each side. However, there were many unrepresented litigants (*pro se*), and a large portion of cases were decided by default when a defendant did not answer or could not be located. Each of these characteristics is problematic for courts. In default cases, judgments are made but individuals must then be tracked down for implementation. Many times this involved simple debt collection, but a portion of these involved "deadbeat daddies" who had not paid child support.

Pro se litigation also presented a major problem to Mountain County. On a national level, this issue has begun to command the attention of the American Bar Association and the American Judicature Society. Civil litigation is procedurally complicated and includes institutional rules and norms that are typically foreign to the average citizen. Pro se litigants, then, are at a great disadvantage when facing a plaintiff or defendant who is represented. The large number of pro se litigants in Mountain County represents a "have nots" problem that civil justice systems need to address, a point addressed later.

Mountain County did seem to have a distinct legal culture. Attorneys and judges went out of their way to emphasize that they interacted often and that their relationships were consensual. A number of attorneys and judges discussed the role of the local bar in fostering communication among attorneys. Relatedly, others mentioned that members of sections of the local bar knew each other very well. Although there was a large number of attorneys from outside the district, in general, repeat players dominated the Mountain County system. These were generally local.

Case settlement norms reflect the importance of attorneys in civil litigation. High levels of settlement seemed to be due to the presence of consensual working relationships among local attorneys. In interviews, attorneys confirmed this as they acknowledged that "burning bridges" with opposing attorneys severed important norms that led to future negotiations and case settlement. The fact that many attorneys were "repeat players" in the system and members of the local bar indicated that future dealings were certain.

Case settlement clearly took place "in the shadow of the law," as Mnookin and Kornhauser (1979) and Erlanger et al. (1987) have emphasized. A number of attorneys and judges mentioned that they often looked to the jury when discussing settlement terms. Judges and attorneys, however, exposed the "shadow of law." They indicated that they would impress on litigants how a typical case might end with a jury, while some attorneys mentioned that previous jury awards and settlements were often used as guides in settlement negotiations.

Civil justice in Mountain County, then, is fairly routine, with domestic cases making up a very large part of the caseload. Like parallel processes on the criminal side, the formal rules of civil procedure and settlement norms aid court actors in processing cases, but these are clearly supplemented by local rules (like mediation) created by the local bar and court. It would be interesting to see if similar legal cultures exist in other civil trial courts.

SUMMARY OF MEDIATION AND ITS EFFECTS

Mediation in Mountain County began and was implemented in "bottom-up" fashion (see Mazmanian and Sabatier, 1989). To be sure, the Supreme Court of Georgia encouraged local judicial circuits to adopt forms of ADR that suited the culture of the locality. However, as interview respondents mentioned, the bench and the local bar met and agreed to adopt court-annexed mediation. It could be argued, then, that this "local legal culture" within the local bar organized in response to the problem of increasing civil dockets and then altered the "norms" of local civil procedure.

This contrasts with the "principal-agent" model of policy making discussed in earlier chapters. In Georgia, the state Supreme Court encouraged the adoption of mediation, but did not require implementation.

There was, then, no higher principal to local mediation "agents." The actual principals, then, are the local legal elites who may have co-opted or regulated community mediation that was already in existence.

The fact that the leaders of the local legal establishment and proponents of mediation met to consider the problem of case processing is also telling as to the amount of "organization" in the civil court system. While civil courts are not closely coupled, bureaucratic agencies, individuals, and groups became "reluctant partners" in order to begin the mediation of civil cases (see Stoker, 1991). The local legal culture observed in Mountain County resembles Stoker's model of policy regimes in which "rules, norms, and procedures...govern the interaction of participants to some collective decision" (1989: 30).[63] Interestingly, though, these rules, norms, and procedures had local origins.

These findings remind one of Harrington's (1985) study of Neighborhood Justice Centers in which she suggests that neighborhood justice centers are a technocratic response to the policy problem of case management within courts. Here, the legal establishment came "on board" with ADR because of its concern with efficiency and bureaucratization. The informality of ADR, then, serves as another way to keep alternative reforms in the justice system within the control of the legal establishment--a coopting of ADR, if you will (see Ellen, 1995; Auerbach, 1983).

Interviews with system actors did not specifically bear out that attorneys were worried that ADR would diminish the legal establishment. There was some evidence that "older" attorneys were not pleased with the changes, but, in general, attorneys supported the program and drew attention to potential benefits. Specifically, attorneys identified benefits from this policy change distinct from the goals of court efficiency. These generally consisted of new options for and in legal practice.

In the course of the research, there was evidence that referrals increased over the time period of the study. Still, mediation constituted a very small proportion of the overall civil caseload. In general, most cases referred to mediation were domestic. The participation of civil actors in mediation, then, was similar to that of general civil cases. For instance, most litigants were individuals who were represented by a single attorney. There were, however, fewer pro se litigants. The number of pretrial actions and case processing time were slightly higher in mediated cases, indicating that court workloads may not have been improved.

As to case disposition, mediated cases did settle at a higher rate than general civil cases, but trial rates were slightly higher for mediated cases.

Conclusion

Apparently, more cases settled in mediation, but fewer pretrial dispositions involved the action of judges. Those cases in mediation that were tried appeared to be more contentious than the average general civil case. So, the fact that trial rates were slightly higher in mediated cases is not surprising since judges seemed to refer "tougher" cases to mediation.

More sustained comparison of mediated and general civil cases was difficult because the types of cases referred to mediation were not the same as those in the general civil caseload. Through a more focused comparison and time-series analysis, hypotheses on the efficiency realized by mediation could be tested.

In this regard, mediation did not have much of an effect on caseloads, court workloads, trial rates, or litigation time in comparisons with the average civil case. However, when more focused comparisons controlling for case type and complexity were considered, mediation was found to have an indirect impact on court efficiency. Specifically, evidence suggested that mediation may remove contested and less routine cases from the system, freeing actors to work on other cases. Mediated cases also settled at higher rates.

Interviews with civil actors highlighted other benefits, albeit unanticipated, to mediation. For instance, the daily work of attorneys and judges changed. Even though the program had little impact on overall caseloads, local actors emphasized that mediation positively affected case processing, increased settlements, and freed up time for other work.

Most interesting was the fact that attorneys thought that mediation saved them and their clients both time and money. Although I assumed that attorneys would be rational and want to increase billable hours by proceeding to trial, this was not the case. Indeed, some attorneys had even begun to add mediation to their fee structure.

Attorneys also noted that mediation was an aid in settling cases, which saved clients' time and money, and made for happier clients who paid their bills. Also, attorneys argued that mediation allowed them to process their own workloads faster. Although they might receive less money per case, processing larger numbers of cases increased profits by "economies of scale." Finally, some attorneys added mediation to the services they offered in their practices by mediating cases themselves.

All court actors clearly recognized that mediation carried several other benefits than efficiency. It helped to save clients money, it increased client satisfaction with the legal system, and it provided new opportunities for attorneys and judges to manage their work.

MEDIATION AS INSTITUTIONAL CHANGE

Earlier, I argued that new institutionalism could serve as a framework for analyzing mediation as institutional change. As outlined earlier, there are at least two variations of the new institutionalist paradigm, rational choice and historical/interpretivist. In addition, some scholars have attempted to reconcile these variations. In general, each approach argues that institutions such as rules, norms, and procedures matter. There is, however, little consensus on just **how** they matter. How are the findings of this study reconciled under these conceptions of new institutionalism?

Under the Rational Choice Paradigm

Under the rational choice variation, institutions are conceived as products of self-interested choices that are, themselves, constrained by existing institutions. A number of the findings of this work seem to illustrate this conception.

The origins of ADR were publicly stated to be the promotion of court efficiency. However, other strategic preferences were clearly on the minds of proponents. Evidence from interviews indicated that self-interest of court actors was an important part of mediation support. Attorneys identified benefits that seemed cooptive, including the incorporation of ADR into their practices and fee structure. For their part, mediators agreed to court-annexed mediation, in part to have more cases to mediate. Furthermore, judges discussed efficiency benefits in general terms but were clearly concerned with their personal workloads.

Interestingly, constraints on institutional choice did not come from the "top." Unlike the traditional "top-down" model of policy implementation, the Supreme Court of Georgia did not mandate, but only encouraged, mediation at the local level. This gave local courts and districts the freedom to adopt the type or style of ADR that suited their locality. Implementation, then, was primarily "bottom-up."

There were, however, constraints at the "bottom." The parameters that constrained the adoption and implementation of mediation were the existing rules and norms of the local legal system. For example, there was a concern about "lay-persons" with little training mediating cases in an unrestricted fashion. Also, the interest of an organized ADR section of the state bar suggested that local legal elites were professionally interested in mediation. Mountain County attorneys were beginning to mediate cases themselves and they expected future opportunity with court-annexed mediation.

Preferences for the preservation of existing legal procedures also constrained the implementation of the mediation program. For example, Mountain County judges were given the discretion to refer cases to mediation. This authority was most often applied to domestic and minor criminal cases, while some judges rarely referred cases at all.

Similarly, judges referred some types of cases to "attorney-mediators" rather than "lay" mediators. Sometimes referral was granted on the request of attorneys managing the case, most often when presented by attorney-mediators. "Lay" mediators, then, were excluded from some cases to the benefit of "attorney-mediators" and the preservation of existing legal traditions.

Rational choice perspectives also help to illuminate results related to program impact. Program impact is, of course, a direct function of implementation (see Mohr, 1988). In Mountain County, it was generally shaped by those who chose the program. The rational choice variation on the new institutionalist paradigm tells us that self-interested pursuits, including the preference for existing institutions and norms, would keep many cases from being referred to mediation. This may help to explain why mediation had little impact on court efficiency. Certainly one could argue that efficiency was not really sought by court actors and that more short-term and self-interested motives prevailed. The bottom line here is that behavioral changes associated with the institutional change of mediation were not directly or solely associated with the publicly stated goal of court efficiency. Other, decidedly rational preferences were at work and these dominated mediation.

Under the Historical/Interpretivist Paradigm

Historical/interpretivist variations on the new institutionalism focus on the relative autonomy of political and legal organizations as products of economic relations or the functional needs of social systems. Here, institutions "prescribe action, construct motives, and assert legitimacy" (Skowronek, 1995: 94) and constrain even rational actors to other pursuits such as their duty and mission (Gillman, 1997). How are the results of this study illuminated by this conception of new institutionalism?

First, mediation was publicly promoted as a response to a functional need of society. Study results indicated that there was a perceived litigation crisis in Mountain County where caseloads (especially domestic) were increasing while court resources remained essentially the same. Program proponents, then, sold the program publicly as a means of achieving court efficiency by settling cases before trial, speeding the processing of cases, and decreasing workloads of court actors.

While the evidence presented earlier showed very limited evidence of success, court actors often focused on the need to improve justice and emphasized that mediation improved litigant satisfaction with the justice system. Also, court actors stated that mediation sped case disposition, led to settlement (even when no agreement was reached in mediation), and improved the workload of courts. Case records did not bear out all of these claims and, in fact, the mediation program was used sparingly in Mountain County. However, there was a sense of "duty" and "mission" that seemed to exist apart from other rational interests that figured in the adoption of mediation.

Did mediation prescribe action, construct motives, or assert legitimacy as Skowronek (1995) suggests in his historical/interpretivist paradigm? This is unclear. The adoption of mediation and its promotion did highlight the importance of courts in the justice system. One could argue that selling mediation to "save" the courts in the midst of crisis promotes legitimacy. Also, bringing mediation formally into courts only enhances the power and legitimacy of courts as the arbiters of disputes. The related institutional change, then, was adopted using the "ceremonies and rituals" of the traditional legal system and as such perpetuated an attachment to the legal system and its mission (Gillman, 1997).

The problem with the historical/interpretivist approach is that mediation in Mountain County did not achieve what proponents had asserted. In fact, judges referred few cases. More rational motives seem to have figured more prominently in the program adoption and implementation, thus lending more support to that new institutional approach. In this sense, it may be that institutions can exist as parameters that both constrain and free actors in their choices. For instance, the institutional change of mediation did not provide the efficiency advanced by proponents. But it did free judges by giving them the option of case referral, which, in turn, was used to encourage settlement and process cases. At the same time, judicial referral helped to preserve and maintain the legitimacy of "the law" as a powerful constraint on societal behavior.

Further evidence supporting this was gleaned from interviews with attorneys and mediators. While constrained vis-a-vis mediation by the judge, attorneys were free to pursue a new avenue for case settlement and even to volunteer their cases for mediation, to act as mediators themselves, and to build mediation into their fee structure. While constrained by the court as to certain types of cases, mediators were free to pursue the overarching mission of mediation to empower individuals to solve their own problems and to transform communities into safer, more peaceful, places to live.

The "new institutionalism," then, helps us to frame the results reported. First, it demonstrates that operative motives can be identified more accurately by behavior than formal policy pronouncements. Also, it forces us to recognize that this behavior can be constrained by institutions. In the final analysis, "new institutionalism" only manages to show that changes in institutions alter the behavior of actors, but does not necessarily insure specific results.

POLICY IMPLICATIONS

Why did mediation fail to live up to its expected efficiency goal? As noted, new institutional approaches help us to answer this question. But what of the characteristics of the change itself?

First, the Office of Dispute Resolution may not have had the capacity to handle large numbers of cases. Serving Hall and fourteen other northeast Georgia counties, the mission was broad. Also, the program was not limited to civil cases, with minor criminal cases included. It may eventually be necessary, then, for Mountain County, as one of the larger court systems in the Ninth District, to adopt its own mediation program and concentrate on a wider number and variety of cases.

One has to recognize, though, that the Mountain County mediation program is in its infancy. At the time of this study, only four years had passed since implementation. The number and types of cases that have been mediated since have expanded. As Mountain County court consumers and participants get more comfortable with mediation, there may be more case referrals even without a separate office and staff.

Although the impact of mediation on case processing efficiency in Mountain County was indirect at best, one cannot conclude that the policy/institutional change had no effect. Interviews suggested that the legal community is satisfied with and benefits from mediation. Other indirect benefits include removing cases from the system, freeing judges to pursue other cases. These indirect benefits may be worth expanding the program and might contribute to future court efficiency.

Finally, this study suggests that mediation may have been oversold as to its effect on court efficiency (see Herrman, 1995). The danger in promising too much, too soon is that negative policy evaluations give fuel to political opponents and even suppress the ambitions of supporters. Proponents of mediation need to be honest about the realities of mediation as a court efficiency tool and emphasize its other potential benefits. Promising too much could do harm to mediation at the expense of these other goals.

HEURISTIC IMPLICATIONS

Limitations of the study reported here insure the need for more research. First and most glaring, this research focused on a single jurisdiction. Generalizations to other programs or regions, then, are limited. Second, this study does not offer any multivariate analyses. It is, indeed, possible that other factors or variables caused the results presented. Finally, the interviews were conducted with a limited number of participants and may not be representative of the population of civil actors in Mountain County.

Given these limitations, where do we go from here? For those who study trial courts, several questions persist. Do distinct local legal cultures exist in civil justice systems? What effects do local institutions have on civil case processing? How and for what reasons do local actors in other courts choose administrative policies for case processing such as those found in Mountain County? Comparative studies of civil courts are clearly needed.

For those who study mediation, an equally important set of questions need to be examined. Does mediation offer indirect benefits to court efficiency such as fewer subsequent actions after agreements? Is mediation being oversold as a method of improving court efficiency? Would a focus on the benefits of mediation to participants (i.e., attorneys, judges, and litigants) be a more honest and appropriate way to sell mediation to the public?

One thing that is clear from this research is that trial court and mediation scholars need to work together to assess the impact of this institutional change. The theoretical framework of this study suggests that

Conclusion

policies often reach unintended and even hidden outcomes that cannot be assessed without closely studying the behavior of local policy agents. We must study the "rules in use" of local policy actors in order to understand the impact of policies (see Sproule-Jones, 1993). Court-annexed mediation, then, cannot be adequately assessed without looking at the entire civil system in which it operates.

Notes

[1] The "private" law distinction existed despite the fact that in many states civil justice is often delivered along with criminal justice in the same court systems.

[2] It should be noted that ADR programs have traditionally been volunteer-based forums with the over-arching goal of community empowerment in addition to problem solving. The current movement by state governments to bureaucratize formally ADR is from a different ideology, with efficient dispute processing as its primary focus. For an excellent discussion of ADR ideology and history, see the introductory chapters of Schwerin (1995) and Hermann (1993).

[3] Examples of grant-funded projects on the criminal side include Eisenstein and Jacob, 1977; and works by Eisenstein, Nardulli, and Flemming published in 1988 and 1992. The study of civil courts includes the Civil Litigation Research Project (CLRP) based at the University of Wisconsin. Spinoffs of this research include Trubek et. al., 1983; and works by Herbert Kritzer, 1990; 1991.

[4] "Author Meet Critics: Martin Shapiro and the Study of Public Law and Judicial Politics," American Political Science Annual Meeting, August 31-September 3, 1995, Chicago, Illinois.

[5] Eisenstein and Jacob (1977) provide theoretical background on courtroom characteristics in chapter 2. Among the patterns of characteristics explored are courtroom authority patterns, courtroom influence patterns, shared goals of courtroom work groups, work group specialization, work techniques of the organization, courtroom tasks, and

work group familiarity. These data were collected primarily through observation and interview, and findings were reported through description.

[6] The ecology of courtroom work groups are explored in chapter 3 of Eisenstein and Jacob (1977). Here, they observed for patterns in courtroom environments which were broken into physical surroundings of the work group and the social networks of the group. Of particular interest is the focus on sponsoring organizations such as police, legislatures, appellate courts, and the partisanship of the environment. Again, the authors generally describe each court work group by focusing on these factors through observation.

[7] Works by Kritzer (1990, 1991) on lawyers in civil litigation has argued that the rationale for settlement may include the need for attorneys to process many cases quickly at lower rates of return. This often generates more income than the time and expenditures necessary for a single large damage case.

[8] In domestic cases as well as others, it is difficult to determine "winners" and "losers" since a defendant who "looses" a jury verdict may have lost less money in damages than earlier settlement offers. In domestic cases, a judgment raising child support for a plaintiff may be less money than the defendant was originally willing to pay. These "stakes" are difficult if not impossible to determine from case files.

[9] Kritzer (1990) argues that his measure of direct involvement of judges still does not take into account whether judges are directly involved in the settlement process (e.g., settlement conferences).

[10] The focus of the San Francisco Community Boards Program, one community mediation center, was to form popular justice that was almost contrary to the legal system (Merry and Milner, 1993). The goal was to overcome the alienation of the adversary system by empowering individuals to settle their own disagreements. The long-term goal was "not so much the settlement of agreements, but the longterm rebuilding of community capacities" (Adler, Lovass, and Milner, 1988: 321; see Neubauer, 1996).

[11] Discussion of the effects of mediation within the legal system has yielded even more drastic possibilities. One such discussion with a mediation expert and a court administrator left the possibility that lawyers (and others) would become certified in mediation and then mediate disputes for larger and larger fees. One conclusion was that eventually there would be two justice systems: one private system for the wealthy and a public justice system for the poor. Ellen's (1995b) work on the North Carolina system has found that court-annexed mediation has begun to move closer to private (and competitive) settlement negotiations and further from the traditional concept of cooperative mediation.

[12] Note that studies of court-ordered arbitration have also provided mixed results on case processing. For example, Hanson and Keilitz's (1991) study of Fulton County, Georgia found evidence that case processing was slower in arbitration when measured as filing of case to disposition. However, like previous studies, arbitration was much speeder than trial courts when measuring time from arbitration referral to disposition.

[13] Note the exceptions of the organizational studies on the criminal side and the recent work of Jacob (1996) on trial courts as loosely coupled organizations.

[14] As Chapter 1 suggests, contemporary study of civil trial courts has been related to a perceived litigation "crisis" that has led to government efforts to reform torts. Much of this research has been directed at testing the nature and extent of this crisis (see discussion in Eaton and Talarico, 1996).

[15] Recent works by scholars of the courts have provided evidence supporting the neo-institutional theory. Brace and Hall's (1995, 1990) work on state courts provides evidence that institutions affect the decisions of judges more so than other explanations of court behavior. Work on Supreme Court decision making has yielded evidence of internal and external institutions affecting behavior and outcomes. See Gely and Spiller (1990) on external influence of president and Congress, and Schwartz (1992) on influence of internal court rules and norms. See also Songer, Cameron, and Segal (1995) on the rational behavior of litigation. Gibson's (1979) view of "roles" as constraining attitudes in judicial decisions also lends support to this theory.

[16] Note that this study is limited to the effects of the program on Mountain County civil justice alone. Criminal cases, then, were counted, but not explored as part of this study. An analysis of both criminal and civil justice in all 15 counties would need the support of a large grant.

[17] A focus on a single jurisdiction allows for triangulation techniques to be used. In this respect, the civil court actors, processes, and institutions can be examined through interviews and elements of case flow and outcomes can be measured by examining case files. The quantification of these data provide the ability to measure the effects of mediation on civil justice over time. Each of these techniques is possible in a multi-site study, but would lack the depth necessary for exploration.

[18] The case records from both state and Superior courts were sampled by searching docket books in the Clerk's Office for appropriate case numbers and selecting every "nth" case. The "nth" case number was calculated by dividing the total caseload for the year by 100. This insured that the systematic sampling method would take me through the entire docket for that year.

[19] Note that dates for these cases are based on the filing date in the Mountain County system. Therefore, some mediated cases were referred in 1992 or 1993, but were actually filed in the Hall system much earlier (as early as 1989). The 1995 mediated cases, then, are cases that were filed in 1995 and also referred in the same year.

[20] See Appendix A for a specific codesheet. It should also be noted that the code format is compatible with those used in recent studies of civil litigation by the National Center for State Courts (e.g., DeFrances et. al., 1995) and research supported by the Georgia Civil Justice Foundation (Dunn, et al., 1995; Eaton and Talarico, 1994, 1995, 1996).

[21] See end of codesheet in Appendix A for additional information drawn from mediated cases.

[22] See appendix B1 through B4.

[23] Note that a study such as this has the primary limitation of generalizability. However, the basis of this study is that of exploration similar to first generation studies such as Neubauer (1974) on criminal courts. One should not discount the importance of similar exploratory research on the civil side (even under the research constraints of generalizability) as a guide to more systematic research in the future.

[24] The findings are similar to those of Eaton and Talarico (1996) in their study of tort and civil trends in four other Georgia counties.

[25] The State of Georgia Department of Human Resources (GADHR) will file for unrecovered child support on behalf of mothers and their dependents. When I encountered these cases, I found that the filing mechanism was quite routine. The GADHR typically filed a form complaint with the courts.

[26] However, costs to society of pro se representation can be quite high in court resources. One judge interviewed in this study commented without prompting that pro se litigants took up a very large amount of time in correcting answers and consent agreements to be legally binding. Sometimes the judge's staff was left with the job of correcting the procedural errors in documentation.

[27] An attorney was coded local if his/her office was located inside the county, otherwise the attorney was coded as an "outsider".

[28] The number of attorneys was much larger among plaintiffs due to the number of unknowns coupled with pro se representation.

[29] As with attorneys, information on judges will be reported in an anonymous fashion as promised to the individuals for their participation in the interviews reported later.

[30] Once the case is assigned to a judge, it is typically sent to the judge's staff (administrative assistant and clerks) where it is formally docketed for a pre-trial hearing.

[31] In Georgia, when a judge retires, dies, or is elevated, the governor appoints a successor to fill out the term of the former judge. The replacement can then choose to run for re-election in a nonpartisan election.

[33] In general, few new judicial seats were created in the State of Georgia during the time period of this study (1989-1995). In fact, only seven new full-time judges were added to the State court system in the time of the study. These were in the counties of Fulton, Cobb, Gwinnett, Brooks, Fayette, McIntosh, and Clarke.

[34] One potential problem with these data is whether all of the events in a case are filed with the courts. In one interview, a local attorney said that many events such as discovery are made informally and are never filed with the court. The data reported hereafter only discuss the events of particular cases that were formally filed with the Clerk of Courts Office and most certainly underestimate total case events.

[35] A number of domestic cases were disposed of by pre-trial orders. Originally, Mountain County court administrators had referred to this large number of dispositions as bench trials. Later, these cases were classified as different because they involved simply signing an order or decree rather than holding full proceedings in chamber or in court. Here, bench trials were strictly coded as situations where full hearing proceedings were held.

[36] Settlements are defined as those cases dismissed with or without prejudice, before or after trial. I collapsed all of these categories into one measure of settlement.

[37] In particular, table 3-4 shows a decrease in domestic case filings in Superior Court in 1993 and 1994.

[38] The simplest divorce cases are generally filed in the Clerk's Office by *pro se* litigants.

[39] There was an unusually high number of cases where information on attorneys was missing or unknown (20%). These cases, of course, could raise the amount of attorney participation or suppress it further.

[40] The "total" category in Table 30 refers to attorneys in mediated cases that had appearances for both plaintiffs and defendants. The category is calculated the same as in Table 11.

[41] Some programs do not give the judge the full power of case referral. In other jurisdictions around the country (and even other programs in Georgia), entire classes of cases (e.g., domestic) are automatically referred to mediation.

[42] Pretrial actions include continuances, discovery attempts (depositions), leaves of absence, and motions (compel, dismiss, etc.). The figures only include the number of actions in the case file itself. It is likely that other actions occurred between attorneys and were not formally filed. Pretrial hearings do not include routine temporary hearings in domestic cases, but represent actual hearings on motions.

[43] In the original data collection, I did not specifically code cases as contested or uncontested. This is certainly a shortcoming for this portion of the study, but I have attempted to remedy this problem here. In the data collection, each case was coded as to whether the defendant had filed an answer in the case. It can be assumed, then, that if a case is formally answered, then the legal issues in the case are contested or at least being defended. I spot checked to see which cases were left out and found that this removed uncontested, routine divorces as well as cases that ended in default. It is possible that some cases that were appropriate to be selected were left out if an answer was missing in the file. This is not a perfect measure, but does go a long way toward a more refined comparison than in Chapter 3.

[44] Most cases, then, had zero pretrial actions but the large number of pretrial actions in some cases resulted in a positive mean.

[45] Note that previous research reviewed here has found that mediated agreements are often modified by litigants, judges, and attorneys prior to final decrees of divorce.

[46] Note that a number of cases referred to mediation were actually filed in the civil court system prior to 1992. Therefore, the figures below show some mediated cases in the years of 1990 and 1991.

[47] The 1995 general civil caseload included a fairly large number of pending cases that most certainly would have settled (on average). This explains the abnormally low 54.9% figure in 1995. Mediated caseloads did not include many pending cases in this year.

[48] This comparison is somewhat problematic given that the general civil cases are measured from filing to disposition. To be fair, some general civil cases involve delay from filing to the time of the first action in the case (before a judge or otherwise). Even so, the comparison is more rigorous than comparing the pace of mediated cases as measured from filing to disposition.

[49] Again, this measure is not perfect as it includes general civil cases that were dismissed on default, or for lack of service. In general, mediated cases are much less likely to be dismissed on default, etc.

[50] Two notable articles do present different arguments. Bryan (1992) and Grillo (1991) both argue that divorce mediation benefits men over women. In each, the argument is that the process benefits the party with the most money and power--typically the man. Additionally, the process is viewed to remove "the fight" from women and influences them to conform.

[51] One potential problem recognized by scholars is that alternatives to court, or informal justice methods, may benefit the "haves" anyway (Abel, 1985; Auerbach, 1983; Harrington, 1985). Abel argues that the formal legal system is the only arena where unequals can hope to achieve justice versus informal systems like the economy or politics (1985). Alternatives to courts may be designed to siphon off those discontented with the justice system and discourage them from seeking litigation that might benefit social change (Auerbach, 1983). Harrington's assessment of the modern ADR movement is similar in that the movement to informalize the justice system is a technocratic movement to decentralize the court system. Informal mechanisms, such as ADR, are not an alternative to the system, but are merely a "shadow" of courts (Harrington, 1985). See also Bryan (1992) and Grillo (1991) on whether divorce mediation benefits men (the powerful) over women in disputes.

[52] The State Court judge had practiced primarily criminal law with some domestic and juvenile cases. Interestingly, the part-time State Court judge

still practiced law on the side and typically handled, business, contracts, and some domestic ("if she has to").

[53] The State Court judge received her bachelor's and JD out of state (B.A., Southern Illinois U.; J.D., University of Chicago). The retired Superior court judge received his B.A. at Davidson College.

[54] This mediator had training as a paralegal and started the largest legal services company in the Southeast. She currently works in the marketing of legal services. Prior to this position, she was a conciliator for the U.S. Department of Housing and Urban Development.

[55] Diversity of population may affect caseloads by weakening community "ties" or norms of collegiality among neighbors. Auerbach (1983) argued that immigrants in the late 19th and early 20th century turned to the courts for redistribution of wealth and for protection of individual rights. As community bonds are fractured by new arrivals, one might expect more use of the courts in civil disputes such as property and torts.

[56] With all of the discussion of a judge's pretrial role, one should not underestimate the amount of time judges spend in hearings and at trial. The assistant judge in State court emphasized that much of her time was spent on the bench in criminal arraignment and sentencing. Additionally, the retired Superior court and State court judges both described trial work, sentencing, and arraignments as very time consuming.

[57] Erlanger, Chambliss, and Melli (1997) even suggest that since most judges essentially rubberstamp the large volume of settlements, a judge's perception of the value of a case may come from settlements and not juries.

[58] The case referral sheet at the time of this study contained the following information: the names of the parties, the names of attorneys, the case's docket number, the type of the case, and if the case included domestic violence. A new form was adopted after the period of this study that included the option of sending the case to mediation, arbitration, or case evaluation.

[59] Some counties in the Ninth District would allow the judge to refer the case through a standing court order for certain types of cases. For

example, in Cherokee County, all divorce cases are referred to mediation by order of the court.

[60] The mediation coordinator told me that her program was supportive of choosing mediators that were outside the program.

[61] Interestingly, some scholars (see Auerbach, 1983) and some practitioners (interview with a Dispute Resolution Coordinator in Southern Georgia) have argued that ADR has been more affordable to the poor and that this could eventually lead to a system where the poor are serviced by ADR and the rich turn to the court system. The interview with the Dispute Resolution Coordinator in South Georgia, though, also argued that the very wealthy could or would turn to private forms of ADR to keep commercial disputes cheaper, private, and out of the realm of legal regulation.

[62] Case files indicated that about a month passed between the time that the mediation office received the initial referral and the actual mediation. These mediation sessions typically lasted approximately two hours.

[63] Stoker (1989; 1991) produced a body of work that made use of game theory to explain policy implementation. Regimes have the characteristics of promoting cooperation through the "alteration of transaction costs, availability of information, or level of uncertainty in the decision process" (1989: 30). The crux of his theory is that cooperative behavior is more likely when actors are engaged in long-term, ongoing relationships (37).

BIBLIOGRAPHY

Abel, Richard L. "The Real Tort Crisis - Too Few Claims." 48 *Ohio State Law Journal* (1987): 443-467.

_____. "Informalism: A Tactical Equivalent to Law." 19 *Clearinghouse Review* (1985): 375.

Adler, Peter, Karen Lovass, and Neal Milner. "The Ideologies of Mediation: The Movement's Own Story." 10 *Law and Policy* (1988): 317-339.

Alchian, Armen A. and Harold Demsetz. "Production, Information Costs, and Economic Organization." *American Economic Review* (1972): 777-795.

Ashman, Allan, and Jeffrey A. Parness, "The Concept of a Unified Court System." 24 *DePaul Law Review* (Fall 1974): 1-41.

Auerbach, Jerold. *Justice Without Law?* New York: Oxford University Press, 1983.

Berk, Sarah F., and Donileen R. Loseke. "'Handling' Family Violence: Situational Determinants of Police Arrest in Domestic Disturbances." 15 *Law and Society Review* (1981): 317.

Berkson, Larry, Carbon, Susan, and Judy Rosenbaum. *Court Unification: History, Politics, and Implementation.* Washington: National Institute of Law Enforcement and Criminal Justice, Law Enforcement Assistance Administration, Department of Justice, 1978.

Black, Donald J. "The Social Organization of Arrest." 23 *Stanford Law Review* (1971): 1087.

Blumberg, Abraham. *Criminal Justice.* Chicago: Quadrangle Books, 1967.

Blumstein, James F., Randall R. Bovbjerg, and Frank A. Sloan. "Beyond Tort Reform: Developing Better Tools for Assessing Damages for Personal Injury." 8 *Yale Journal on Regulation* (Winter 1991): 171-212.

Boersema, Craig, Roger Hanson, and Susan Keilitz. "State court Annexed Arbitration: What do Attorneys Think?" 75 *Judicature* (June/July 1991).

Bohmer, Carol and Marilyn Ray. "Divorce Mediation and Gender: A Solution to the Domination and Disempowerment Theory of Law or Just Another Example of it?" A Paper Presented at the Law and Society Annual Meetings, Philadelphia, PA, May 1992.

Brace, Paul, and Melinda Gann Hall. "Neo-Institutionalism and Dissent in State Supreme Courts." 52 *Journal of Politics* (1990): 54-70.

_____. "Studying Courts Comparatively: The View From the American States." 48 *Political Research Quarterly* (March 1995): 5-29.

Bryan, Penelope E. "Killing Us Softly: Divorce Mediation and the Politics of Power." 40 *Buffalo Law Review* (1992): 441.

Bush, Robert A. Baruch, and Joseph P. Folger. *The Promise of Mediation: Responding to Conflict Through Empowerment and Recognition.* San Francisco: Jossey-Boss, 1994.

Canon, Bradley C., and Lawrence L. Baum. "Patterns of Tort Law Innovations: An Application of Diffusion Theory to Judicial Doctrines." 72 *American Political Science Review* (1981): 774-788.

Carter, Lief H. *The Limits of Order.* Lexington, MA: D.C. Heath, 1974.

Catenacci, Richard D. "Hyperlexis or Hyperbole: Subdividing the Landscape of Disputes and Defusing the Litigation Explosion." 8 *Review of Litigation* (1989): 297-324.

Clarke, Richard N., Frederick Warren-Boltan, David D. Smith, and Marilyn J. Simon. "Sources of the Crisis in Liability Insurance: An Economic Analysis." 5 *Yale Journal on Regulation* (1988): 367-395.

Clarke, Stevens H., Laura Donnelly, and Sara Grove. "Court-Ordered Arbitration in North Carolina: Case Outcomes and Litigant Satisfaction." 14 *Justice System Journal* (1991): 154-182.

Clarke, Stevens H., Elizabeth D. Ellen, and Kelly McCormick. "Court-Ordered Civil Case Mediation in North Carolina: An Evaluation of Its Effects." Report prepared for the North Carolina Administrative Office of the Courts, June 1995.

Cole, George F. "The Decision to Prosecute." 4 *Law and Society Review* (1970): 313-343.

Daniels, Stephen. *Caseload Dynamics and the Nature of Change: The Civil Business of Trial Courts in Four Counties, 1870-1960*. Chicago: American Bar Association, 1988a.

_____. *The Discontinuous Nature of Change: Institutional Constraints and Caseload Dynamics in Illinois Courts, 1880 to 1960*. Chicago: American Bar Association, 1988b.

_____. "Caseload Dynamics and the Nature of Change: The Civil Business of Trial Courts in Four Illinois Counties." 24 *Law and Society Review* (1990): 298.

Davis, Robert C., Martha Tichane, and Deborah Grayson. *Mediation and Arbitration as Alternatives to Prosecution in Felony Arrest Cases: An Evaluation of the Brooklyn Dispute Resolution Center*. New York: Vera Institute of Justice, 1980.

DeFrances, Carol J., et al. *Bureau of Justice Statistics, Civil Justice Survey of State courts, 1992: Civil Jury Cases and Verdicts in Large Counties* (1995).

Depner, Charlene, K. Cannata, and M. Session. "Building a Uniform Reporting System: A Snapshot of California Family Court Services." 30 *Family and Conciliation Courts Review* (1992).

Duquesnel, Joseph. *Client Satisfaction Survey: A Consumer Evaluation of Mediation and Investigative Services.* Report to Judicial Council of California, March 1991.

Dunn, Richard E., Thomas A. Eaton, Roger E. Hartley, and Susette M. Talarico. "Tort Litigation in Georgia: A Descriptive Profile and Preliminary Analysis." Paper Presented at the 1995 Meetings of the Southern Political Science Association, Tampa, Florida, November 4, 1995.

Dunn, Richard E., Thomas A. Eaton, Roger E. Hartley, and Susette M. Talarico. "Patterns of Tort Litigation in Georgia: 1990 - 1993 An Analysis of Disposition Type." Paper Presented at the 1996 Meetings of the American Political Science Association, San Francisco, California, August 28 - September 1, 1996.

Eaton, Thomas A., and Susette M. Talarico. *A Profile of Tort Litigation in Georgia and Reflections on Tort Reform.* A Report Submitted to the Georgia Civil Justice Foundation (Manuscript), 1995.

_____. "A Profile of Tort Litigation in Georgia and Reflections on Tort Reform." 30 *Georgia Law Review* (Spring 1996): 627-729.

Eisenberg, Theodore. "Section 1983: Doctrinal Foundations and an Empirical Study." 67 *Cornell Law Review* (1982): 482.

_____. "Testing the Selection Effect: A New Theoretical Framework with Empirical Tests." 19 *Journal of Legal Studies* (1990): 337-358.

Eisenberg, Theodore and James A. Henderson, Jr. "Inside the Quiet Revolution in Products Liability." 39 *UCLA Law Review* (1992): 732-810.

Eisenstein, James, and Herbert Jacob. *Felony Justice: An Organizational Analysis of Criminal Courts*. Boston: Little, Brown and Company, 1977.

Eisenstein, James, Roy B. Flemming, and Peter F. Nardulli. *The Contours of Justice: Communities and their Courts*. Boston: Little, Brown and Company, 1988.

Ellen, Elizabeth D. "Mediation Meets the Legal Establishment: Using ADR as Court-Reform." Paper presented at the Midwest Political Science Association Annual Meeting, Chicago, Illinois, April 7, 1995a.

_____. "Tinkering With the Adversary System: The ADR Movement and Other Court Reforms." Paper presented at the Southern Political Science Association Annual Meeting, Tampa, Florida, November 4, 1995b.

Elliott, Euel, and Susette M. Talarico. "An Analysis of Statutory Development: The Correlates of State Activity in Product Liability Legislation." 10 *Policy Studies Review* (Spring/Summer 1991): 61-78.

Emery, R. and M. Wyer. "Child Custody Mediation: An Experimental Evaluation of the Experience of Parents." 55 *Journal of Consulting and Clinical Psychology* (1987): 179-186.

Epstein, Lee. *Contemplating Courts*. Washington, DC: CQ Press, 1995.

Epstein, Lee and Jack Knight. *The Choices Justices Make*. Washington, DC: CQ Press, 1998.

_____. "The New Institutionalism, Part 2." 8 *Law and Courts* (Spring 1997): 4-13.

Erlanger, Howard S., Chambliss, Elizabeth, and Marygold S. Melli. "Participation and Flexibility in Informal Processes: Cautions from the Divorce Context." 21 *Law and Society Review* (1987): 585.

Ethington, Philip J. and Eileen L. McDonagh. "The Common Space of Social Science Inquiry." 28 *Polity* (1995): 85-90.

Felstiner, William L.F., and Lynne Williams. *Community Mediation in Dorchester, Massachucetts.* Washington, D.C.: U.S. Department of Justice, 1980.

Felstiner, William L.F., Richard K. Abel, and Austin Sarat. "The Emergence and Transformation of Disputes: Naming, Blaming, Claiming ..." 15 *Law and Society Review* (1980-81): 631-654.

Fix, Michael and Philip J. Harter. *Hard Cases, Vulnerable People: An Analysis of Mediation Programs at the Multi-Door Courthouse of the Superior court of the District of Columbia.* The Urban Institute, June 2, 1992.

Flemming, Roy B. "Review Essay: Ordinary Litigation in America's Civil Courts: Images of Lawyers and Bargaining." 26 *Law and Society* (1992): 669-687.

Flemming, Roy B., Peter F. Nardulli, and James Eisenstein. *The Craft of Justice: Politics and Work in Criminal Court Communities.* Philadelphia: University of Pennsylvania Press, 1992.

Folberg, Jay and Allison Taylor. *Mediation: A Comprehensive Guide to Resolving Conflicts Without Litigation.* San Francisco: Jossey-Boss, 1984.

Galanter, Marc. "Why the Haves Come Out Ahead: Speculations on the Limits of Legal Change." 9 *Law and Society Review* (1974): 95-160.

_____. "Reading the Landscape of Disputes: What We Know and Don't Know (and Think We Know) About Our Allegedly Contentious and Litigious Society." 31 *UCLA Law Review* (1983): 4-71.

_____. "The Day After the Litigation Explosion." 46 *Maryland Law Review* (Fall 1986): 3-39.

Galanter, Marc, and Thomas Palay. *Tournament of Lawyers: The Transformation of the Big Law Firm.* Chicago: University of Chicago Press, 1991.

Gates, John B. "Theory, Methods, and the New Institutionalism in Judicial Research." In *The American Courts: A Critical Assessment*, ed. John B. Gates and Charles A. Johnson. Washington, DC: CQ Press, 1991.

Gates, John B., and Charles A. Johnson. *The American Courts: A Critical Assessment*. Washington, DC: CQ Press, 1991.

Gely, Rafael, and Pablo T. Spiller. "A Rational Choice Theory of Supreme Court Statutory Decisions with Applications to the *State Farm* and *Grove City* Cases." 6 *Journal of Law, Economics, and Organization* (Fall 1990): 263-300.

Gibson, James L. "A Role Theoretic Model of Criminal Court Decision-making." In *The Study of Criminal Courts: A Political Perspective*, ed. Peter F. Nardulli. Cambridge: Ballinger Publishing, 1979: 83-99.

Gillman, Howard. "The New Institutionalism, Part 1: More and Less than Strategy; Some Advantages to Interpretive Institutionalism in the Analysis of Judicial Politics." 7 *Law and Courts* (Winter 1996-97): 6-11.

Goggin, Malcolm L., et al. *Implementation Theory and Practice: Toward a Third Generation*. Glenview, IL: Scott, Foresman/ Little, Brown, 1990.

Goldberg, Stephen B., Frank Sander, and Nancy Rogers. *Dispute Resolution: Negotiation, Mediation, and Other Processes*. Aspen, CO: Aspen Law and Business, 1992.

Goldman, Sheldon. "Bush's Judicial Legacy: The Final Imprint." 76 *Judicature* (1993): 285.

_____. "The Bush Imprint on the Judiciary: Carrying on a Tradition." 74 *Judicature* (1991): 295.

Goldstein, Joseph. "Police Discretion Not to Invoke the Criminal Process: Low-Visibility Decisions in the Administration of Justice." 69 *Yale Law Journal* (1960): 543.

Grafstein, Robert. *Institutional Realism: Social and Political Constraints on Rational Actors.* New Haven, CT: Yale University Press, 1992.

Grillo, Trina. "The Mediation Alternative: Process Dangers for Women." 100 *Yale Law Journal* (1991): 1545.

Hanson, Roger. "An Assessment of Florida Fourth District Court of Appeal Settlement Conference Program." 18 *Florida State University Law Review* (Summer 1990).

Hanson, Roger, and Susan Keilitz. "Arbitration and Case Processing time: Lessons from Fulton County." 4 *Justice System Journal* (1991).

Harrington, Christine B. *Shadow Justice: The Ideology and Institutionalization of Alternatives to Court.* Westport, CT: Greenwood Press, 1995.

Harrington, Christine B., and Sally E. Merry. "Ideological Production: The Making of Community Mediation." 22 *Law and Society Review* (1988): 709.

Heinz, John P., and Edward O. Laumann. *Chicago Lawyers: The Social Structure of the Bar.* New York: Russell Sage Foundation and American Bar Foundation, 1982.

Hensler, Deborah R. *Court-Ordered Arbitration: An Alternative View.* Santa Monica, CA: Rand, 1992.

Hensler, Deborah R., Mary E. Vaiana, James S. Kakalik, and Mark A. Peterson. *Trends in Tort Litigation: The Story Behind the Statistics.* Santa Monica, CA: Rand, 1987.

Herrman, Margaret S. "On Balance: Promoting Integrity Under Conflicted Mandates." 11 *Mediation Quarterly* (Winter 1993): 123-138.

Howard, Jr., J. Woodford. Comment from "Roundtable on Looking Backward at the Study of Judicial Politics." Panel at the 1997 American Political Science Association Meetings, Washington, D.C., Friday, August 29.

Jacob, Herbert. "Decision Making in Trial Courts." in *The American Courts: A Critical Assessment*, ed. by John B. Gates and Charles A. Johnson. Washington, DC: CQ Press, 1991: 213-234.

_____. "The Elusive Shadow of the Law." 26 *Law and Society Review* (1992): 565.

_____. *Silent Revolution: The Transformation of Divorce Law in the United States*. Chicago: University of Chicago Press, 1988.

_____. "Trial Courts as Loosely Coupled Organizations." Paper presented at the 1996 Meetings of the American Political Science Association, San Francisco, California, August 28 - September 1, 1996.

_____. "Urban Trial Courts -- A Different Vision." Paper presented at the 1995 Meetings of the American Political Science Association, Chicago, Illinois, August 31 - September 3, 1995.

Judicial Council of Georgia. "Untitled Website Introduction and Purpose", (http://www.doas.state.ga.us/courts/supreme/aocfrhp.htm).

Keating, Michael and Lela Love. "CUNY Faculty Mediation Workshop." The City University of New York Dispute Resolution Consortium, John Jay College of Criminal Justice, New York, May 8, 1998.

Keilitz, Susan. "Civil Dispute Resolution Processes." in *National Symposium on Court-Connected Dispute Resolution Research*, ed. National Center for State Courts. Williamsburg, VA: National Center for State Courts, 1994: 5-33.

Keilitz, Susan, Henry Daley, and Roger Hanson. *Multi-State Assessment of Divorce Mediation and Traditional Court Processing*. National Center for State Courts, 1992.

Kelly, Joan. "Is Mediation Less Expensive? A Comparison of Mediated and Adversarial Divorce Costs." 8 *Mediation Quarterly* (Fall 1990).

_____. "Mediated and Adversarial Divorce: Respondents' Perceptions of Their Processes and Outcomes." 7 *Mediation Quarterly* (Summer 1989).

Knight, Jack. *Institutions and Social Conflict.* New York: Cambridge University Press, 1992.

Kobbervig, Wayne. *Mediation of Civil Cases in Hennepin County: An Evaluation.* Judicial Center, February, 1991.

Krehbiel, Keith. *Information and Legislative Organization.* Ann Arbor, MI: University of Michigan Press, 1991.

Kressel, Kenneth, et al. *Final Report of the Essex County Custody Mediation Project: Obstacles to Intervention, Effective Mediator Strategies, and Recommendations.* New Brunswick, NJ: Rutger's University, June 1991.

Kritzer, Herbert M. *The Justice Broker: Lawyers and Ordinary Litigation.* Oxford: Oxford University Press, 1990.

_____. *Let's Make a Deal: Understanding the Negotiation Process in Ordinary Litigation.* Madison, Wi: University of Wisconsin Press, 1991.

_____. "Rhetoric and Reality...Uses and Abuses...Contingencies and Certainties: The American Contingent Fee in Operation." Working paper originally presented at the Conference on the Law and Economics of Litigation Reform, John M. Olin Law and Economics Program, Georgetown University Law Center, October 28-29, 1994, (1996 Version).

Kritzer, Herbert M., and J. Mitchell Pickerill. "Contingent Fee Lawyers as Gatekeepers in the American Civil Justice System." Paper Presented at the Annual Meeting of the American Political Science Association, August 28 - September 1, 1996.

Kritzer, Herbert M., and Francis Kahn Zemans. "Local Legal Culture and the Control of Litigation." 27 *Law and Society Review* (1993): 535-555.

Landon, Donald D. *Country Lawyers: The Impact of Context on Professional Practice.* New York: Praeger, 1990.

Levin, Martin A. *Urban Politics and the Criminal Courts.* Chicago: University of Chicago Press, 1977.

Lippincott, Ronald C., and Robert P. Stoker. "Policy Design and Implementation Effectiveness: Structural Change in a County Court System." 20 *Policy Studies Journal* (1992): 376-387.

Maccoby, E. and Robert Mnookin. *Dividing the Child: Social and Legal Dilemmas of Custody.* Cambridge, MA: Harvard University Press, 1992.

Macauley, Stewart, Friedman, Lawrence M., and John Stookey. *Law and Society: Readings on the Social Study of Law.* New York: W.W. Norton, 1995.

MacCoun, Robert J., E. Allan Lind, and Tom R. Tyler. *Alternative Dispute Resolution in Trial and Appellate Courts.* Santa Monica, CA: Rand, 1992.

March, James G., and Johan P. Olsen. "The New Institutionalism: Organizational Factors in Political Life." 78 *American Political Science Review* (1984): 734-749.

_____. *Rediscovering Institutions: The Organizational Basis of Politics.* New York: Free Press, 1989.

Martin, Elaine. "Men and Women on the Bench: Vive la Difference." 73 *Judicature* (1990): 204-208.

_____. "The Representative Role of Women Judges." 77 *Judicature* (1993): 166-173.

Mather, Lynn. "Policy Making in State Trial Courts." In *The American Courts: A Critical Assessment*, ed. John B. Gates and Charles A. Johnson. Washington, DC: CQ Press, 1991.

_____. "Dispute Processing and a Longitudinal Approach to Trial Courts." 24 *Law and Society Review* (1990): 357.

_____. "The Fired Football Coach (Or, How Trial Courts Make Policy)." In *Contemplating Courts*, ed. Lee Epstein. Washington, DC: CQ Press, 1995.

Mazmanian, Daniel A. and Paul A. Sabatier. *Implementation and Public Policy: With a New Postscript*. Lanham, MD: University Press of America, 1989.

McCann, Michael W. *Rights at Work: Pay Equity Reform and the Politics of Legal Mobilization*. Chicago: University of Chicago Press, 1994.

McEwen, Craig. *An Evaluation of the ADR Pilot Project: Final Report*. Bowdoin College, January 1992.

_____. "Note on Mediation Research", in *Dispute Resolution: Negotiation, Mediation, and Other Processes* by Stephen B. Goldberg, Frank Sander, and Nancy Rogers. Aspen, CO: Aspen Law and Business, 1992: 155-157.

McEwen, Craig, and Richard Maiman. "Mediation in Small Claims Courts: Achieving Compliance Through Consent." 18 *Law and Society Review* (1984).

McEwen, Craig, Lynn Mather, and Richard Maiman. "Lawyers, Mediation, and the Management of Divorce Practice." 27 *Law and Society Review* (1993).

McIsaac, Hugh. "Mandatory Conciliation Custody/Visitation Matters: California's Bold Stroke." 19 *Conciliation Courts Review* (1981).

Menkel-Meadow, Carrie. "Pursuing Settlement in an Adversary Culture: A Tale of Innovation Co-opted or 'The Law of ADR'." 19 *Florida State University Law Review* (1991): 1-45.

Merry, Sally E., and Neal Milner (eds.). *The Possibility of Popular Justice: A Case Study of Community Mediation in the United States.* Ann Arbor: University of Michigan Press, 1993.

Miller, Richard E., and Austin Sarat. "Grievances, Claims, and Disputes: Assessing the Adversary Culture." 15 *Law and Society Review* (1980-81): 525-566.

Mnookin, Robert, and Lewis Kornhauser. "Bargaining in the Shadow of the Law: The Case of Divorce." 88 *Yale Law Journal* (1979): 950.

Moe, Terry. "The New Economics of Organization." 28 *American Journal of Economics* (1984): 739-77.

Mohr, Lawrence B. *Impact Analysis for Program Evaluation.* Pacific Grove, CA: Brooks/Cole Publishing, 1988.

Munger, Frank. "Trial Courts and Social Change: The Evolution of a Field of Study." 24 *Law and Society Review* (1990): 217-226.

Myers, Martha A. and Susette M. Talarico. *The Social Contexts of Criminal Sentencing.* New York: Springer-Verlag, 1987.

Nardulli, Peter F. "Organizational Analyses of Criminal Courts: An Overview and Some Speculation." In *The Study of Criminal Courts: Political Perspectives,* ed. Peter F. Nardulli. Cambridge: Ballinger Publishing, 1979: 101-130.

_____. *The Study of Criminal Courts: Political Perspectives.* Cambridge: Ballinger Publishing, 1979.

Nardulli, Peter F., James Eisenstein, and Roy B. Flemming. *The Tenor of Justice: Criminal Courts and the Guilty Plea Process.* Urbana-Champagne, IL: University of Illinois Press, 1988.

National Center for State Courts. *State Court Caseload Statistics, Annual Report, 1984.* Williamsburg, VA: National Center for State Courts, 1986.

_____. *State Court Caseload Statistics: Annual Report 1990.* Williamsburg, VA: National Center for State Courts, 1992.

National Center for State Courts, and State Justice Institute. *National Symposium on Court-Connected Dispute Resolution Research: A Report on Current Research Findings - Implications for Courts and Future Research Needs.* Williamsburg, VA: National Center for State Courts, 1994.

Neubauer, David W. *Criminal Justice in Middle America.* Morristown, NJ: General Learning Press, 1974.

_____. *Judicial Process: Law, Courts, and Politics in the United States.* Pacific Grove, CA: Brooks/Cole Publishing Company, 1991: Chapters 10-11.

_____. *Judicial Process: Law, Courts, and Politics in the United States.* Draft of 2nd. Edition of text, 1996.

Neubauer, David W., and Stephen Meinhold. "Too Quick to Sue? Public Perceptions of the Litigation Explosion." 16 *Justice System Journal* (1994): 1-14.

Olson, Walter. *The Litigation Explosion: What Happened When America Unleashed the Lawsuit.* New York: Truman Talley Books/ E.P. Dutton, 1991.

Ostrom, Elinor. "New Horizons in Institutional Analysis." 89 *American Political Science Review* (March 1995): 174-178.

Pearson, Jessica. "Child Custody: Why Not Let the Parents Decide?" 20 *The Judges Journal* (Winter 1981).

_____. "The Equity of Mediation Divorce Agreements." 9 *Mediation Quarterly* (Winter 1991).

_____. "Family Mediation." in *National Symposium on Court-Connected Dispute Resolution Research* by National Center for State Courts and State Justice Institute. Williamsburg, Va.: 1994.

Pearson, Jessica and Nancy Thoennes. "Mediating and Litigating Custody disputes: A Longitudnal Evaluation." *Family Law Quarterly* (Winter 1984).

_____. *The Child Custody and Child Support Project*. Final Report to the Federal Office of Child Support Enforcement, AFCC/Research Unit, Denver, CO, November, 1985.

_____. *Reflections on a Decade of Divorce Mediation Research: The Process and Effectiveness of Third Party Intervention*. Jossey-Bass Publications, 1989.

Pressman, Jeffrey L. and Aaron Wildavsky. *Implementation*. Third edition. Berkeley, CA: University of California Press, 1984.

Priest, George L. "The Current Insurance Crisis and Modern Tort Law." 96 *Yale Law Journal* (1987): 1521-1590.

Ray, Larry. *Dispute Resolution Program Directory*. Washington, D.C.: American Bar Association, 1981.

Ray, Marilyn. "Divorce Settlements: Comparing Outcomes of Three Different Processes for the Resolution of Disputes." A Paper Presented at the Law and Society Annual Meetings, Vail, Colorado, June 9-12, 1988.

Reiss, Jr., Albert J. "Longitudinal Study of Trial Courts: A Plea for Developments of Explanatory Models." 24 *Law and Society Review* (1990): 345.

Richardson, C. *Court-Based Divorce Mediation in Four Canadian Cities: An Overview of Research Results*. A Report Prepared for the Department of Justice, Canada, 1988.

Rodgers, Harrell R., Jr.,and Charles S. Bullock,III. *Law and Social Change: Civil Rights Laws and their Consequences*. New York: McGraw-Hill, 1972.

Ross, H. Lawrence. *Settled Out of Court: The Social Process of Insurance Claims Adjustment*. 2nd Edition. New York: Aldine Publishing, 1980.

Rottman, David B. "Tort Litigation in the State courts: Evidence from the Trial Court Information Network." 1990 *State Court Journal* (1990): 4-18.

Saks, Michael J. "Do We Really Know Anything About the Behavior of the Tort Litigation System - And Why Not?" 140 *University of Pennsylvania Law Review* (April 1992): 1147-1292.

Sander, Frank and S.B. Goldberg. AFitting the Forum to the Fuss: A User Friendly Guide to Selecting an ADR Procedure. 10 *Negotiation Journal* (1994): 49-68.

Sanders, Joseph, and Craig Joyce. "Off to the Races: The 1980s Tort Crisis and the Law Reform Process." 22 *Houston Law Review* (1990): 207.

Sarat, Austin, and William L. F. Felstiner. "Law and Strategy in the Divorce Lawyer's Office." 20 *Law and Society Review* (1986).

Sarat, Austin, and Joel B. Grossman. "Courts and Conflict Resolution: Problems in the Mobilization of Adjudication." *American Political Science Association* 69 (Dec. 1975): 1200-1217.

Schultz, Karl. *Florida's Alternative Dispute Resolution Demonstration Project: An Empirical Assessment*. Florida Dispute Resolution Center, 1990.

Schwartz, Edward P. "Policy, Precedent, and Power: A Positive Theory of Supreme Court Decision-Making." 8 *Journal of Law, Economics, and Organization* (1992): 219-252.

Schwerin, Edward W. *Mediation, Citizen Empowerment, and Transformational Politics*. Westport, Ct: Praeger, 1995.

Segal, Jeffrey A., and Harold J. Spaeth. *The Supreme Court and the Attitudinal Model*. Cambridge: Cambridge University Press, 1993.

Seron, Carroll. "The Impact of Court Organization on Litigation." 24 *Law and Society Review* (1990): 451.

Shapiro, Martin. "Public Law and Judicial Politics." In *Political Science: The State of the Discipline II*, ed. Ada Finifter. Washington, D.C.: The American Political Science Association, 1993.

Shepsle, Kenneth A. "Studying Institutions: Some Lessons from the Rational Choice Approach." 1 *Journal of Theoretical Politics* (1989): 131-147.

Shepsle, Kenneth A., and Barry R. Weingast. *Positive Theories of Congressional Institutions*. Ann Arbor, MI: University of Michigan Press, 1995.

Skocpol, Theda. "Why I am a Historical Institutionalist?" 28 *Polity* (Fall 1995): 103-106.

Skolnick, Jerome. "Social Control in the Adversary System." 11 *Journal of Conflict Resolution* (1967): 52-70.

Smith, Christopher E. *Courts and the Poor*. Chicago: Nelson-Hall Publishers, 1991.

Smith, Rogers M. "Political Jurisprudence, the 'New Institutionalism,' and the Future of Public Law." 82 *American Political Science Review* (1988): 89-108.

_____. "The New Institutionalism and Normative Theory: A Reply to Professor Barber." In *Studies in American Political Development*, vol. 3, ed. Karen Orren and Stephen Skowronek. New Haven: Yale University Press, 1989.

Smith, Steven K., Carol DeFrances, Patrick A. Langan, and John Goerdt. *Bureau of Justice Statistics, Civil Justice Survey of State Courts, 1992: Tort Cases in Large Counties* (1995).

Songer, Donald R., Charles M. Cameron, and Jeffrey A. Segal. "An Empirical Test of the Rational-Actor Theory of Litigation." 57 *Journal of Politics* (November 1995): 1119-1129.

Songer, Donald R., Jeffrey A. Segal, and Charles M. Cameron. "The Hierarch of Justice: Testing a Principal-Agent Model of Supreme Court-Circuit Court Interactions." 38 *American Journal of Political Science* (1994): 673-96.

Sproule-Jones, Mark. *Governments at Work: Canadian Parliamentary Federalism and Its Public Policy Effects*. Toronto: University of Toronto Press, 1993.

Stoker, Robert. *Reluctant Partners: Implementing Federal Policy*. Pittsburgh: University of Pittsburgh Press, 1991.

Stookey, John A. "Trials and Tribulations: Crises, Litigation, and Legal Change." 24 *Law and Society Review* (1990): 497 - 520.

Stumpf, Harry P. *American Judicial Politics*. San Diego, CA: Harcourt Brace Jovanovich Publishers, 1988: Chapter 8.

Thoennes, Nancy, and Jessica Pearson. "Predicting Outcomes in Divorce Mediation: The Influence of People and Process." 41 *Journal of Social Issues* (1985).

Thoennes, Nancy, Jessica Pearson, and Julie Bell. *An Evaluation of the Use of Mandatory Mediation*. Final Report to the State Justice Institute, Center for Policy Research, Denver, CO, October, 1991.

Tomasic, Roman, and Malcolm Feeley. *Neighborhood Justice -- Assessment of an Emerging Idea*. New York: Longman, 1992.

Trost, Melanie R. and Sanford L. Braver. *Mandatory Divorce Mediation: Part I: The Impact of Mandatory Mediation on the Court System*. Tuscon, AZ: Arizona State University, February 1987.

Trubek, David, William Felstiner, Joel Grossman, Herbert Kritzer, and Austin Sarat. *Civil Litigation Research Project Final Report*, Three Volumes. Madison, WI: University of Wisconsin Law School, 1983.

Umbreit, Mark, and Robert Coates. "Cross-Site Analysis of Victim-Offender Mediation in Four States." 39 *Crime and Delinquency* (1993).

Weaver, R. Kent and Bert A. Rockman. *Do Institutions Matter? Government Capabilities in the United States and Abroad.* Washington, DC: Brookings, 1993.

Welsh, Wayne N. "The Dynamics of Jail Reform Litigation: A Comparative Analysis of Litigation in California Counties." 26 *Law and Society Review* (1992): 591-625.

Yngvesson, Barbara. "Contextualizing the Court: Comments on the Cultural Study of Litigation." 24 *Law and Society Review* (1990).

APPENDIX A
CIVIL AND MEDIATED CASE CODESHEET

VARIABLE NAME/DESCRIPTION	CODES
CASE_#	9-10 Digit Clerk# (e.g. 92CV1335C)
YEAR--Year case filed	4 Digit Year
YEARREF--Yr. Case Ref. to Med.	4 Digit Year
COUNTY--County of Case	1 = Hall 2 = Other
TYPECRT--Type of Court	1 = Superior 2 = State 3 = Criminal 4 = Magistrate 5 = Juvenile 6 = Other
JUDGE--Judge Case Ref. to	1 = Gosselin (D) 2 = Girardeau (C) 3 = Smith (A) 4 = Story (B) 5 = Kenyon (Ret.) 6 = Fuller 7 = Crawford 8 − Joliff 9 = Others

PLAINTI--# of Plaintiffs   Total Number

LITTYPP1--Type of Plaint. 1   1 = Individual
                                        2 = Insurance
                                        3 = Bank/Financial
                                        4 = Hospital/Med.
                                        5 = Other Business
                                        6 = Govt. Agency

LITTYPP2--Type of Plaint. 2   Codes 1-6 Above

LITTYPP3--Type of Plaint. 3   Codes 1-6 Above

LITTYPP4--Type of Plaint. 4   Codes 1-6 Above

DEFEND--# of Defendants   Total Number

LITTYPD1--Type of Defend. 1   Codes 1-6 Above

LITTYPD2--Type of Defend. 2   Codes 1-6 Above

LITTYPD3--Type of Defend. 3   Codes 1-6 Above

LITTYPD4--Type of Defend. 4   Codes 1-6 Above

TYPECASE--Type of Civil Case   1 = Tort
                                        2 = Contract/Comm.
                                        3 = Real Property
                                        4 = Domestic
                                        5 = Govt. Benefits
                                        6 = Bus. Regulation
                                        7 = Criminal
                                        8 = Other
                                        9 = Combo. 1-8

MAGAPP--Appeal from Mag. Court?   0 = No
                                        1 = Yes

Appendix A

TYPETORT--Type of Tort
1 = Auto
2 = Med. Mal.
3 = Premise Liab.
4 = Products Liab.
5 = Other Prof. Mal.
6 = Combo. 1-5
7 = Other/Unknown

TYPECONT--Type Contract/Commercial
1 = Debt: Suit on Acct/note/contract
2 = Garnishment Wage
3 = Contempt of Debt
4 = Cont/Comm. Fraud
5 = Poor Work/Breach
6 = Unspec. Breach

(Note: 1-3 collapsed as "Debt Collection in some tables)

TYPEPROP--Type Real Property
1 = Condemnation of Land (by Govt.)
2 = Condemnation of Land (by Utility)
3 = Repo of Property
4 = Eviction
5 = Asset Forfeit (Drug Case)
6 = Zoning
7 = Other

TYPEDOM--Type of Domestic
1 = Divorce
2 = Mod. of Divorce/ Child Sup./Visit
3 = Change/Mod. Cust
4 = Contempt Child Sup. (deadbeat dad)
5 = Family Violence
6 = Combo. Above
7 = Other

TYPEGOVB--Type of Govt. Benefits	1 = Welfare Fraud 2 = Workers Comp. 3 = Other
TYPEBRG--Type of Business Reg.	1 = Any Business? 2 = Add any addition
RELATION--Attorney Opposition	1 = Local v. Local 2 = Loc. v. Outsider 3 = Outsider v. Out. 4 = Local v. *Pro se* 5 = Out. v. *Pro se* 6 = *Pro se* v. *Pro se*
PLATATT--Total Plaint. Attorneys Total Number	
BAR#PL--Plaint. Att. Bar # (1st list)	6-7 Digit Number 999999 = missing 000000 = *pro se*
PLATTGEO--Pl. att. from Jud. Circuit	1 = Off. in Circ. 2 = Off. Outside 3 = Unknown
TYPPATT1--Type of Plain. Att. 1	1 = *pro se* 2 = Private 3 = Legal Aid 4 = Govt. 5 = In House Att. 6 = Other
TYPPATT2--Type of Plain. Att. 2	Codes 1-6 Above
TYPPATT3--Type of Plain. Att. 3	Codes 1-6 Above
TYPPATT4--Type of Plain. Att. 4	Codes 1-6 Above
DEFATT--# of Defense Att.	Total Number

BAR#DEF--Def. Att. Bar #	6-7	Digit Number 999999 missing 000000 *pro se*
DEFATTGE--Def. Att. from Jud. Circ.		1 = Off. In Circ. 2 = Off. Outside 3 = Unknown
TYPDATT1--Type Def. Att. 1		See Codes 1-6 for Plaint. Att. Above
TYPDATT2--Type Def. Att. 2		Codes 1-6 Above
TYPDATT3--Type Def. Att. 3		Codes 1-6 Above
TYPDATT4--Type Def. Att. 4		Codes 1-6 Above

REMEDIES SOUGHT BY PLAINTIFF/DAMAGES ASSESSED

COMPDAM--Type Compensatory Dam.	1 = Monetary 2 = Property 3 = Combo. 1-2 4 = Other 5 = N/A
MONCOMP--Amt. monetary compensation?	enter best value
SEEKPUN--Puntive Damages sought?	0 = No 1 = Yes
AMTPUNIT--Amt. of punitive damage?	enter best value
INJ_DECL--Injunction/declaratory rel.?	0 = No 1 = Yes
REMDOM--Remedy in domestice dispute?	1 = Div. only 2 = Div+ prop/assets/debts 3 = #2 including child

Support
4 = Custody only
(incl. mod. of vis.)
5 = Child Supp. Only
6 = Restraining ord. Family Violence
7 = Combo.
8 = Other

COMDEM--If Condemn/Repo., what rem.? 1 = Condemn of land
2 = condemn of House
3 = condemn of Money
4 = Condemn of Guns
5 = Condemn of Car
6 = Other Prop.
7 = Combo.

DATEFILE--Date filed if diff from comp.   Six digit date

CROSSCLAIM--Was cross or counter filed? 0 = No
1 = Yes

DATECROS--Date of crossclaim?   Six digit date

ANSWER--Was Answer filed?
0 = No
1 = Yes
2 = No/Lack serv
3 = Default
4 = cons. agree.
5 = other

DATEANS--Date of first answer?   Six Digit Date

DATETRIA--Date trial started?   Six Digit Date

DATEVERD--Date of Verdict?   Six Digit Date

DATECMPL--Date of Complaint?   Six Digit Date

Appendix A

DATEDISP--Date of Disposition	Six Digit Date
TIMEDISP--Days from Comp. to disp. (datedisp-datecmpl)	Total # of Days
DATEAPP--Date Notice of Appeal	Six Digit Date
DATAPPDI--Date Appeal disposition	Six Digit Date
APPOUTCO--If Appeal, Outcome?	1 = Appeal Denied 2 = Appl Hrd/Affirm 3 = Reversed 4 = Rev. and aff. in part
DISPDF1--Disp. Type Def. #1	See Codes Item #14
DISPDF2--Disp. Type Def. #2	See Codes Item #14
DISPDF3--Disp. Type Def. #3	See Codes Item #14
DISPDF4--Disp. Type Def. #4	See Codes Item #14

ITEM #14 DISPOSITION CODES FOR 4 ABOVE:

1=Jury Trial   6=Dismiss w/o prej. b/f trial   11=Consent Agree/decree
2=Bench Trial   7=Dismiss w/p prej. a/f trial   12=Dis. lack Prosecution
3=Jud. n/with verd   8=Summary Judgement   13=Transfer/Removal
4=Dismiss w/Prej.   9=Default Judgement   14=Dismiss/Other
15=Pending   16=Pending Also   17=Divorce Decree/Pretrial Order

***Anything coded 2/11 (div. decree consent) was collapsed into #11.
#17 equals divorce decree...judge ordered...pretrial.

SUMMJUDG--If Summary Judg., who won?
1 = Plaintiff
2 = Defendant
3 = Mixed

VERDICT--If trial verd., who won?
1 = Plain./Leans Pl.
2 = Def./Leans Def.
3 = Mixed

SETTREL--Type of Settlement relief?
1 = Monetary only
2 = Child Supp.
3 = Divide Property
4 = Child Custody
5 = Combo.
6 = Other

MONETSUM--If Monetary, Sum?   Enter Best Value

CUSTODY--Who Gets Children?
1 = Father
2 = Mother
3 = Other Fam. Memb.
4 = Joint Custody

SETTWIN--Who "won" settlement?
1 = Plaintiff
2 = Defendant
3 = Unclear

TRIALREL--Type of Trial Relief?
1 = Monetary Only
2 = Child Support
3 = Property
4 = Child Custody
5 = Combo.
6 = Other

TRIALMON--How much money at trial?   Enter Best Value
TRLCUST--If trial custody, who won?
1 = Father
2 = Mother
3 = Other Fam. Memb.

PTRLCON#--# of Pretrial Conferences?   Enter #

PRTRLHR#--# of Pretrial Hearings?   Enter #

Appendix A

PSTRLHR#--# of Posttrial Hearings?	Enter #
PTRLM0T#--# of Pretrial Actions?	Enter #
PSTRLMT#--# of Postrial Actions?	Enter #
CONT#--# of Continuances?	Enter #
MOTDIS#--# of Motions to Dismiss?	Enter #
DISCOV#--# of Motions for Discovery?	Enter #
OTHMOT#--# of Other Motions/Actions?	Enter #
MEDIATED--Was Case Referred to Mediat?	0 = No 1 = Yes

***IF Answer above is "NO", skip all following variables!

DATEREFM--Date of Referral to mediat?	Date
DATEREC--Date Referral Received?	Date
DATEMED--Date of Mediation?	Date
TIMEMED--Total Time Spent in Mediat.?	enter hours/quarters
MEDAGRE1--Was agreement reached in Med?	0 = No 1 = Partial 2 = Yes 3 = No Mediation (Settled prior/No Show)
DISPOSMD--If no, How case disposed?	0 = NA 1 = Scttlcd 2 = Pretrial Judge./Consent

	Decree 3 = Trial/Bench Trl. 4 = Settled Aft. Trl
MEDWINN--Who won med., if clear?	1 = Plaintiff 2 = Defendant 3 = Unclear
MEDATTPT--More than one attempt?	0 = No 1 = 1 addt. 2 = 2 addt. 3 = 3 addt. 4 = 4 addt. etc.
ATTMED--Were attorneys pres. in Med?	0 = No 1 = Plaintiff 2 = Defendant 3 = Both
FOLLOWME--Agreement in Followup Med.?	0 = NA 1 = No 2 = Yes

MEDIATI--If monetary agree., how much? Total Amount

CASEREF--If Med., where in lifespan was case referred?

1 = After filing
2 = Before Disc.
3 = During Disc.
4 = After Disc.
5 = Prior to Trial
6 = During Trial
7 = After Trial

Appendix A

CASEDISP--If Med., where in lifespan was case disposed of?
    1 = Aft ref./bf med.
    2 = During Mediation
    3 = Aft med./bf trl.
    4 = During Trial
    5 = After Trial

ATTORMED--Was Mediator a lawyer?
    0 = No
    1 = Yes
    2 = Non-Lawyer w/JD

DTRFDISP--Date Referral to Final Disp.   Time in Days

DTRFMED--Date Referral to Mediation   Time in Days

APPENDIX B1
Attorney Interview Schedule

Background

Where do you live? How long?

Why or how did you become an attorney?

Employment History? (Firm size, clerk..who, etc)

Education? (where how much?)

Political Leanings?

Profile of Work

What do you do in your job? (what types of cases, etc.)

Who do you routinely work with? (judges, other lawyers, opposing)

How would you describe your relationship with opposing attorneys? In town/out of town?

Are there advantages/disadvantages to these relationships?

What part of your job takes up most of your time?

Describe your legal practice?

Impressions of Civil Justice

How would you describe the Civil Justice system in Mountain County?
-Is it similar/different than other places you've worked?

What are the most instrumental pieces of the justice system?
-Who are the most important actors? What rules dominate? What norms (informal)? Does the local bar play a role? How? Do you act strategically in managing cases? What tools help in strategy? (forum shopping, delay, settlements)

What kinds of cases dominate the system? Any changes over time?
How does civil justice compare with the criminal variety? Does the environment differ? Norms? Rules? Actors?
Some argue that criminal justice has an "organizational structure" because of pub def/district attorn/etc. Does civil justice system have an organizational structure (similar/different)
How does plea bargaining differ from civil case settlement?
How well does civil system work?
How well is it understood?
Who has the most effect on the civil justice system?

Can you think of any reforms that you would favor or find interesting?

Impressions of Mediation

Have you had much involvement in mediation?

What are your experiences? What do you think of it?

How do you think it works? What are its goals? Strengths/Weaknesses

Is it living up to expectations? Whose? How?

Do you find it a useful tool in your practice? Why or Why not?
(Does it pose financial gains? Do cases settle quicker? Easier? Is another hurdle?

How has mediation changed the civil system as a whole? (case

Appendix B1

processing, attorney/client relations, attorney/attorney relations, attorney/judge relations)

Has the new program changed your work environment? How? Why?

Has mediation, in your experience, formalized the process of civil justice (or imposed more structure)? Who gains most from this new procedure (power-wise)?

-Has mediation sped up case processing time? Do Cases settle earlier or easier during mediation? What about after mediation? Are trial rates decreased by mediation? Do clients feel better in mediation than in settlement? Is there any difference?

-Are there fewer contempts of mediated agreements than in normal settlements?

Summary

What else do I need to know to understand civil justice? The affect of mediation on the civil system?
Who else should I speak with?

APPENDIX B2
Attorney/Mediator Interview Schedule

<u>Background</u>

Where do you live? How long?

Why or how did you become an attorney?

Why did you become a mediator?

What training did you go through to become a mediator?

Employment History? (Firm size, clerk..who, etc)

Education? (where how much?)

Political Leanings?

<u>Profile of Work</u>

What do you do in your job? (what types of cases, etc.)
-Describe attorney work? Mediator work? How do they differ/relate?
-What are advantages/disadvantages of your mediator role in your work?

Who do you routinely work with? (judges, other lawyers, opposing)
-How would you describe your relationship with opposing attorneys? In town/out of town?
-Are there advantages/disadvantages to these relationships?

What part of your job takes up most of your time?

Impressions of Civil Justice

How would you describe the Civil Justice system in Mountain County?
-Is it similar/different than other places you've worked?
What are the most instrumental pieces of the justice system?
-Who are the most important actors? What rules dominate? What norms (informal)? Does the local bar play a role? How? Do you act strategically in managing cases? What tools help in strategy? (forum shopping, delay, settlements) Is the court system efficient?

Since most cases settle, how/why are judges important?

What kinds of cases dominate the system? Any changes over time?

How does civil justice compare with the criminal variety? Does the environment differ? Norms? Rules? Actors?
Some argue that criminal justice has an "organizational structure" because of pub def/district attorn/etc. Does civil justice system have an organizational structure (similar/different)
How does plea bargaining differ from civil case settlement?

How well does civil system work?
How well is it understood?
Who has the most effect on the civil justice system?

Can you think of any reforms that you would favor or find interesting?

Impressions of Mediation

How many cases have you mediated? How many have you represented in mediation?

What are your experiences? What do you think of it?

How do you think it works? What are its goals? Strengths/Weaknesses

Is it living up to expectations? Whose? How?

Do you find it a useful tool in your practice? Why or Why not?

(Does it pose financial gains? Does it make civil justice more or less efficient?)

How has mediation changed the civil system as a whole? (case processing, attorney/client relations, attorney/attorney relations, attorney/judge relations). Has mediation formalized the process of civil justice (imposed more structure)? Who gains most from mediation?

Has the new program changed your work environment? How? Why?

Specific Follow-ups

-Has mediation sped up case processing time? Do Cases settle earlier or easier during mediation? What about after mediation? Are trial rates decreased by mediation? Do clients feel better in mediation than in settlement? Is there any difference?

-Are there fewer contempts of mediated agreements than in normal settlements?
-What types of cases are best to mediate? What affects whether an agreement is reached or not? (attorneys present/absent, referred early or late/mediator skill/etc.)

Summary

What else do I need to know to understand civil justice? The affect of mediation on the civil system?

Who else should I speak with?

APPENDIX B3
Judge/Administrator Interview Schedule

Background

Where do you live? How long?
Why and how did you end up in this field?

What training did you go through to become a/n clerk/court administrator/mediation coordinator?

Employment History? (Firm size, clerk..who, etc)

Education? (where how much?)

Political Leanings?

Profile of Work

What do you do in your job? (what types of cases, etc.)

Who do you routinely work with?

What part of your job takes up most of your time?

Describe your role in case processing?

Impressions of Civil Justice

How would you describe the Civil Justice system in Mountain County?
-Is it similar/different than other places you've worked?

What are the most instrumental pieces of the justice system?
-Who are the most important actors? What rules dominate? What norms (informal)? Does the local bar play a role? How? Do you act strategically in managing cases? What tools help in strategy? Is the court system efficient?

What factors lead a case to settle or go on to trial?

Since most cases settle, how/why are judges important?

What kinds of cases dominate the system? Any changes over time?

How does civil justice compare with the criminal variety? Does the environment differ? Norms? Rules? Actors?
Some argue that criminal justice has an "organizational structure" because of pub def/district attorn/etc. Does civil justice system have an organizational structure (similar/different)
How does plea bargaining differ from civil case settlement?

How well does civil system work?
How well is it understood?

Can you think of any reforms that you would favor or find interesting?

Impressions of Mediation

What are your experiences with mediation? What do you think of it?

How do you think it works? What are its goals? Strengths/Weaknesses

Is it living up to expectations? Whose? How?

Who gains most from mediation? Do attorneys find it advantageous/disadvantage? How/why?

How has mediation changed the civil system as a whole? (case processing, attorney/client relations, attorney/attorney relations, attorney/judge relations).

Has mediation formalized the process of civil justice (imposed more structure)?

Has the new program changed your work environment? How? Why?

What factors do you use to judge whether a case should be referred or not? Are they old cases/new? Complex/simple?

Specific Followups

Does mediation free up court resources in Mountain County? Significant?

-Has mediation sped up case processing time? Do Cases settle earlier or easier during mediation? What about after mediation? Are trial rates decreased by mediation? Do clients feel better in mediation than in settlement? Is there any difference?

-Are there fewer contempts of mediated agreements than in normal settlements?

-What types of cases are best to mediate? What affects whether an agreement is reached or not? (attorneys present/absent, referred early or late/mediator skill/etc.)

Summary

What else do I need to know to understand civil justice? The affect of mediation on the civil system?

Who else should I speak with?

APPENDIX B4
Mediator Interview Schedule

Background

Where do you live? How long?

Employment History? (Firm size, clerk..who, etc)

Education? (where how much?)

Political Leanings?

Why did you become a mediator?

What training did you go through to become one?

Profile of Work

Describe your work as a mediator? Describe how you fit into the civil justice system?

Who do you routinely work with? (judges, other lawyers, opposing)
-How would you describe your relationship with attorneys? In town/out of town?
-Are there advantages/disadvantages to these relationships?

What part of your job takes up most of your time?

Impressions of Civil Justice

How would you describe the Civil Justice system in Mountain County?
-Is it similar/different than other places you've worked?

What are the most instrumental pieces of the justice system?
-Who are the most important actors? What rules dominate? What norms (informal)? Is the court system efficient?

What types of cases do judges most refer to you? Are they complex? Simple? Old/new?

What kinds of cases dominate the system as a whole? Any changes over time in the civil system? What cases do you least mediate?

How does civil justice compare with the criminal variety? Does the environment differ? Norms? Rules? Actors?

Some argue that criminal justice has an "organizational structure" because of pub def/district attorn/etc. Does civil justice system have an organizational structure (similar/different)

Can you think of any reforms that you would favor or find interesting to improve civil justice?

Impressions of Mediation

How many cases have you mediated?

What are your experiences? What do you think of it?

How do you think it works? What are its goals? Strengths/Weaknesses

Is it living up to expectations? Whose? How?

How has mediation changed the civil system as a whole? (case processing, attorney/client relations, attorney/attorney relations, attorney/judge relations). Has mediation formalized the process of civil justice (imposed more structure)? Who gains most from mediation?

Appendix B4

Has the program changed since you began work? How has your work changed in Mountain County?

How does mediation compare in other counties?

What changes or reforms might improve mediation in Mountain County?

<u>Specific Followups</u>

-Has mediation sped up case processing time? Do Cases settle earlier or easier during mediation? What about after mediation? Are trial rates decreased by mediation? Do clients feel better in mediation than in settlement? Is there any difference?

-Are there fewer contempts of mediated agreements than in normal settlements?

-What types of cases are best to mediate? What affects whether an agreement is reached or not? (attorneys present/absent, referred early or late/mediator skill/etc.)

<u>Summary</u>

What else do I need to know to understand civil justice? The affect of mediation on the civil system?

Who else should I speak with?

Index

ADR 1, 2, 4, 12, 13, 15, 19, 20, 21, 22, 24, 26, 29, 35, 36, 37, 38, 39, 40, 41, 42, 43, 44, 95, 96, 97, 99, 125, 126, 138, 139, 140, 141, 142, 143, 161, 162, 163, 173, 181, 186, 192, 193, 195, 201, 202, 204, 232
Alternative Dispute Resolution 19, 26, 177
arbitration.... 13, 19, 21, 22, 26, 99, 162
attorney/mediator 165, 182, 185, 186, 191, 192
attorneys.....3, 5, 6, 8, 9, 10, 11, 14, 15, 16, 17, 18, 19, 22, 24, 25, 26, 30, 43, 44, 47, 48, 52, 53, 54, 55, 56, 57, 60, 61, 62, 63, 64, 77, 90, 91, 92, 93, 94, 100, 101, 111, 113, 127, 134, 137, 145, 160, 161, 162, 163, 164, 165, 167, 168, 170, 171, 172, 173, 174, 175, 176, 177, 178, 179, 180, 181, 182, 183, 185, 186, 187, 188, 189, 190, 192, 193, 194, 195, 196, 200, 201, 202, 203, 204, 205, 207, 208
Auerbach, Jerold 19, 20, 202
Axelrod, Robert 30
Blumberg, Abraham 4, 5, 6, 16, 30
caps on damages 13
case management .. 3, 6, 20, 29, 167, 181, 192, 202
case processing . 12, 14, 15, 21, 23, 24, 43, 57, 60, 62, 63, 64, 99, 123, 125, 126, 129, 130, 137, 140, 143, 162, 171, 172, 181, 194, 196, 202, 203, 208
case processing time 62
caseloads... 5, 9, 13, 14, 15, 17, 20, 40, 44, 47, 48, 49, 52, 57, 58, 59, 87, 88, 89, 90, 95, 125, 129, 130, 131, 133, 135, 136, 139, 141, 142, 143, 167, 168, 181, 200, 203, 206
Cases
  commercial .. 48, 49, 50, 51, 88, 89, 99
  contracts. 40, 49, 61, 63, 98, 165, 169
  divorce ... 11, 51, 53, 54, 56, 61, 63, 81, 88, 89, 90, 97, 98, 117, 124, 128, 131, 132, 134, 138, 140, 145, 163, 170, 182, 188, 193
  government benefits. 49, 61, 63
  real property. 49, 50, 51, 61, 88, 89, 98, 99, 169
  torts .. 13, 17, 40, 48, 49, 50, 51, 52, 61, 63, 88, 89, 98, 99, 130, 131, 132, 165, 169, 170, 179, 183
civil justice 4, 9, 10, 13, 15, 16, 17, 18, 19, 20, 23, 24, 25, 26, 27, 29, 30, 36, 38, 39,

269

43, 44, 47, 52, 53, 54, 55, 56, 57, 60, 63, 64, 123, 129, 141, 142, 159, 164, 166, 167, 169, 171, 172, 173, 176, 178, 180, 193, 194, 195, 196, 197, 199, 200, 208
civil justice systems . 15, 19, 25
civil litigation 11, 12, 13, 26, 47, 48, 49, 51, 52, 57, 62, 64, 90, 96, 98, 101, 123, 126, 139, 170, 180, 201
civil procedure .. 10, 11, 22, 47, 90, 91, 129, 167, 172, 201
Community Justice 20
court actors 1, 9, 15, 19, 25, 26, 37, 40, 43, 44, 47, 62, 100, 159, 163, 164, 168, 169, 171, 172, 173, 175, 178, 189, 190, 192, 194, 196, 197, 199, 200, 201, 203, 204, 205, 206
court administrators 3, 196
court reform 19, 36
court workloads 23, 96, 124, 134, 141, 202, 203
Court-Annexed ADR 12
criminal courts .. 2, 3, 4, 5, 6, 7, 16, 24, 25, 29, 30, 52, 92, 101, 196
Daniels, Stephen 13
debt collection... 49, 50, 51, 52, 54, 56, 61, 62, 63, 88, 89, 91, 97, 99, 131, 183, 200
default judgement 75
defense attorneys 55, 56, 91, 94
domestic cases 4, 10, 16, 20, 40, 42, 48, 49, 50, 51, 52, 53, 57, 61, 62, 63, 88, 89, 94, 95, 98, 99, 100, 117,

124, 125, 126, 130, 131, 132, 134, 135, 138, 139, 140, 142, 149, 160, 161, 165, 168, 169, 170, 171, 175, 178, 179, 183, 184, 185, 186, 193, 195, 199, 200, 201, 202, 205, 206
Dunn, Richard... 1, 2, 5, 13, 14, 16
Eaton, Thomas 9, 13, 14, 26, 47, 49, 51, 60, 97
Eisenstein, James 4, 5, 6, 7, 16, 30, 92
Ellen, Elizabeth 22, 23, 24, 202
filings 13, 15, 40, 47, 48, 49, 50, 51, 59, 60, 63, 87, 88, 123, 130, 131, 199
Flemming, Roy 4, 5, 6, 7, 8, 16, 26, 29, 92
Galanter, Marc . 13, 48, 54, 162
Gibson, James 4, 16, 30
Gillman, Howard 32, 33, 34, 37, 205, 206
Grafstein, Robert 34, 35, 37, 38, 172
Harrington, Christine 20, 21, 38, 96, 124, 130, 202
Hermann, Margaret. 20, 22, 24, 96
Historical/Interpretivist Institutionalism 33, 34, 204, 206
implementation 2, 3, 26, 37, 38, 39, 40, 42, 44, 59, 63, 101, 123, 128, 129, 140, 141, 200, 201, 204, 205, 206, 207
institutional change ... 4, 27, 35, 37, 38, 39, 44, 55, 93, 101, 128, 143, 159, 196, 197,

199, 204, 205, 206, 208, 209
Institutional constraints 16
institutions ... 1, 2, 3, 5, 8, 9, 11, 12, 15, 16, 17, 19, 24, 26, 29, 30, 31, 32, 33, 34, 35, 36, 37, 38, 39, 40, 45, 52, 54, 143, 166, 172, 175, 204, 205, 206, 207, 208
Jacob, Herbert ... 1, 2, 3, 4, 6, 7, 11, 12, 15, 16, 25, 30
judges .. 3, 4, 5, 6, 9, 11, 15, 16, 17, 19, 20, 22, 24, 25, 26, 30, 32, 33, 42, 43, 44, 47, 57, 58, 59, 61, 62, 63, 64, 87, 88, 89, 90, 93, 94, 95, 96, 98, 100, 101, 116, 124, 125, 130, 131, 132, 135, 137, 143, 145, 160, 161, 162, 163, 164, 167, 168, 169, 170, 171, 172, 173, 174, 175, 176, 177, 179, 181, 182, 183, 184, 186, 187, 192, 194, 195, 196, 200, 201, 203, 204, 205, 206, 208
Kornhauser, Lewis .. 10, 11, 17, 18, 25, 176, 201
Kritzer, Herbert ... 9, 11, 12, 16, 17, 18, 19, 24, 25, 26, 30, 56, 57, 61, 171
Landon, Donald 8, 17, 55
legal change 1
Levin, Martin 6, 7, 9, 16
litigants ... 3, 11, 13, 16, 23, 30, 41, 43, 47, 51, 52, 53, 54, 56, 57, 58, 60, 62, 64, 90, 91, 92, 94, 98, 142, 160, 162, 163, 171, 172, 173, 176, 178, 182, 196, 200, 201, 202, 208
local legal culture 16, 36, 55, 57, 64, 95, 100, 126, 196, 201, 202
March, James 31, 32, 36, 38, 129, 224
Mather, Lynn 2, 14
mediation .. 1, 9, 13, 15, 19, 20, 21, 22, 23, 24, 26, 27, 39, 40, 41, 42, 43, 44, 47, 48, 59, 63, 64, 87, 88, 89, 90, 91, 92, 93, 94, 95, 96, 97, 98, 99, 100, 101, 103, 123, 124, 125, 126, 127, 128, 129, 130, 131, 132, 133, 134, 135, 136, 137, 138, 139, 140, 141, 142, 143, 145, 151, 159, 160, 161, 162, 163, 164, 166, 173, 175, 177, 180, 181, 182, 183, 184, 185, 186, 187, 188, 189, 190, 191, 192, 193, 194, 195, 196, 197, 199, 201, 202, 203, 204, 205, 206, 207, 208, 209
mediators 22, 23, 26, 41, 43, 44, 93, 98, 160, 161, 162, 163, 164, 165, 166, 180, 183, 185, 186, 187, 188, 189, 190, 191, 192, 193, 194, 196, 204, 205, 207
Merry, Sally E. .. 20, 21, 38, 96
Mnookin, Robert 10, 11, 17, 18, 25, 128, 176, 201
Myers, Martha 7, 8
Nardulli, Peter. 4, 5, 6, 7, 8, 16, 30, 92
National Center for State Courts ... 10, 13, 15, 22, 124, 126

negotiation 9, 18, 41, 126, 128, 138
neighborhood justice 21
Neighborhood justice 20
neighborhood justice centers 202
Neighborhood Justice Centers 20, 124, 202
Neo-institutional 24
Neubauer, Abraham 2, 5, 13, 20, 25
New Institutionalism 31, 32, 33, 34, 35, 36, 38, 39, 127, 204, 205, 207
norms 3, 5, 8, 9, 10, 12, 19, 25, 26, 27, 31, 33, 39, 44, 57, 127, 143, 171, 172, 174, 175, 178, 196, 200, 201, 202, 204, 205
Olsen, Johan 31, 32, 36, 38, 129
Ostrom, Elinor 35
pace of litigation ... 14, 44, 130, 137, 139, 140, 141, 142, 143, 174
Pickerill, Jo Mitchell 18, 30, 56, 171
plaintiff attorneys 14, 53, 55, 93
plea bargaining .. 4, 7, 9, 16, 57, 92, 94, 101
Principal-Agent Theory 38
pro se representation 54, 57, 64, 100
public law 3, 5, 32
Public law 1
Rational Choice ... 3, 31, 32, 33, 34, 204, 205
reforms .. 12, 13, 22, 26, 35, 47, 51, 59, 202
reluctant partners ... 36, 37, 202
repeat player . 8, 14, 17, 18, 43, 52, 53, 55, 64, 93, 178
Ross, Lawrence 11, 17, 25
rules 3, 9, 10, 12, 31, 32, 33, 34, 35, 36, 37, 39, 40, 41, 58, 127, 171, 172, 175, 177, 178, 179, 181, 185, 196, 200, 201, 202, 204, 209
settlement rates . 23, 64, 97, 98, 123, 124, 126, 133, 134, 135, 136, 141, 142, 143, 200
settlements 9, 11, 12, 16, 18, 23, 24, 57, 61, 62, 98, 126, 128, 129, 131, 134, 135, 136, 145, 148, 151, 175, 176, 177, 180, 201, 203
shadow of the law ... 10, 11, 18, 201
Shapiro, Martin 1, 3
Shepsle, Kenneth 32, 33, 37
Smith, Rogers 9, 14, 15, 31, 32, 39, 49, 54, 129, 241
Sproule-Jones, Mark 34, 35, 39, 209
State Courts 29
summary judgement ... 64, 151, 173
Talarico, Susette 7, 8, 9, 13, 14, 26, 47, 49, 51, 60, 97
TRIAL 1, 3, 5, 7, 9, 15
trial courts . 1, 2, 3, 4, 5, 6, 7, 9, 10, 14, 15, 16, 25, 26, 29, 30, 39, 40, 94, 97, 127, 201, 208
wrongful death 14
Zemans, Francis 9, 57